The Right to Exploit

The Right to Exploit

Parasitism, Scarcity, Basic Income

Gijs van Donselaar

OXFORD
UNIVERSITY PRESS
2009

OXFORD
UNIVERSITY PRESS

Oxford University Press, Inc., publishes works that further
Oxford University's objective of excellence
in research, scholarship, and education.

Oxford   New York
Auckland   Cape Town   Dar es Salaam   Hong Kong   Karachi
Kuala Lumpur   Madrid   Melbourne   Mexico City   Nairobi
New Delhi   Shanghai   Taipei   Toronto

With offices in
Argentina   Austria   Brazil   Chile   Czech Republic   France   Greece
Guatemala   Hungary   Italy   Japan   Poland   Portugal   Singapore
South Korea   Switzerland   Thailand   Turkey   Ukraine   Vietnam

Published by Oxford University Press, Inc.
198 Madison Avenue, New York, New York 10016

www.oup.com

Oxford is a registered trademark of Oxford University Press

Library of Congress Cataloging-in-Publication Data
Donselaar, G. van.
The right to exploit : parasitism, scarcity, basic income / Gijs van Donselaar.
p.   cm.
Includes bibliographical references.
ISBN 978-0-19-514039-2
1. Right of property—Moral and ethical aspects.   2. Exploitation.
3. Distributive justice.   I. Title.
HB701.D66   2008
174—dc22   2007052452

1 3 5 7 9 8 6 4 2
Printed in the United States of America
on acid-free paper

For Madelon and Jonas

ACKNOWLEDGEMENTS

Many people have supported me in various ways during the period that I have been working on this book. They read and discussed earlier drafts, criticized my ideas, made suggestions, or just encouraged me to proceed. Or they went out of their ways to provide or arrange the (economic) space I required. Or they did all of this.

To one man (who did all of this) I am grateful more than to anybody else: Govert den Hartogh, my friend and supervisor from the early days, who simply refused to despair even though my progress was sometimes so slow as to challenge the patience of a snail. I cannot put it otherwise: his faith in the project was what saw it through.

I am indebted to Paul van den Berg, Jelle de Boer, Marianne Boenink, John Cunliffe, Marc Davidson, Jan and Lies van Donselaar, Ewald Engelen, David Gauthier, Nathalie Glauser, Loek Groot, Bastiaan Hoorneman, Frans Jacobs, Jeroen Knijff, Will Kymlicka, Peter Lammers, Ned McClennen, Dorota Mokrosinska, Philippe Van Parijs, Peter Rijpkema, Peter Vallentyne, Robert van der Veen, Bruno Verbeek, Stuart White, Karl Widerquist, Theo van Willigenburg, Han van Wietmarschen, Jürgen de Wispelaere, Henri Wijsbek, Frans and Alison van Zetten, and Ross Zucker.

And, of course, my very special thanks go to my friends Chris and Elissa Morris, without whom this book would not have seen the light of day.

CONTENTS

The Right to Exploit

CHAPTER I

❦

ABUSE OF RIGHTS, ABUSE OF PEOPLE

1.1 Nuisance and its Value

In 1895 the Judges of the House of Lords allowed Mr. Pickles to get away with a vicious trick he had played on the community of Bradford, England. The year before, Pickles had deliberately diverted the course of a stream that was flowing through his land so that now it no longer supplied the municipal water reservoir. In an earlier stage of the lawsuits that followed, it was established by the Trial Judge, that the object of Pickles's conduct had been "to injure the plaintiffs [Mayor of Bradford] by carrying off the water and to compel them to buy him off in order to avert it" (Voyame, Cottier, and Rocha 1990: 39; O'Sullivan 1955: 68. The Trial Judge, J. North, is quoted).

Notwithstanding the apparent evidence of Mr. Pickles's intention to do harm, the Judges involved in this case agreed that his action had not been illegal, as it was held that "no use of property which would be legal if due to a proper motive can become illegal because it is prompted by a motive which is improper or even malicious" (O'Sullivan 1955: 68). The ruling on *Mayor of Bradford v. Pickles* has been regarded as a piece of "good English law" ever since; English law knows no such thing as an "abuse of rights" (O'Sullivan 1955: 69).

Forty years earlier the Court of Colmar in France had been less "legalistic" in a case, which also involved intent to do harm. It ruled in favor of the plaintiff. Two neighbors, Mr. Keller and Mr. Doerr, had been in an argument before and took a strong dislike to each other.

3

One day the upper storey of Doerr's house burned down. Keller, whose house had already been higher than that of his neighbor, had always enjoyed a magnificent view over the rooftop of Doerr's house. The latter, however, now decided to take the opportunity to annoy his adversary and, instead of rebuilding the upper storey of his house, erected a huge, but false, chimney right in front of the other's window, with the single purpose of spoiling the view. In its decision on *Keller v. Doerr* the court argued that "the principles of morality and equity oppose that justice sanctions an action that is inspired by malice, carried out under the reign of an evil passion, that is not justified by a single personal interest and yet does serious damage to someone else" (quoted in O'Sullivan 1955; my translation from the French). The demolition of the offensive chimney was ordered in 1855, and the ruling on *Keller v. Doerr* is regarded as a highlight in the development of the (continental) legal doctrine of *l'Abus des Droits*.[1]

The concept of "the Abuse of Rights" is controversial, and not only between English and continental legal scholars. Research in comparative law on this point reveals "that there are almost as many conceptions of the abuse of rights as there are member states of the Council of Europe. . . . doctrinal disputes and contradictory judgements are commonplace" (Voyame, Cottier, and Rocha 1990: 23). And I believe there is no reason to assume that other countries will not have still other judgments to offer.

This book is not about the law, and it does not intend to make a contribution to the doctrinal disputes among legal scholars in particular. It has nothing to say on the question of how existing law should be taken. Rather it is about principles of justice that may serve as a basis for legislation and policy making. I have chosen to introduce cunning Mr. Pickles from Bradford because I believe that his conduct, whatever its legal status as an abuse of rights, is an instance of abusing other people. He is trying to be a parasite; he is trying to exploit other people.

From the book of David Gauthier, *Morals by Agreement* (1986), which is the main subject of chapter 2, I derive a conception of parasitism (or exploitation),[2] which, I believe, goes a long way in capturing what is objectionable in it: a parasitic (property rights) relation exists between two persons A and B if in virtue of that relation A is worse off than she would have been had B not existed or if she would have had nothing to do with him, while B is better off than he would have been without A, or having nothing to do with her, or vice versa.

Although I shall not frame my arguments in this terminology in the rest of this book, we may also say that what is essentially lacking from the parasitic relation is an element of "reciprocity." Some gain through others while the others lose out. Evidently many offences that form the hard core of the criminal law can be characterized as parasitic: theft, robbery, and also fraud and extortion consist in inflicting harm to persons by other persons who, by their harmful act or subsequently, gain what they could not have had without their victims. Slavery, likewise, is parasitic. Societies that allow these things allow parasitism, and if just societies should be "cooperative enterprises for mutual advantage" as Gauthier, following Rawls, thinks they should be, then just societies cannot tolerate such blatant and stark violations of reciprocity. Obviously, our types of society, the Western liberal democracies, and many other types of society, do not.

But, as I shall argue, the objection to parasitic relations, and the concept of a just society as mutually advantageous, should have further reaching consequences and, as I shall also argue, these consequences are not always fully appreciated in the philosophy of justice. Pickles's case of parasitism is more subtle and complicated than the common cases of downright robbery. He is not involved in some direct assault on other people's person or property, and indeed the thing he is doing— diverting a stream to which he evidently has some entitlement—might be thought of differently if he did it for other than his present purposes. Suppose that Pickles, like Hercules a long time ago, changed the course of the stream in order to clean out his dirty stables. The diversion of the stream in itself would be as large a nuisance or harm to the community of Bradford as it is now. But would we characterize Pickles's conduct as abusive of other people in that case? I think not. Undoubtedly, we may think that Pickles the Hercules would be very inconsiderate by cutting off Bradford's water supplies, and we may even judge that the Bradfordians deserve a more considerate treatment, but such judgments would have nothing to do with our objection against exploitative action. The act of Pickles the Hercules would be harmful to his neighbors, but he himself would not be doing better, through his action, than he would have done without the existence of his victims. He ignores the others, which is rude, but he does not abuse them.

So the point of the objection against parasitism is not that people may not be a nuisance to each other, or that their existence may not be harmful, for in circumstances of scarcity they cannot but be a nuisance to each other, and harm is unavoidable if two persons want to use a single thing, like a river, for conflicting purposes. Sometimes all of us cannot enjoy what each of us would have enjoyed in the absence of the others, and surely this fact should by itself raise the question how scarce resources ought to be distributed, and we shall meet answers to that question in the course of this book.

But here the point is rather that a man like Pickles seeks to turn his capacity for annoying others into a benefit to himself. Somehow, as he believes, his unrestricted property right to the stream does not only allow him to be a nuisance to others, but it also allows him to exploit his capacity to be a nuisance to others. Pickles's type of parasitism, then, consists in deliberately exploiting his nuisance value. His obstructive behavior, his deliberate act of sabotage, can only be explained by his desire to obtain a benefit to which Bradford is instrumental and for which Bradford receives nothing in return. Making money out of being a nuisance to others is exploiting others. And the right to market one's nuisance value, even if masqueraded as a property right, would just be the right to be a parasite.

The transaction Pickles proposes, by which he would abstain from being a nuisance in return for cash, is markedly different from the normal case. Normally, people who transact, or who agree to cooperate, both make something available to the other, something that would not be obtainable otherwise, and both benefit. Through exchange they are both better off than they would have been without the other.

1.2 A Short Course Through the Book

The phenomenon of *marketable (or exploitable) nuisance*, as a structural feature of economic relations, will be the focal point of this book. I will try to point out how marketable nuisance is dealt with, if at all, by several theories of justice in the distribution of rights to resources. The proposals under scrutiny will be those of David Gauthier, John Locke, Robert Nozick, Ronald Dworkin, and Philippe Van Parijs. Occasionally I will be referring to others as well. All these authors have worked in the broadly liberal tradition of normative philosophy, and their work reveals, in various measures, a commitment to the typical values of liberalism, such as freedom, equality, and impartiality. The challenge, then, will be to see how an objection to exploitation fits in with, or upsets, their interpretations of these values.

Obviously, if property rights are what the Lord Justices took them to be in 1895, then the institution of unconstrained private property rights in external things, such as a river, paves the way to, indeed invites, parasitic action. It will legally empower individuals to use their exclusive and protected access to resources in such a fashion that they may get free access to the "benefit of another's pains" as well. Indeed in the first chapter, on David Gauthier, I argue against Gauthier's own position that a system of unrestricted and "fixed" private property rights in external resources (such as land, rivers, oil, minerals, and fishing grounds) is not consistent with the idea of society as a mutually advantageous enterprise.

In *Morals by Agreement* David Gauthier wants to demonstrate that compliance with what he calls "the Lockean proviso," which prohibits taking advantage of other people, is individually rational. This doctrine is only a part of Gauthier's many-faceted and subtle theory of rationality. He argues that rational persons have a capacity to constrain their straightforwardly utility-maximizing actions and that they will choose to do so where such constraint would be necessary, and effective, to establish a basis for mutually advantageous cooperation. Compliance with a prohibition on parasitic action—worsening the position of others in bettering one's own—is one such requirement of rational constraint. It will establish what each may regard as his personal endowment prior to the interaction he might seek with others. In the first half of chapter 2, I try to evaluate Gauthier's argument for this claim and conclude that he has failed to demonstrate the rationality of complying with the Lockean proviso. But a failure of Gauthier's ambitious project of reconciling rationality and morality should not keep us from agreeing that he has captured, by his formulation of the Lockean proviso, a sound principle of justice in its own right. I then proceed to argue, as indicated, against the idea that private endowments as unrestricted property rights can be consistent with the Lockean proviso. And taking the argument just a step further I conclude that the Lockean proviso warrants a system of flexible (even "evanescent") and restricted use rights in resources—more like "concessions" or "franchises"—such that those who produce most efficiently will be secured access to productive opportunities. Arranging things otherwise would be giving parasites a chance. But flexible and adjustable access rights to resources are still individual rights. In the last section of chapter 2, I compare the "Lockean" definition of parasitism to the socialist definition of "exploitation," and I conclude that they are markedly distinct, conceptually and in their normative consequences. The proviso warrants restrictions in the bargaining power, as based in property rights as private endowments that individuals hold against each other, but it is no justification for a doctrine of a collective ownership of resources.

Modern systematic thought on how individuals may legitimately acquire property rights in external resources has been developed by

John Locke. In chapter 3, which is devoted to a short course through the proto-history of Gauthier's "Lockean proviso," I begin with an interpretative discussion of the proviso as John Locke himself first formulated it. Although people acquire the right to their own person, that is the right of self-ownership, upon birth, or, arguably, upon reaching adulthood, legitimate rights in external resources, says Locke, are established by "mixing them with labor." The much-debated proviso in this doctrine of appropriation is that in making acquisitions through labor something "as good" should be "left for the others in common." Odd things have been said about this clause in Locke's *Second Treatise of Government*. I dismiss Jeremy Waldron's observations concerning the grammar in the precise phrasing of the proviso even though I grant him, and others, that the proviso is bound to raise problems under conditions of scarcity, when no appropriation can be made without somehow leaving something less good for others. Some commentators have argued that the proper interpretation of Locke's text would not allow any restriction on acquiring property through labor at all—with or without conditions of scarcity. I oppose that interpretation and point out a certain ambiguity in Locke's position that may be accountable for it. I argue that the least we should accept as a restriction following from the proviso is a prohibition on appropriations that are intended to put others in the position of a coerced buyer. Failing to give the proviso that meaning would be failing to understand Locke's fundamental reason for having a theory of property with a central role for labor in the first place. It was after all he who said that we have no right to "the benefit of another's pains."

In the second half of chapter 3, I discuss some aspects of Robert Nozick's "historical entitlement theory of justice," which has been formulated in *Anarchy, State, and Utopia* (1974). Nozick, a declared Lockean in spirit, is aware of the systematic problems in Locke's doctrine of appropriation and the proviso that goes with it. But through making a distinction between use rights and property rights, he seeks a way around them. According to Nozick, the proviso should imply that we may not run ahead of all others to appropriate the only water hole in the desert and then sell the water to those who arrive later. The others maintain a right to "use" the water—though they can no longer "appropriate" it. But I argue, and give examples to demonstrate, that the distinction between use and appropriation fails to do what it seemingly purports to do: to restrict the right of original acquisition in such a fashion that it cannot serve to exploit one's nuisance value, hence to serve the parasite.

Other parts of Nozick's theory, however, not developed in relation to the problem of original acquisition (but readily applicable to it) are more direct in their rejection of parasitism, and of the institution of rights that would support the parasite. The distinction, this time, is between types of transaction: "productive" transactions, says Nozick, leave both parties better off than they would have been without their partner, "(partially) unproductive" transactions however leave one of the parties worse off and one of the parties better off, than he or she would have been without the other. Obviously there is a very close fit between our Gauthier-style definition of parasitism and Nozick's definition of unproductiveness, and indeed Nozick defends a legitimate prohibition of unproductive transactions. But again, as in Gauthier, there seems to be a certain lack of awareness in Nozick of the tension between his objection to unproductive transactions and his libertarian rhetoric about inviolable property rights. Eric Mack has pointed out this tension, but he in his turn proceeds to argue that the objection to unproductiveness is wholly unwarranted, since such an objection would apply equally to "peaceful boycotts." I argue that Mack is wrong, that peaceful boycotts are not parasitic, and that he has misstated Nozick's argument. Nozick is our third case of an abortive effort to make the objection against taking advantage consistent with a commitment to originally acquired and fixed property rights in resources.

The second half of this book, chapters 4, 5, and 6, is devoted to a critical discussion of a proposal to radically reform the social arrangements of modern democratic industrialized states. That proposal is to introduce a so-called unconditional basic income. A basic income is a monetary provision, in regular installments, to which every citizen would be entitled unconditionally, by virtue of being a citizen, and without a corresponding obligation to accept suitable work if available. The idea of a basic income has a history, but recently it has found renewed and indeed powerful support in the book *Real Freedom for All: What (if Anything) Can Justify Capitalism?* (1995) by Philippe Van Parijs.

In chapter 4, I try to analyze Van Parijs's argument and to lay bare its philosophical foundations. One essential element in these foundations is Ronald Dworkin's doctrine of "equality of resources." Roughly the argument runs as follows: once we reject the idea, as indeed I do in the first chapters of this book, that property rights in natural resources can be justified by historical privilege, by birth rights, or by the arbitrary fact that one was the first to take possession, how then should resources be divided and distributed among all individuals? Ronald Dworkin's argument is that they should be divided equally: we are to imagine ourselves as bidding, at an auction, for the various resources the world has to offer, each of us commanding an equal amount of token money. Units of resources will then go to those who care, and hence bid, most for them, and the resulting "competitive" allocation will be free of envy. Van Parijs then goes on to argue on the basis of Dworkin's position that all individuals are in fact entitled to an equal share of the value of the resources of the world. Suppose indeed, he reasons, that each of us were the owner of an equal share of resources, then it is quite imaginable that those among us who wish to work very hard, the "Crazies," would be willing to buy additional resources to their own equal share, and suppliers would then be those among us who do not care for very high incomes and prefer to have leisure instead, the "Lazies." So people who do not want to work are still entitled to the market value of the equal share of resources that is legitimately theirs, and hence to an income that is not generated through their own labor. Those who have large shares of resources and work hard should be the suppliers of that labor-free income. The possession of resources, Van Parijs concludes, should be taxed, the proceeds distributed equally among all; and that would be a basic income.

I object to basic income on the ground that it would be exploitative. The relations that basic income would establish between the Lazies and the Crazies (the net beneficiaries of a basic income policy and the net suppliers of the benefit) satisfy the definition of parasitism. However, the real target of my criticism of basic income is the underlying idea, Dworkin's idea, of equality of resources. I point out that nothing in the idea of the resource auction, or in the idea of envy-freeness, excludes that some persons, probably the Lazies, will want to obtain resources only with the purpose of selling them to others later on. The auction allows individuals to regard and freely acquire resources as merchandise. What the Lazies spend is token money, but what they acquire has real value. The Lazies exploit the fact that resources are scarce; they make a nuisance of themselves by taking what others want, and then they sell it. This is a serious flaw in Dworkin's doctrine because it implies that the resulting allocation of resources will not reflect each individual's "independent interest" in an opportunity to supply herself with an income. Instead it will reflect the interest that some have in the proceeds of other people's labor. Indeed, the concept of resources as pseudo-merchandise proves to be the one essential assumption in the argument for basic income that should be rejected. I point out a similar flaw in John Roemer's recent reinterpretation of the Marxist concept of exploitation.[3]

In chapter 5, I discuss an important extension of Philippe Van Parijs's argument for basic income. As he argues, recent theories of unemployment warrant the idea that jobs should in fact be regarded as scarce external assets that, just as natural resources, have been appropriated by some and from which others have been excluded. He then concludes that all citizens have a right to an equal share of the value of jobs, that the "employment rents" associated with the possession of a job should be taxed, and that the proceeds would serve to boost basic income into something really significant. Support for Van Parijs's view can be found in an argument by Bert Hamminga. Hamminga proposes, in order to "liberalize the labor market," to issue an equal amount of so-called Labor Rights to all adult citizens, which they may then trade amongst each other—those wanting full-time employment purchasing, the lovers of leisure selling. I have no quarrel with the idea that jobs should be regarded as scarce assets and that they may be treated on an equal footing with natural resources. But, of course, in my view this cannot lead to a legitimate unconditional basic income, since what is true for resources is also true for jobs: regarding them as merchandise, and then distributing them equally to Lazies and Crazies alike, fails to appreciate the reason why we would want to give a person access to a job in the first place. Why should a person not willing to work have a share in jobs that others want? Access to work itself, like access to resources, should not be unconditional. It should depend on a person's willingness to work.

Instead of the introduction of basic income, I argue, the justice of the labor market requires that we consider the possibilities of labor-time reduction and job sharing much more seriously. I discuss some objections raised by Van Parijs to such a policy and find them unconvincing.

In chapter 6, finally, I begin by pointing out a serious further but related difficulty in the argument for basic income, based on equality of resources, namely that it cannot rank larger stocks of resources as more "socially desirable" than smaller stocks of resources without violating the liberal principle that justice ought to be neutral regarding the interests of all. If resources were to be more plentiful and assuming all initially to hold an equal and tradable share, then basic income would go down. Extending the stock of resources would therefore not be in the interest of the Lazies. The set of bundles of leisure and income that we can choose on a smaller island only intersects with the set of such bundles that we can choose on a larger island, and therefore it cannot be maintained that our so-called "real freedom" would be greater on the larger island.

I explicate Van Parijs's fundamental notion of real freedom and identify the fundamental value real freedom is supposed to protect: our capacity for autonomous choice. But I conclude that, on a proper understanding of it and contrary to his own view, the tradability of resources does not realize an extension of our real freedom. It is therefore not correct to assume that bundles of leisure and income that can only be obtained through the sale of resources, such as, for instance, full-time leisure on revenues at the level of basic income, are part of our real freedom. Such tradability realizes Pareto optimality in the distribution of bundles of leisure and income that people acquire, and that is desirable, but not on account of a commitment to equality of real freedom.

My analysis avoids the awkward result that larger stocks of resources cannot be ranked as superior, and, more importantly, it clears the way to seek for an alternative distributive principle that combines a commitment to the value of autonomous choice, protected equally for all, and Pareto optimality in the allocation of bundles of leisure and income. I offer (at least the contours of) such an alternative. It is called "the principle of equality-based progressive satiation" or, for short, "the rule of Maimonides." Its great merit is that it avoids exploitation.

1.3 So Be It

Sometimes a writer must refrain from trying to cast off all loose ends, or he will keep on knitting forever. An inherent danger of such a decision is that once people start pulling the loose ends, and they are always tempted to do so, the whole fabric of the work may come apart. So be it. I must face this danger, since the present study cannot be exhaustive. Of course, it cannot. Indeed, I am well aware that there are many important questions and considerations that I have ignored or put between brackets, either because they, though relevant, could not be discussed given the limited space and time allowed by this book, or, which is more serious, because they would lead me to tread into fields beyond my present competence.

There is however one important issue that I do not consider a mere loose end, and that should be discussed before I proceed, and I will do so briefly for the remainder of this introductory chapter. It is perhaps best addressed by turning our attention for a while to the work of the great American revolutionary Thomas Paine. In 1796 Paine wrote a pamphlet, *Agrarian Justice*, in which he unfolded an idea quite similar to

Van Parijs's proposal for a basic income (the indebtedness being recognized by the latter). That plan was to tax the intergenerational transfer of wealth, inheritances, and to redistribute the proceeds unconditionally among all in the form of a substantial grant upon reaching the age of maturity. The point of this tax and transfer system was to compensate those who had been disadvantaged by having lost their access to natural resources. According to Paine "civilization...or that which is so called, has operated two ways: to make one part of society more affluent, and the other more wretched, than would have been the lot of either in a natural state"; and "on the one side, the spectator is dazzled by splendid appearances; on the other, he is shocked by extremes of wretchedness."

But then, further on, he goes on to claim as one of the great merits of the plan that it "will immediately relieve and take out of view three classes of wretchedness—the blind, the lame, and aged poor."

So, evidently, Paine includes the lame and the blind among those whose wretchedness is explained by their lack of access to natural resources. But once we ask how the lame and the blind would presumably have fared in a "natural state," it is obvious that such inclusion is odd. He stresses, repeatedly, that the systematic transfer of wealth according to his plan is a matter of historical redress, or, as he puts it, a matter "of right, not of charity," but if we take the fate of the individual in the state of nature as the benchmark for a distinction between right and charity, then, most plausibly, taxes and transfers in support of the lame and the blind should count as charity, not as right. The assumption behind the requirement of redress or compensation is, of course, that in the absence of the prior appropriations by the presently wealthy those who are now wretched would have been willing and able to make their own use of the world's resources and that therefore they would have been less wretched, or perhaps even wealthy themselves. The first appropriators in this sense cause the wretchedness of the others, and that calls for reparation. But clearly, the lame and the blind face constraints in making use of external resources that have nothing to do with the (prior) behavior of others, and it seems that if their wretchedness is a matter of concern to us, as it obviously was to Paine, a mere principle of redress by "historical" right could never suffice.

Obvious as Paine's mistake may be, I believe that many modern-day followers of the basic income idea, or something like it, fall victim to a similar inconsistency. What they ultimately care about, and what they want to mend, is the wretchedness of some, but what they come up with in arguing for the required transfers, meanwhile apparently desiring to evade the accusation of arguing for charity, is a quasi-historical principle of redress, justifying a right to behavior that is relevantly similar to that of farmer Pickles: the exploitation of nuisance value. But Pickles, as far as we know, was not wretched, and neither need a "lazy" person who prefers to sit in the sun rather than work-and-consume a lot, for that reason be wretched.

So much is however true: those who want to argue for solidarity with the wretched as a fundamental moral principle will need to argue that the Lockean proviso, on Gauthier's interpretation of it, is of limited moral significance or at least not exhaustive of all that is of moral weight. They will have to argue against those who hold that the objection against the (involuntary) transfer of value from one person to another cannot be compromised for any reason. Among those is Gauthier himself: "the proviso says nothing about meeting needs. The rich man may feast on caviar and champagne, while the poor woman starves at his gate. And she may not even take the crumbs from his table, if that would deprive him of his pleasure in feeding them to his birds" (Gauthier 1986: 218). Although he describes this situation as "distressing," it is clear that Gauthier's philosophy is not intended to address the concerns of Thomas Paine. Similar observations can be made, of course, about Robert Nozick.

But whichever way we look at this problem, I think that those who want to argue for solidarity with people who need support should not try to secure such support by granting every person an a priori and unconditional right to a share of the earth, which can then be commercially exploited, thus jumbling together the "wretched" and the "lazy" as equally deserving beneficiaries of a tax and transfer system.

It is, for one thing, strategically unwise to do so, for it invites the opposition's response (of which it will not easily become weary) that the wretched are not really wretched, but actually lazy. But more importantly, the roundabout via original claims to resources will ultimately obscure the real nature of a moral requirement of solidarity. It makes the fate of the wretched vitally, and perhaps fatally, dependent on the contingent value of natural resources. That value may in theory sink to zero, in which case the a priori claims of those in need would be empty. They would be left as badly off as they would be in the state of nature. That, it seems to me, should count as an awkward result, even if only theoretical, for those who believe in solidarity.

I believe there are sound arguments for the moral requirement to help those in distress, even arguments for the political enforcement of that requirement. But there is no denying that in order to provide such arguments altogether different sources must be tapped from the ones that are considered in this book. The provision will have to wait for another occasion. But my remarks on this issue cannot be completed without referring the reader to *The Civic Minimum* (2003), the book by Stuart White in which he develops an attractive view of social justice, reflecting both a strong commitment to policies that protect the vulnerable and an equally strong commitment to a "reciprocity principle" that precludes that people exploit their fellow citizens.

The present work is not intended to achieve something as comprehensive. It is merely about farmer Pickles (and his likes) who believes that his property rights entitle him to a transfer of value from others regardless of any assessment of his situation as distressful or not. It is my purpose to demonstrate how amazingly tolerant theories of justice, both from the right and the left, have been in dealing with his claims.

Let me make one concluding remark to this chapter. Though obviously the purpose of this book is primarily academic, I have tried not to write the kind of jargon that would discourage rather than inspire interest in a wider audience. After all, some of the subject matter, such as the legitimacy of basic income, is very relevant to the ongoing public debate on social policies, and that debate concerns each of us.

However, there are also some pages where I have not been able to avoid a somewhat more technical language, and where my points partly rely on the explanatory force of graphics. These passages, I am sure, are less attractive to read. Unfortunately, some of the very first paragraphs of the next chapter, dealing with David Gauthier's highly abstract approach to justice, are precisely of this nature, and they might provoke some people's disenchantment with the book as a whole. But I hope they will not put it aside at such an early stage. In any event, the point of individual chapters, or even of clusters of paragraphs within chapters, often can be grasped without having appreciated the full details of all that has preceded in the structure of the book. So those who feel that I have been erecting obstacles to their continuing interest are advised just to skip what they do not like, and to go on where the prose regains accessibility.

CHAPTER 2

WITHOUT ME, WITHOUT YOU: COOPERATION AND SCARCITY

Because political economy loves Robinsonades.

Karl Marx

2.1 Gauthier: The "Lockean Proviso": Bargaining and the Market

Conventionalist theories of morality seek to establish that it is individually rational to comply with just moral rules and that just moral rules should be identified as those with which it is rational to comply. The conventionalist approach can be traced as far back as Hobbes, and Hume has made his contributions to it. But a recent, and powerful, attempt to argue for this tight relation between reason and morality has been made by David Gauthier in *Morals by Agreement* (1986). One of the central issues of this book is the following: if compliance with principles holding between essentially self-interested rational individuals can constitute a cooperative practice that is advantageous to all, how should the surplus that is produced through the cooperative effort be distributed? How do we divide the benefits of our cooperative activities in such a way that it is advantageous to all to cooperate in the first place, and also that it is rational to consent to this division rather than another? The question, then, is twofold. Compared to what situation should the cooperative advantage of each be measured? And: given this status quo point or initial bargaining point of comparison, how large a share should each of the parties get of the total surplus produced jointly, in relation to the share of the others? Phrased in a different way: how do we establish what it is that each of the parties brings to the bargaining table, and how do we establish what each should take from the bargaining table (given what he or she has brought)?

Gauthier's answers are the following. Given a certain fixed initial bargaining position the "principle of minimax relative concession" (MRC) leads us to a Pareto optimal distribution of the substance we are bargaining about, which it is rational to accept for all parties. Loosely stated, MRC implies that, for each agent involved, the contribution to a cooperative effort must be in the same proportion to the benefit from that effort. And the initial bargaining point from which to measure each person's relative benefit from and contribution to the cooperative effort is established by what Gauthier calls the "Lockean proviso": advantageous, in the relevant sense, are those increases in my utility that make me better off than I would have been in the absence of the other parties or in the absence of the possibility to interact with them. Likewise, the others are considered to be better off with me, if through my actions they are better off than they would have been in my absence. "[T]he base point for determining how I affect you, in terms of bettering or worsening your situation, is determined by the outcome that you would expect in my absence. Worsening, and equally bettering, are judged by comparing what I actually do with what would have occurred, *ceteris paribus*, in my absence" (Gauthier 1986: 204). And since the proviso fixes the initial position of all parties, it prohibits taking advantage of other persons through the worsening of their position.

> [T]he proviso prohibits bettering one's situation through interaction that worsens the situation of another. This, we claim, expresses the underlying idea of not taking advantage.... no one is free to better his own situation through interaction worsening the situation of another. To allow that, in order to better one's own situation, one may worsen that of others, would be to allow one to be a *parasite*. (Gauthier 1986: 205–6)

Once we start cooperating, we measure our benefits from the position I would have been in without you and you would have been in without me. The Lockean proviso establishes what things are not subject to the bargain, it establishes what is ours prior to the bargain. It establishes our rights that are to serve as a basis for cooperation.

> [T]he proviso introduces a rudimentary structure of rights into natural interaction. It converts the predatory natural condition described by Hobbes into the productive natural condition supposed by Locke. But its primary role is to make possible the further structures required for the forms of social interaction. (Gauthier 1986: 208)

Neither of Gauthier's two answers is uncontested. Rational solutions for the division of bargaining surpluses have been determined in different ways, along lines different from Gauthier's principle of MRC. Nash, Zeuthen, and Harsanyi have made rival proposals,[1] and others have even denied that there is a single and rational method for solving bargaining problems at all, at least as long as there are no previously established mutual expectations among the bargainers.[2] Of course, this issue is of paramount importance for any theory of social justice of the type that Gauthier has presented, but nevertheless I shall not pursue it here. My main purpose is to consider and discuss the merits (and shortcomings) of Gauthier's argument for accepting the Lockean proviso as the way to fix the initial bargaining position. I will subject Gauthier's claim that compliance with the Lockean proviso would be rational to scrutiny. In the following, I shall even assume more than can perhaps be warranted concerning the question of the rational division of surpluses; I shall assume that there is a method to fix a single distribution of the object of the bargain, which it is uniquely rational to accept, given that we have a certain initial point from which to assess what the object of the bargain actually is.

There is a second general target of *Morals by Agreement*. Besides offering the proviso as the proper method for fixing the point from which to start bargains, Gauthier claims that it is also the proper method to establish what it is that individuals bring to the market. Markets are not cooperative practices the surplus of which must be divided independently through negotiations, since everyone only brings to the market what she may withhold when expected returns do not sufficiently move her to produce or sell. Yet markets, like forms of cooperation, do offer the prospect of mutual benefit, if they function properly, since then all traders will be better off with each other than they would have been without each other. Both bargains and markets must satisfy the general condition of being beneficial to us compared to our position in the absence of the ones we cooperate or trade with, but the difference between the two contexts is in the way that returns are determined. In the case of bargains, we have the principle of MRC (or one of its rivals) to lead us to a division of the returns, but in the case of the market, returns are to be determined by the free play of demand and supply, ideally fixing an equilibrium price for all transfers. Hence, the difference is also that, since the spontaneous outcome of the market is mutually beneficial, it needs no constraints on individually utility-maximizing behavior except for compliance with the proviso. The market is what Gauthier calls a "morally free zone"; anyone may act as he or she wants, provided that the initial endowments of each in entering the market are constrained by the Lockean proviso. Only if market distributions reflect, for instance, pre-existing coercive relations do such distributions violate the proviso.

Let me, tentatively, break down Gauthier's theory of the rationality of morality as follows:

1. it points out why, and under what conditions, it is rational to comply with the Lockean proviso as the starting point for cooperative practices and markets;
2. it points out why, and under what conditions, it is rational to comply with (to keep, to honor, to respect) agreements the content of which it is rational to accept; and
3. it points out the content of agreements that it is rational to accept—given that they will be kept and given that the proviso has been respected.

The latter part of the theory has, what we may call, two distinct contexts of application:

The bargaining situation: Given that the proviso is respected and given that agreements will be kept, there is room for negotiations about the content of the agreement; in this case, the rational acceptable content is specified by MRC.

The competitive market: Given that the proviso is respected and given that agreements will be kept, there is *no* room for negotiations about the content of the agreement; in this case, the rationally acceptable content of the agreement is simply given by the (equilibrium) market prices of the goods or services the exchange of which happens to be under consideration.

2.2 Moral Anarchy?

As for the difference between these two contexts of application, I will first try to clarify a certain confusion, and this will lead us to a refinement of Gauthier's claims. It is not directly relevant to our assessment of the value of Gauthier's arguments for the rationality of complying with the Lockean proviso, but it helps to put in perspective the type of morality that he is concerned with. Competitive markets, according to Gauthier, are "morally free zones," and that claim strongly suggests that if all the world were a market we would not have any purpose for the type of moral constraint on our utility-maximizing behavior as pointed out under (2). It would then never be rational to accept such constraints. The market is a place of "moral anarchy." Gauthier even goes so far as to claim that the market provides each individual agent with a context of *parametric* choices; she may simply assume the behavior of others to be given, she need only respond to fixed data in the way that maximizes her utility. She can act as an unconstrained rational utility maximizer. But this claim, in itself, would be completely unwarranted unless one takes the existence of external contract enforcement as a defining characteristic of markets as such. This is, of course, what economists tend to do, but it is also, of course, what a moralist cannot legitimately do. Once we deny ourselves the economist's convenience, it is immediately obvious that the possibility of fraud, and its temptation, is as real in the context of the market, and as destructive for its success, as it is in the context of bargains.[3] We can only take the behavior of other agents as fixed when we recognize them as trustworthy or when we know that they fear the punishing fury of the "sovereign"—in the manner meant by Thomas Hobbes. Although the determination of the price we agree on—in a given market transaction—is not dependent on negotiations between us, we must nevertheless agree on it and keep that agreement. I agree to deliver, you agree to pay, but each of us is "tempted" to break his part of the agreement if he expects the other not to do so. Clearly, then, in the absence of a sovereign "to hold us all in awe," the possibility of a properly functioning market would require us to stick to the deals we strike through internal constraint, to comply with agreements, in the same way as the possibility of successful cooperation requires us to do so. To think that, in the absence of internal constraint, there can be an invisible hand without a visible foot is a mistake. Or, to make the point the other way around: if we may assume the presence of an external enforcer of agreements, then cooperative practices are as "morally free" as markets are, in the sense that neither would require us to accept constraints on our utility-maximizing behavior. This would be so, since offering or seeking a service or good for the market price as well as "bargaining is a straightforwardly maximizing activity leading to agreement on a joint strategy" (Gauthier 1986: 151).

Both in the context of the market and in the context of a bargain, the process of determining the content of agreements is the result of straightforwardly utility-maximizing behavior. And both contexts require either a rational acceptance of constraints in keeping the agreements or the presence of their external enforcement. It is not very helpful to specify such a presence as characteristic of the one context and not of the other.

So the essential difference between bargains and markets is not in the moral anarchy of the latter, at least not in this sense. What, then, is there to Gauthier's claim that markets are morally distinct from bargaining problems? Of course, the fact itself that the one context requires bargains while the other does not is an important distinction. But is it a moral distinction? I think we have to look in another direction. Gauthier argues that markets cannot always be had. Markets fail to optimally supply so-called public goods, or to optimally suppress the supply of public bads. It turns out that the production of public goods has the structure of an (n-person) bargaining problem and therefore MRC, assuming its rational acceptability, would require each to agree to do his bit in the production of the good relative to his benefit, and ex ante rational agents would agree to such terms for its production. Yet it is difficult to imagine the hundreds of thousands, perhaps millions, who are involved in producing public goods, or avoiding public harms, gathered around a single bargaining table, all individually consenting ex ante to contribute in return for, and in MRC-proportion to, their benefit. Public goods the production of which would depend on actual agreement being reached, on a true understanding among all beneficiaries, would never come into being. Their coming into being requires a constraint other than the simple one of keeping actual agreements. It requires one to contribute even in the absence of one's explicit consent to contribute, that is: in the absence of agreement proper.

If we take a "contractarian morality" to imply, as Robert Nozick argues, that no obligation to contribute can arise without some form of consent, then the obligation to abstain from free riding is beyond the scope of contractarian morality. The simple fact that one benefits from the contributions of others cannot constitute an obligation to contribute as well. This is indeed Nozick's conclusion (Nozick 1974: 90–95).

But it is clear from *Morals by Agreement* that Gauthier is more ambitious. In seeking a way from Hobbes to Locke he is not only trying to argue for the rationality of complying with actual agreements in the sense of "being as good" as one's word, one's nod, or one's signature but also for the rationality of complying with distributions of benefits and contributions one would have agreed to if (counterfactually) these distributions had been the object of a bargain. He is arguing for the legitimacy of an MRC-version of the notorious "principle of fairness."

Why, on the other hand, is it not difficult to think of the hundreds of thousands, yes the millions, who are involved in the market

as consenting to their transactions? It is not difficult at all to think
of them like that because the millions who deal with each other in
the market place do not have to agree with all the others at the same
time on a single cooperative enterprise. Standardly, they deal with
only one of the others at a time. Mr. X buys bread from the baker,
and so does Mrs. Y. The baker sells bread, and she buys flour from the
miller; the miller purchases wheat from the farmer; the farmer buys
tools from the smith, and so on (lack of space does not allow me to
continue until I have listed a million market agents, but it could be
done). All these agents transact on the basis of a one-to-one agreement. They all consent to their transactions, and even though many of
their contracts may not be explicit and documented, they are mutually confirmed and recognized. Market transactions proceed on an
understanding between two agents. If you want to exploit another
market agent you will have to lie to her, or at least you will have to
try to mislead her.

It is here, then, that we find a significant difference between market
morality and non-market morality. Effective external (legal) contract
enforcement (if it could be had) would be sufficient to make the market work, at least if we take the conventional ways of consenting and
agreeing (a word, a nod, a signature) as constitutive of legally binding
contracts. But the presence of positive contract law would be of little
help in the production of public goods, since, typically, there are no
contracts to enforce in this sphere. Even the constrained utility maximizer who rationally accepts that he should stand by his word can be
a perfect free-rider in his enjoyment of a public good when he never
actually gave his word to contribute. He need not deceive in order to
exploit. The free-rider can do without fraud. He can always, and truth-
fully, say: "I never led you to expect that I was going to contribute, so
what are you complaining about?" In this sense, then, there is a special
kind of moral constraint related to the production of public goods,
which we can do without in markets. I guess it is this type of morality
that Gauthier must have had in mind. Ultimately, his claim has nothing
to do with the difference between parametric and strategic choices.
The difference is rather between constraints that make agreements
work and constraints that make cooperation work in the absence of
agreement. The point is simply that the market consists in bilateral
(one-to-one) interactions in which actual consent to agreements is
easily to be had, while the production of public goods requires cooperation among numbers of agents that virtually exclude actual agreement. The market, distinctively, is the great *bilateralizor* of economic

relations. It is therefore also the great facilitator of agreements. I guess we should add to the list above that Gauthier is in fact trying to:

2. point out why, and under what conditions, it is rational to comply with distributions of contributions and benefits one would have rationally agreed to (ex ante), had they been the subject of a bargain.

In this light "Morals by Agreement" may appear to be a misnomer, at least if we take "agreement," as contract law does, as essentially referring to some expression of will.[4] I will put further considerations on this issue aside and proceed to discuss the main topic: the moral requirement not to take advantage of one's fellows, that is, the Lockean proviso.

2.3 Overview

The next sections are structured as follows: first, it will be important to get a clear grasp of the difference between, on the one hand, what it is that the proviso prohibits, and, on the other hand, why and under what conditions Gauthier believes that it is rationally required to comply with this prohibition. As we saw, the proviso prohibits taking advantage of others, but Gauthier is only interested in compliance with the proviso if, and in so far as, such compliance would be necessary to establish a rationally acceptable basis for cooperation. Where (some of) the parties cannot expect a benefit from constraining themselves compared to the outcome of their most effective noncooperative activities (even if these are predatory and coercive) they are not required to comply with the proviso.

Second, I will argue that, even if we take the Lockean proviso as a principle for the establishment of a bargaining point only, and not as an unconditional principle of justice, some conclusions drawn by Gauthier do not in fact follow from its definition. Notably, his idea that "no person has the right to impose uncompensated costs on another" (prior to mutually advanageous cooperation or prior to market relations), is inconsistent with the proviso's actual requirements.

Third, and most importantly, I will try to assess, and criticize, Gauthier's central claim that compliance with the Lockean proviso, even under the appropriate conditions, is rational. Even if Gauthier is right, as I believe he is, that people who face a prospect of mutually advantageous cooperative or market relations must be concerned to find a rationally acceptable demarcation of the "endowments" with which each enters cooperative practices or the market, it has not been established that the proviso gives this rationally acceptable demarcation. Gauthier gives us two reasons for his claim.

The first is that it would be irrational to dispose oneself to accept agreements that invite prior predation or coercion. This may be a valid claim in its own right, and it would exclude a number of actions as irrational, but it fails to pin down the proviso point for "status quo." Notably, it also fails to exclude the so-called "natural distribution" against which Gauthier is explicitly arguing.

The second reason is that agreements based on uncompensated prior costs or benefits cannot be rationally acceptable, since rational agreements require that benefits relate to contributions in the same way for each, as is specified by the principle of minimax relative concession. This argument is invalid as an argument for the rationality of compliance with the proviso, because the problem that this argument tries to solve is how to establish the position in relation to which benefits and contributions should be measured. The argument tries to establish a point from which to measure benefits and contributions, and then proceeds to use a measure of benefits and contributions, which presupposes that we already have a point such as the one we are searching for.

Finally I will conclude this chapter by pointing out some implications of the Lockean proviso with regard to the notion of private property. I will argue that, despite Gauthier's own adherence to the institution of ownership rights in external resources, the Lockean proviso can never allow the establishment of exclusive rights to external objects. People's holdings in natural resources, however they came into being, are always liable to adjustment in light of the justice of economic outcomes.

2.4 Equilibrium and the Proviso

Suppose that cooperation were technically impossible, or suppose that the agents we met were unwilling to cooperate with us under any condition. What would then be the rational thing for us to do? In chapter 3 of *Morals by Agreement* ("Strategy: Reason and Equilibrium"), Gauthier argues that in the absence of the possibility of cooperation rational agents will choose their so-called (non-cooperative) equilibrium strategies. A set of equilibrium strategies is a set of strategies such that neither agent has reason to change her strategy given the strategy that is chosen by the other. To each set of strategies belongs a certain outcome. An outcome is a set of (expected) utility pay-offs. To the set of equilibrium strategies belongs the equilibrium outcome. The equilibrium outcome, then, consists of the utilities that rational agents may expect in the absence of the possibility to cooperate. Another term for the equilibrium outcome that is used by Gauthier (following James Buchanan) is "the natural distribution."[5]

In real life, more often than not, the natural distribution will be suboptimal. Both agents might do better if they both chose some other strategy than their equilibrium strategy. Typically, the utilities granted in the absence of cooperation are the utilities that belong to lives that are "solitary, poor, nasty, brutish and short." Moreover, they will also reflect the costs that the agents have invested in predatory and defensive activities, since, as Thomas Hobbes took pains to point out, only these state-of-nature activities are in equilibrium: if both invest in aggression neither will have reason to change his strategy; if one of them invests in aggression while the other does not, then the one who does not has good reason to change his strategy; and if both do not invest in aggression, then both have reason to start doing so. Only mutual aggression is in equilibrium. Other strategy sets are not. Yet, the agents could avoid the cost of mutual aggression if they somehow managed to agree on and commit themselves to a cooperative strategy of non-aggression, thus perhaps also paving the way for "cooperation" in the more conventional sense of "doing things together."

What is the role of the natural distribution in Gauthier's theory of rational agreement? He believes, as we saw, that rationality requires that cooperative agreements and market relations ought to proceed from an initial (bargaining) point, and from a definition of personal endowments, that is constrained by the Lockean proviso. The Lockean proviso would allow each a utility level equal to his expectations in the absence of the other. And, of course, there is little reason to presume that the distribution of utility between us as granted by mutual compliance with the proviso will coincide with the natural distribution (though, further on, we will meet with a suggestion to the contrary). Besides being suboptimal, the natural distribution is bound to be below the proviso-level for at least one of us.

Of course, the fact that the natural distribution is suboptimal does not in itself imply that the existence of each of us is a nuisance to the other. It does not imply that both of us must suffer compared to the absence of the other, it does not imply that investment in predation on another person is unprofitable compared to the absence of the other. If I, say, because of my vastly superior strength, manage to enslave you and force you to work for me, it may well be that my utility is substantially higher than it would have been had you not existed at all. Of course, your utility will then be lower than it would have been had I not existed. Nothing in the definition of the natural distribution excludes that it is parasitic. But even as a parasitic distribution, the natural distribution can be suboptimal, because both of us might be doing better, say, in an arrangement such that you continued to do part (but not all) of your slave work for me while I stopped pressing you to do more. We could both do better if we agreed to change your status from a permanently monitored serf who has to work all day to a tributary farmer to whom some leisure is allowed.

So, given that the proviso point and the natural distribution do not coincide, what role is there for the natural distribution in Gauthier's theory of rational agreement? Should it be ignored completely, and should bargaining and cooperation always proceed from the proviso point regardless of the natural distribution? No. The rationality of complying with the constraint of the proviso, in its turn, is conditional on the prospect of mutual advantage compared to the natural distribution. "The proviso constrains the initial bargaining position to the extent, but only to the extent, that such constraint is compatible with the cooperative outcome affording each person the expectation of a utility greater than that afforded by the non-cooperative outcome" (Gauthier 1986: 229–30).

In order for compliance with the Lockean proviso to be rational, such compliance followed by an MRC-distribution of the benefits of cooperation must lead to a better outcome than the natural distribution. If agreements subjected to the Lockean constraint were to have worse results for me than my most effective non-cooperative strategy, then compliance with such agreement cannot be rational. Note that two concepts of "benefit" are at work here: the benefits that are shared according to MRC are benefits measured from the proviso point. It is only when such benefits are also benefits compared to the natural distribution that compliance with the proviso is required.

Graphically we can represent Gauthier's idea as in figure 2.1: the proviso point ("pp") represents the set of your utility and mine that we might expect in the absence of the other (or if we had nothing to do with each other). If we cooperated with pp as the initial bargaining point, and shared the benefits according to MRC, then the "proviso outcome" on the Pareto frontier would represent the utility distribution between us. The points marked nd1, nd2, and nd3 represent three possible natural distributions between us, and to each belongs

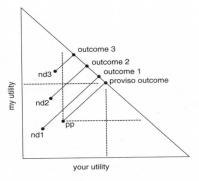

Figure 2.1. Proviso point and natural distribution

a Pareto optimal outcome that would occur if we cooperated, and shared according to MRC, with that natural distribution as the initial bargaining point. Gauthier's condition for rational compliance with the Lockean proviso can be stated as follows: if, and only if, the "proviso outcome" is Pareto superior to the natural distribution, is it rational to accept the proviso point as the initial bargaining point and hence rational to agree on the proviso outcome as the result from cooperation. In figure 2.1 this is the case if the natural distribution happens to be nd1 or nd2, since only then will compliance with the proviso be compatible with mutual advantage. The proviso outcome is not Pareto superior to nd3 however; in this case I would be the one to do worse by accepting pp as the basis for cooperation between us. Yet, both nd2 and nd3 as natural distributions are parasitic. They allow me a utility that is higher than it would have been in your absence, while your utility will be lower than it would have been in my absence. Only if nd2 is the natural distribution am I required to give up my parasitic gain as a prelude to cooperation. We may summarize: only if cooperation not preceded by parasitic action is better for me than parasitic action not followed by cooperation, am I required not to engage in parasitic action.

However, there appears to be an ambiguity in Gauthier's formulation of the requirement to comply. It is apparent when the natural distribution happens to be nd1. In nd1 our mutual investment in aggression has mutually worsened our positions compared to solitary existence, which means that neither of us has actually taken advantage of the other—though perhaps one or both of us has tried to do so. As neither of us is in actual violation of the proviso, why shouldn't we bargain from nd1? In that case, we would not accept an initial bargaining point, which reflects parasitic behavior prior to cooperation. A similar problem might arise if the natural distribution happens to be Pareto superior to the proviso point. This might occur, for instance, if two persons, otherwise unconnected, both unintentionally produce some external positive effect on each other, and yet arrive at a position that might be improved by cooperative strategies. Again, in that case, the natural distribution would not be parasitic and hence might seem to be unproblematic as an initial bargaining point. The response, I guess, must be the following: not being in actual violation of the proviso is not the same thing as having complied with the proviso. Gauthier's condition does not state that in order to proceed with MRC it is sufficient if all parties happen not to be in violation of the proviso, it requires that they accept bargaining results that coincide with MRC, and as if these were reached when proceeding from the proviso point. Gauthier often argues that the proviso requires agents to proceed from the "non-coercive non-cooperative point" and that certainly warrants this interpretation. Nd1 may not be predatory and parasitic, but it is (mutually) coercive. So, agents are required to accept pp as their initial bargaining position, even if the natural distribution is mutually harmful and not parasitic.

2.5 Acquiescence

What are rational cooperators required to do when Gauthier's condition for compliance with the Lockean proviso is not satisfied? Should they, in that case, proceed from the natural distribution? Should they accept the natural distribution as the initial bargaining point, just sharing cooperative benefits according to MRC from there? Not quite. It is for these cases that Gauthier introduces the notion of "acquiescence." Rationally acquiescent persons accept that in some cases (of extreme differences of power between them) mutual compliance with the proviso is not rationally attainable, but this does not mean that they will then just accept MRC-improvements of the natural distribution. Rational cooperators will still insist that cooperation is beneficial to them compared to the absence of the other. As we may say: they will accept that they are bargaining from the natural distribution, but they will no longer accept MRC as a bargaining principle. In figure 2.2 we can see such an extreme case.

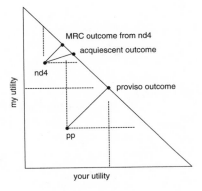

Figure 2.2. Acquiescence

If the natural distribution would relate to pp as in figure 2.2, the rationally acquiescent agent would accept that she could not bargain from pp. Yet she will not bargain for the "MRC outcome from nd4" either. Instead she will rationally insist that the outcome will allow her some improvement of utility compared to pp. Of course, a person's power disadvantage may be so extreme that even rational acquiescence is no longer helpful. If the natural distribution moves still further into the upper left corner of the outcome space it might just be that no cooperative outcome affording me benefit compared to the natural distribution would also afford you benefit compared to my absence. Sometimes we cannot both be glad that the other is a rational cooperator and also that he exists in the first place. Gauthier makes no comment on this possibility. Perhaps he despairs of the viability of cooperative efforts in such a case.

2.6 Scarcity, an Underdeveloped Part of the Theory

So far, we have only considered interactive situations where mutual improvements of the proviso position were technically possible. But what if cooperation could only improve the natural distribution to such a limited extent that neither would be as well off as, or better off than, he or she would have been without the other, in solitary existence. In that case pp would simply be non-existent; it would then be situated outside the outcome space of the interaction, as in figure 2.3.

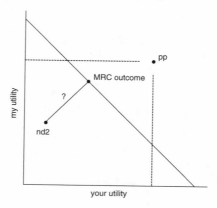

Figure 2.3. An extra-optimal proviso point

Clearly, in such a case, agents cannot comply with the Lockean proviso prior to cooperation (since pp is "extra-optimal," so to speak), and there are no feasible bargaining results between them that might be compatible with such compliance. Yet, nd is suboptimal and it would require cooperation to produce an outcome on the Pareto frontier. How should they proceed, and from where should they proceed? From nd? MRC-wise? One would expect this to be the solution under conditions of such severe scarcity that agents, through cooperation, will not even be able to improve on their proviso utility levels.

Even if we are both going to stay hungry anyway, we may still be rationally interested in preventing a fight over what little food there is. One would expect a theory of rational bargaining to provide a solution for all logically possible bargaining problems, and hence also for cases where the presence of company, even if fully cooperative, will be a burden rather than a benefit. But Gauthier leaves his theory underdeveloped in this respect. He tells us how the benefits of society ought to be rationally shared, but he does not tell us how the burden of company may be ameliorated through cooperation. Instead he more or less waves aside the real possibility of such restricted cooperative advantages and stipulates that our cooperative efforts can always be expected to leave us better off than we would have been in solitary existence. Seeing it otherwise would be seeing it like the Dobu:

> (...suppose that) the Dobu believe that the world offers only a fixed supply of the goods they treasure—primarily yams. The more yams in my garden, the fewer in yours. There is no place in the Dobuan scheme of things for co-operation directed at the increase of benefits, for more

yams cannot be grown... The Dobuan world may have its sophisticated
defenders.... But we shall suppose that the Dobuan view of the world is
false. And given variable supply we may be aware of each other as potential co-operators in increased production. (Gauthier 1986: 115–16)

Now, apart from the question of what experiences caused the Dobu to
entertain such a wildly exotic and false view of the scheme of things,
it seems to me that Gauthier is simply making an empirical claim here:
the possibility of proviso improvement is always present. Compared to
a solitary existence, society is always more beneficial than company is
burdensome.

But this claim is strong and unsatisfactory. Avoiding mutual nuisance
is as much a cooperative effort as finding mutual benefit. Suppose we
live along the borders of a lake and have nothing to do with each other
except for the fact that each of us throws our waste in the water. Thus,
together, we destroy the lake as a resource for the fish we like to eat.
We produce a public harm, which might be prevented by accepting
some sensible restriction in our polluting behavior. Are we now tied to
this suboptimal outcome because we cannot find a definition of what
a "sensible restriction" would be? Would cooperation only be viable if
it would secure each of us a utility at least as high as if we had been
alone and had the lake all to ourselves? Can the Dobu only cooperate
if each of them may expect a return at least equal to all the yams in all
the gardens, as each of them would have had if he had been the Dobu
island's sole inhabitant? If there were one thousand Dobu and one
thousand yams, would it be required that cooperation would result in
the production of at least 999,000 yams, for each Dobu to cooperate
rationally? If so, it seems too strong a condition. But if not, from which
point are the Dobu required to proceed in bargaining. What may each
of them regard as his private endowment? These are questions left open
by Gauthier's theory, but they deserve an answer.

However, for the present purpose of a further evaluation of Gauthier's argument I shall put such cases aside as well.

2.7 Compensating for Costs

So, for the sake of argument, let us assume that cooperation will "over-
take" the utility levels that any one of us might have expected in the
absence of partners. Have we now dismissed the problem of natural
scarcity? Not yet, I think. I will argue that the problem of scarce natural resources, the problem of how to divide them and how to establish

individual rights to them is not solved but, in a sense, complicated by the Lockean proviso. This can be brought out by considering the way in which Gauthier handles the problem of so-called (negative) externalities, that is: cases where agents' activities produce a cost to others. I believe he misconstrues the implication of the Lockean proviso for such cases.

Let me illustrate right away. Gauthier believes that compliance with the proviso, prior to cooperation, requires that agents shall "internalize" the costs of their activities, prior to cooperation. If we face the possibility of mutually beneficial cooperative outcomes compared to the natural distribution, then the actual distribution of cooperative benefits may not reflect my "natural" nuisance value to you, or vice versa. According to Gauthier we should proceed as follows: first I compensate you for the cost that I have imposed on you, then we proceed to cooperate and share the benefits according to MRC. Gauthier's own example is the following: we are to picture ourselves as "fisher folk" living alongside a river (Gauthier 1986: 223ff.). You live upstream, I live downstream. For some reason, it is profitable for me to buy some of your fish in addition to my own catch, and, as it happens, it is profitable for you to sell some. So there is a possibility of mutually beneficial trade between us. However, you dispose of the waste you produce by throwing it into the river; thus you pollute the part of the stream that I depend on so that I can catch fewer fish myself than I would have caught if you had not existed (or had lived somewhere else). And thus you also increase my demand for your fish, since that demand is dependent on what I can catch myself, so that you have changed the terms of trade between us to your own advantage. Now, in the language of the previous section, the natural distribution, in the absence of the prospect of cooperation, is the one permitting you to continue to pollute the downstream area. But if we cooperatively trade from that position and share the benefit according to MRC, then we will be trading from an initial bargaining position that is worse for me than it would have been in your absence. My gain in trading with you, though it may be some improvement compared to your absence, will not be an MRC-improvement compared to my position in your absence. Hence, the proviso is violated although the condition for the rationality of complying with it is satisfied. And hence you, the proviso violator, are required to compensate me for the pollution you produce. And you will comply with that requirement if you are rational. "If interaction is to be fully co-operative, it must proceed from an initial position in which costs are internalized, and so in which no person has the right to impose uncompensated costs on another" (Gauthier 1986: 225).

But there is something suspect (fishy?) about this conclusion. Suppose you do compensate me for the pollution you produce or you seek a more expensive non-polluting way of waste disposal (you may choose whichever alternative is cheaper); we then proceed to trade and share according to MRC. Have we now proceeded, by trading, from an initial distribution that allowed each of us a utility equal to the utility to be expected in the absence of the other? Of course not. You are now required to make costs (compensation, expensive methods for waste disposal) that would have been wholly uncalled for in my absence. Surely, you may still gain somewhat from trading with me, compared to my absence, but you will certainly not be gaining an MRC-share. So, if compliance with the Lockean proviso would imply that costs of activities that fall on others must be fully internalized, then those who pay the compensation will be bargaining with their fellows from a substantially worse position than the position in which they would have been without the other. The proviso, thus interpreted, would just switch the full weight of the burden of natural scarcity from "downstreamers" to "upstreamers." And that would introduce an entirely new problem between us because it would mean that living downstream is relatively cheap and living upstream relatively expensive. Downstreamers will be allowed to dispose of their waste as cheaply as they can, upstreamers will have to be cautious not to be a nuisance, or else they will have to pay compensation. How are we going to determine who shall live where? How are we going to determine who has the right to live where? What does the proviso tell us about these questions?

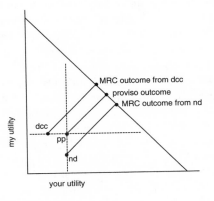

Figure 2.4. Internalizing costs

In figure 2.4 the point is illustrated: as before, pp represents our utilities as they would have been in the absence of the other, and nd represents the natural distribution as it would occur in the absence of the possibility of cooperation, in which case polluting the river would just be your non-cooperative equilibrium strategy. Dcc represents the utility distribution with compensated costs, that is: the distribution that results if you internalize all costs of your activities that fall on me. Nd is worse for me than pp, but dcc is worse for you than pp. If the proviso implied the requirement to compensate prior to cooperation, it would simply reverse the asymmetry of the natural distribution. So it turns out that the cost-internalization requirement cannot be consistent with the requirement to proceed from an initial position allowing each a utility as high as one could have expected in the absence of the other.

Instead, consistency would require that we proceed from pp. However, we cannot proceed from pp. Pp has no physical existence. There is no way that we can both use the river in such a way that both of us are equally well off as we would have been in the absence of the other. The river, as a provider of fish and as a waste dump, is scarce between us, and that fact cannot be altered because there exists a possibility of mutually advantageous trade between us.

It seems we have a persistent problem of externalities. The requirement to fully internalize their costs is not consistent with the Lockean proviso, but neither is there another way of distributing endowments such that the proviso is satisfied prior to negotiations between us.

Now, the reader may feel that I am being too formalistic in my treatment of Gauthier's doctrine here: even though, admittedly, the cost-internalization requirement is not consistent with the proviso, and even though, admittedly, we cannot really proceed from a distribution of endowments in external objects which is consistent with the proviso, we may, and should, accept a bargaining result that reflects compliance with the proviso nevertheless. We should in fact proceed in such a fashion that a Pareto optimal distribution results between us as if we had proceeded MRC-wise from the proviso point. After transaction the upstreamer should pay "compensation" to the downstreamer such that the net distributive result in revenues will be equal to the MRC outcome as it would have been if reached from pp.

I will grant this objection. But I have insisted on splitting some hairs here because I believe that the point is related to a really substantive issue: if the opportunities for use provided by so-called "natural resources" are seriously restricted, such as in the case of the river as a fishing opportunity and a waste dump, then individual property or use rights to such resources cannot be distributed without reference to the bargaining power that such rights would allow their owners. Resources being scarce, there is no way that individual rights can be defined, distributed, or justified, without taking account of the effect that such rights will have on the actual final outcome of cooperative or market processes. Where such outcomes would divert from MRC applied to an (only virtually existent) proviso point, there it must be the case that the distribution of rights has allowed some too much bargaining power, and others too little. The "cost-internalization" requirement—you bother me, you pay me—would have been an easy way around this problem if it had been consistent with the proviso. But it is not. The following picture would be far too simple to capture the implications of the proviso. Initially we divide the world in such a fashion that no one takes advantage of another, and that no two persons are in each other's way, so that each is endowed with those things he would have enjoyed in the absence of the others. And then we let people, so endowed, enter a mutually beneficial cooperative or market relation. There is no such initial division of the world. We may think of "private endowments" in a concrete fashion as the rights that are uncontroversially ours independently of what we (intend to) do with them, from which we may deprive all others if we so wish, and which we may give up in exchange for desirable goods or services that others have in their legitimate control. But the Lockean proviso will exclude such a sphere of individual "sovereignty" in external objects. To be more precise: the Lockean proviso will restrict the notion of private property to just those things the possession of which does not and cannot worsen the position of another person compared to my absence. Hence, it will restrict the right to private property to my own person in the narrow sense of those things that would have been absent in my absence. All other things in my "possession" are potentially subject to evaluation in the light of the bargaining or market power they allow me.

The effects of state-of-nature scarcity may be overcome by the enormous gains of cooperation. Adam Smith's analysis of the gains from labor division (1,000 pins!) strongly suggests this. Indeed it is the claim underlying Gauthier's criticism of the Dobu philosophy of life. But that fact in itself will not resolve any conflict over natural resources. In anticipation of the gains of cooperation state-of-nature scarcity may reappear in a perhaps even more ferocious conflict over resources as resources of bargaining power. And, according to the theory under consideration here, this conflict can only be settled rationally by reference to economic outcomes. "Initial" rights over external assets can only be defined in the light of an evaluation of the justice of economic outcomes that makes use of the proviso. The justice of economic outcomes determines the justice of individual rights, not vice versa. This I believe to be an important implication of Gauthier's theory, and one, which, perhaps, he has not fully appreciated himself. For one thing it brings him somewhat closer to the Marxist view of the collective ownership of the means of production (if we take resources in that way), somewhat closer than his quasi-libertarian vocabulary often suggests, and I surmise, also somewhat closer than he might like to be. I shall return to this matter in section 2.11, where I want to discuss Gauthier's remarks about so-called "original acquisition," and about the "evanescence of rights."

Intermezzo: The Shadow of Tort Law

Before turning to Gauthier's arguments as to why it would be rational to comply with the Lockean proviso, I would like to demonstrate the relevance of my last two points for the reality of a legal system. The first of these points was that the problem of the real (Dobu-type) scarcity of so-called external opportunities cannot be neglected, the second point was that Gauthier's requirement of full cost internalization is arbitrary and not warranted by the Lockean proviso. I will briefly discuss how the problem of negative externalities has been treated in the so-called law and economics tradition, notably the application of economic insights to tort law. It may further illuminate the type of problem we are concerned with.

Consider an example that is used by A. M. Polinsky (discussed and quoted in Bottomley and Parker 1997: 301, 302) to illustrate how the so-called Coase theorem works for interactions involving no transaction costs. A factory pollutes the air by its emissions of smoke, dirtying the laundry that neighboring residents leave to dry in the open air. Depending on the liabilities as specified by the law of torts, these damages may have to be fully internalized by either the factory or its neighbors. But there may also be several cheaper ways to solve the problem, e.g. the factory may install a smokescreen in its chimney or the residents may use electric dryers. In that case the liabilities, and this was one of Coase's basic insights, will determine who will pay for the cheapest of these solutions. In case the residents are liable and if the smokescreen is cheaper than the dryers, the residents will buy the smokescreen for the factory; otherwise they will buy dryers for themselves. If, on the other hand, the factory is liable while the smokescreen is cheaper, it will install the smokescreen; otherwise, it will buy dryers for the residents. No matter how the liability is assigned by law, the available resources (air, smokescreen, dryers) will be used in the same way, namely the way that is most efficient. The only thing that is determined by the legal liability is how the costs and benefits of these uses will be allocated between the factory and its neighbors. As Polinsky concludes: "[T]he choice of legal rule redistributes income by the amount of the least-cost solution to the problem."

But we must be very careful not to misread Polinsky's discussion of the case and his conclusion. They might be taken to suggest that Coase's theorem implies that the liable party will never pay more than the exact price of the least-cost solution (given, of course, that transaction costs are indeed zero). And that would be a mistaken inference. Assume, to use Polinsky's figures, that the aggregate damages to the laundry would be $375, that the smokescreen would cost $150 to install, and that the electric dryers would cost $250. Let us now look what would happen if there were no legal right to clean air, so that the residents would have to find their cheapest way out of the problem. Naturally they would want to buy the smokescreen for the factory. So much is obviously true. But the factory knows that if it refuses to install and use the smokescreen, the residents will have to buy the dryers in order to avoid the damages. By agreeing to have the smokescreen installed, the factory allows the residents to gain $100 compared to their next best alternative, while the factory itself will gain nothing by being cooperative. Now what kind of rational agreement would that be? The factory would merely do its neighbors a $100 favor, and nothing in the law of torts seems to imply that it should do so. Is not the factory still the legal owner of its own facilities, including its chimney, and should it not therefore be the factory, and nobody else, who shall determine whether or not an additional device will be installed in its chimney? The factory has the right to deny the smokescreen. And if it is smart enough, the factory will be aware of this and try to bargain for a share of those $100 that would be gained if it complies with the residents' wishes. And the residents, if they are smart enough, should be ready to pay a certain sum in addition to the cost of the smokescreen to induce the factory to actually install it.

But clearly, in that case, the residents, being the liable party, would pay substantially more than the price of the least-cost solution, the difference being a parasitic benefit for the factory, to which it would not have had access in the absence of its neighbors with their need for clean clothes. Taken in Coase's way, then, legal liabilities do not just tell us who should pay for damages that follow from interactions under natural conditions of scarcity or for the real cost of avoiding them. With the relevant "inviolable" property rights in the background, tort law fixes the bargaining positions of the parties in such a manner that, depending on the circumstances, some may successfully seek to exploit the others (note that the residents would have been in a position to exploit the factory if the relative prices of the smokescreen and the dryers as well as the liabilities were reversed). In such cases, then, the law of torts would have nothing to do with the intuitive idea that the burden of company must be legally allocated somewhere, and that we may trust the market, operating "in the shadow of the law," to reduce that burden anyhow.

But as in earlier cases, one would hope that the exploited residents would be able to find a court, sensitive to the idea of the abuse of rights, that would not go along with those who want to turn the law of torts into an instrument for taking advantage of others. Such a court would rule that the factory ought to accept the installation of the smokescreen, now that the residents have offered to pay for it in full. Thus, the factory would be enabled to continue its activities unaffected by the interaction, no gains, no losses, while the residents would be allowed to minimize the harm inflicted on them. But, reasonable as such a tort-related constraint on market behavior may seem, it is rather depressing to find that the master himself, Ronald Coase does not quite seem to share this view of how the law should ideally operate.

In his famous article "The Problem of Social Cost" (Coase 1960), he sets out by opposing the traditional view (that is Pigou's view) that harms should always and fully be paid for by those who inflict them. Coase rightly identifies the standard problem (of negative externalities) as one "of a reciprocal nature," explaining that if we do not allow A to inflict a harm on B, we inflict a harm on A. This should remind us of my earlier criticism of Gauthier's argument for the full internalization of negative externalities.

By professional nature, economists, it seems, are aggregationists of some sort (income, utility), so Coase subsequently states (but does not argue) that the real problem for the legislator of torts is to avoid the more serious harm. Then follows the argument that, with zero transaction costs involved, this more serious harm will be avoided anyway, by which I assume we may infer that in such cases there would be no grounds for finding a particular assignment of liabilities more "socially desirable" than another. But Coase uses an example that should puzzle us, as it is even starker than the one already encountered, in its exploitative implications, and therefore also because it highlights a fatal ambiguity of this very phrase: "the more serious harm."

The case in question involves, again, neighbors: a rancher raising cattle and a farmer growing crops. Damages may result from straying cattle trespassing on the farmer's property, destroying the crops, and it so happens that the law stipulates that the cattle-raiser is responsible and that he should compensate the farmer for the value of the crops his herd destroys. Coase considers the following possibility.

> Suppose...that the value of the crop that would be obtained by cultivating this strip of land would be $10 but that the cost of cultivating it is $11. *In the absence of the cattle-raiser*, the land would not be cultivated. However, given the presence of the cattle-raiser, it could well be that if the strip was cultivated, the whole crop would be destroyed by the cattle. In which case, the cattle-raiser would be forced to pay $10 to the farmer. It is true that the farmer would lose $1. But the cattle raiser would lose $10.... The aim of the farmer would be to induce the cattle-raiser to make a payment in return for an agreement to leave this land uncultivated. (Coase 1960: 4, my italics)

He then points out that the bargaining space that the farmer seeks to ascertain for himself would, of course, be constrained by the income the cattle-raiser makes of his activities and by the cost of the cattle-raiser's alternatives for avoiding the damages (such as fencing his property), but if space remains within such restrictions, "what payment would in fact be made would depend on the shrewdness of the farmer and the cattle-raiser as bargainers." Upon which the conclusion follows that the liability as assigned by law will again not obstruct the achievement of the most efficient, or least socially costly, use of the available resources: whatever the bargaining result, no fence will be built, no crops will be grown, and cattle will be raised.

But how should we assess the claim that the "more serious harm" will be avoided by this legal arrangement? What is the harm in this case to begin with? Did not Coase tell us that the farmer's land was in fact worthless to him, since it was more costly for him to cultivate it than the value he could obtain by selling the crops, so that in fact he did not suffer any harm at all from his neighbor's trespassing cattle? It would seem, then, that the cattle-raiser's activities in Coase's example are perfectly harmless, in any plausible sense of the word "harm," and that a requirement for him to "compensate" his victim would be absurd, since there is no victim. There is no harm, let alone serious harm. There are no negative externalities, and this is not a case in which forbidding A to harm B would imply harming A.

The cattle-raiser's liability enables the farmer to force the cattle-raiser to pay him for stopping to do something that he would not have done unless he would be paid for stopping to do it. Do you still follow? The only harm that can be identified in this case is a harm that is produced by the law of torts, not avoided, if it assigns liabilities in this particular (silly) way: it is the harm inflicted by the farmer on the cattle-raiser in enforcing a unilateral net transfer of value. And it is a harm to the cattle-raiser that would only be avoided by a law assigning the liabilities the other way around, which would not thereby inflict a harm on the farmer (and which would, in the aggregate, be equally efficient, as Coase recognizes). Again, the "farmer" in Coase's example is a parasite, who, on Coase's own interpretation of it, would be legally empowered to turn the formal liability of his neighbor into an instrument of taking advantage, and this time he need not merely refuse to cooperate as the factory did in not allowing the installment of the smokescreen. In order to cash out his "market position," he must actually (threaten to) engage in an activity—growing crops—that would be wholly unproductive, considered in itself, exactly like Pickles's diversion of the stream.

So, the law of torts may have a shadow indeed, if by that we mean a dark side. I offer the *shadow theorem*:

> Whenever the liable party requires the non-liable party's agreement to implement the least-cost solution, the liable party will be exploitable, even in the absence of negative externalities, if the non-liable party's market behavior is legally unconstrained.

The theorem might carry some weight with the legislator. He might try to constrain the non-liable party's market behavior in the manner already indicated, or he might want to assign liabilities in such a way as to reduce exploitative opportunities to begin with, that is to assign liability to the party who has the private power to realize the least-cost solution without the consent of the other.

There is, however, also some consolation for the aggregationist. Assigning liability to the party who has the private power to realize the least-cost solution avoids exploitation, which is desirable with or without transaction costs involved, but in many real-life situations it would also have the further advantage of avoiding transaction costs that might actually exist if the other party were liable, since in that case bargaining would be necessary to achieve the most effective use of the available resources, and bargaining may cost substantial amounts of time and resources. That procedure would therefore not be most cost-effective. This is already apparent in Coase's own example: the losses the farmer and the cattle-raiser suffer before they reach an agreement about the payment that should stop the farmer from growing crops would have been avoided if the farmer had been liable from the beginning. In the long run, outcomes will be efficient in any case, which is Coase's point, but some runs are longer than others. Avoiding exploitation and realizing aggregate efficiency may therefore both point in the direction of an adjudicating principle like: whenever a least-cost solution is available, assign liability to the party who may realize it privately.

But let us put aside speculation for the moment. Fortunately, there is some good news from practice. Robert Ellickson (1991) has conducted a very thorough and interesting study of how neighboring ranchers and farmers in fact handle liability problems that are connected with the damages resulting from trespassing cattle. In Shasta County (California) he found, in otherwise similar conditions, two formal tort regimes next to each other: either the ranchers or the farmers were legally required to internalize the damages or to bear the cost of avoiding them by putting up and maintaining fences between their properties. But he also found that independently of the legal stipulations, neighbors would quite consistently fail to appeal to the law and preferred to resolve their disputes according to informal norms of "good neighborliness," almost always implying that, where cattle trespasses were serious, the costs of fencing would be shared, e.g. one of them supplying the materials, the other doing, or hiring, the labor. Non-compliers with these and other such informal norms, according to Ellickson, would have to fear for their reputations and were mainly held in check by a sophisticated machinery of gossip.

Ellickson's explanation of these reciprocal settlements, constituting a stable social order "beyond the shadow of the law" (and apparently violating Coase's predictions), was that neighbors tend to need each other on other, future, occasions, and that maintaining a cooperative attitude, even where the legal system would not require it, would still in the long run pay off for all. Another explanation, compatible with my earlier observations of what the Lockean proviso would require in the face of natural scarcity (but not therefore incompatible with Ellickson's explanation), might be that neighbors realize that the law of torts tends to arbitrarily put the full burden of company, and perhaps even more than that, on one of the parties' shoulders, and that they fail to see the reason as to why a problem of a reciprocal nature should be resolved in such an arbitrary way. Neighbors in general may have, more acutely than the judiciary, a sense of proviso-related fairness, which not only keeps them from exploiting the law in order to exploit each other but also actually induces their willingness to share social costs.

To sum up the results so far: we have identified Gauthier's condition for the rationality of compliance with the Lockean proviso—it must be compatible with mutual benefit compared to the natural distribution. We have detected one fallacious generalization of the requirement to comply with the proviso: it does not require us to compensate for all costs that fall on others. And, along the way, we have pointed out some problems related to the scarcity of natural resources. Of course, we have not yet discussed why, the relevant condition being satisfied, it would be rational to comply with the Lockean proviso. We know the when of rational compliance, not yet the why of its rationality. Let us now turn to that question.

2.8 The Rationality of Compliance, 1: No Invitations

In the opening sections of his chapter on the Lockean proviso (ch. 7), Gauthier argues against James Buchanan's view that rationally acceptable cooperative outcomes must reflect an underlying natural distribution (Buchanan 1975: 75). Considering such agreements, Gauthier says:

> [C]learly an individual would be irrational if she were to dispose herself to comply, voluntarily, with an agreement reached in this way. Someone disposed to comply with agreements that left untouched the fruits of predation would simply invite others to engage in predatory and coercive activities as a prelude to bargaining. She would permit the successful predators to reap where they had ceased to sow, to continue to profit from the effects of natural predation after entering into agreements freeing them from the need to invest in further predatory effort. (Gauthier 1986: 195)

It is irrational to be disposed to comply with agreements in a way that invites others to manipulate the initial bargaining point in anticipation of such agreement. This I take to be the essence of the argument, which I shall therefore call the "no-invitation argument." It is an argument for rationally insisting on compliance with the proviso. Of course, an argument for the rationality of insisting that others, successful predators, comply is not yet in itself an argument for the successful predators to comply. The completing step, suppressed in the passage above, but explicit in Gauthier's theory of rationality throughout, is that if it cannot be rational for one agent to accept a certain bargaining outcome, then neither can it be rational for the other. One's rationality must be compatible with the rationality of the others. Rationality, if shared, cannot fail to determine an outcome to agree on. We shall return to this argument in more detail in the next section. So, given that agreements reached from the natural distribution would not be rationally acceptable for those who are victimized in the natural distribution, it cannot be rationally acceptable for those who are the victimizers in the natural distribution either.

It may seem plausible that one should not, by a permissive attitude in bargaining, invite others to predate or coerce, but unfortunately the no-invitation argument fails to exclude what it explicitly purports to exclude, namely the natural distribution as an initial bargaining position. Why is this so? Well, let us consider again how the natural distribution is defined. It is the distribution that the agents will reach if they play their non-cooperative equilibrium strategies, as they will do when no agreement is possible. Hence, it is also the distribution they will reach when there is no question of invitations to manipulate bargaining points, since, by definition, in the absence of the possibility of agreements to cooperate no account can be taken of (potential) bargaining advantages. True enough, the natural distribution will come about as the result of a struggle, and it will allow the strugglers differential bargaining powers. But the no-invitation argument proceeds on the assumption that the natural distribution comes about as the result of a struggle for bargaining power. And this is not true.

How then could it be that the natural distribution reflects the agents' anticipation of bargaining results? It cannot. Non-cooperative distributions that may be reached with an eye on one's bargaining power in a subsequent deal with other agents cannot be what we have called the natural distribution. I am not saying that such distributions do not exist, or that they should not be ruled out by the bargainers' rationality; the claim is only that they cannot be described as the natural distribution. The non-cooperative equilibrium as such cannot reflect people's strategic considerations in bargaining.

One convincing example to support my objection against the no-invitation argument is provided by Gauthier himself. We discussed it in the previous section. You worsen my bargaining position because you, living upstream, pollute the fishing waters that I, living downstream, depend on. Because of your activity, I need to purchase more fish, which allows you a greater advantage in bargaining with

me. But has my willingness to buy (more of) your fish invited you
to pollute the stream? No. You just do it. For you it is the cheapest
way to get rid of your waste, and the unintended, hence uninvited,
effect of your non-cooperative behavior is that it allows you additional gain in trading with me. The anticipation of that gain is not
what motivated you to pollute in the first place. In this case you have
won the "struggle" for the scarce opportunities of the stream (as a
dump and as a provider of fish) at no cost to yourself at all—you
being conveniently settled upriver—but that is a particularity of the
example which is of no conceptual consequence. Equilibrium strategies are just those strategies one rationally chooses in the absence
of cooperation.

So the no-invitation argument may exclude a number of distributions as suitable initial bargaining positions, but the natural distribution
is not among them. And it certainly does not pin down the proviso
point as the rationally acceptable initial bargaining point. The suggestion from the latter inference would be that in the absence of the possibility to cooperate agents would have nothing to do with each other,
or would have no motives at all to coerce each other. Of course, this
might be the case accidentally, e.g. in the complete absence of natural
scarcity, but it would be a matter of empirical contingency if the proviso position happened to coincide with the natural distribution. There
is no reason to assume such coincidence, and anyway, the assumption
would do no work conceptually unless we could argue for some systematic identification of people's proviso positions with state-of-nature
relations between them.

We know of one man, however, who tried to argue for such a
systematic identification: John Locke. And perhaps, then, we find an
echo here of Locke's rosy view of the peace and quiet of the state of
nature—so markedly different from Hobbes's view. For, after all, it was
Locke who believed that without our anticipation of the possibility of
hoarding up gold and silver, that is before the invention of money (and
money is but instant agreement), there would be neither reason nor
occasion to be in any other man's way. Previously, all gain beyond one's
immediate consumptive needs would decay, so why bother to coerce
others in the pursuit of more? Indeed, in his conception of the history
of mankind, people were moved to controversy, "invited" to engage in
fights over resources, only in anticipation of getting a (lion's) share in
the benefits of cooperation. Scarcity would thus be generated by the
prospect of cooperation, and therefore, scarcity and conflict would be
characteristic of society, not of natural man.

Of course, there is something disturbing, and romantic, in Locke's idea that we cannot be united for mutual benefit without at once loosing our "natural" innocence. Money makes us rich, but it perverts everything else. Progress, not poverty, breeds the "bellum omnium contra omnes," and the need for tough moral constraint. If we are "wolves" to one another, then it is only because we are so wealthy.[6]

Romantic or not, the Lockean view does not strike me as completely absurd. Although it is certainly too far-fetched to assume that conflict over natural resources would be completely absent in (or between) societies with a low level of labor division and with little interdependent specialization in productive activities, it is also obvious to see that economic progress consisting in the development of an ever more complicated and successful fabric of mutually beneficial relations will disclose new areas of conflicting interests. If all the world were merely involved in what Marx called "petty production," primarily self-supportive activities with no division of labor extending beyond the members of the family or at most to the members of small village communities, one might expect some conflict over things like land, timber, pastures, fishing and hunting grounds, but the warfare that we are acquainted with over oil or mineral resources, or, for that matter, the struggle for outlets, presupposes an enormous increase in the scale of cooperative interdependency. It presupposes *vergesellschaftlichte Arbeit*. No small community or family or individual can afford to drill for oil or dig for iron on its own and just for its own consumption. That would simply require a larger investment of labor, to be withdrawn from self-supportive food production, than small communities can manage. It makes no sense to hold, or to contest, a claim to an oil field, and invest labor in its exploitation, unless such a claim gives access, perhaps privileged access, to profitable trade relations with others. One wants oil fields because one wants to sell oil, not because one needs all the oil for oneself and one's next of kin. In making such claims, then, one seeks to establish an advantageous bargaining position, and one is "invited" to do so by other people's readiness to buy.

Note that the Lockean claim here is considerably stronger than Gauthier's claim about the Dobu being wrong in their view of the world, as we reported in section 2.6. There we showed that Gauthier explicitly assumes that, however miserable the natural distribution, cooperators will always be able to improve on what they could expect as solitary beings. This is, as we showed, a presupposition of the feasibility of complying with the proviso as an initial bargaining point. But the stronger Lockean claim, which is nowhere endorsed by Gauthier, identifies the natural distribution with the proviso distribution, and hence implies that people in the state of nature would be as well off as when in a solitary existence.[7] And that claim is required as a presupposition of the rationality of complying with the proviso, at least if the no-invitation argument is going to work.

The no-invitation argument will only select the proviso point as the rationally acceptable bargaining point as a matter of coincidence, that is: if we conveniently stipulate, as Locke did, or show empirically, as Locke did not, that the natural distribution and the proviso distribution must coincide. But Gauthier cannot have access to these conveniences because, in arguing explicitly against Buchanan's proposal, he is trying to give us reasons to accept the proviso point instead of the natural distribution as the initial bargaining point. He rightly regards them as conceptually distinct. It is certainly odd to argue that x ought to be accepted instead of y on the (suppressed) assumption that x and y are the same thing.

I conclude that, so far, Gauthier has not given an argument for the rationality of compliance with the Lockean proviso. He has given an argument not to submit to people who, by coercive or other methods, seek to establish their own greater bargaining (or market) power, in the expectation of a greater advantage from a subsequent deal. But people who play their non-cooperative equilibrium strategy prior to negotiation and agreement are just not doing that.

The implication is not that the no-invitation argument is without significance. Bargaining power or market power, e.g. in the form of exclusive rights to oil reserves or mineral resources, is indeed what people are often fighting about, and if the no-invitation argument is valid, then rationality would put an end to that type of fight. Indeed, the first feature of a rational system of individual rights, moral or legal, would seem to be that it should not allow, let alone invite and encourage, their bearers to do what Mr. Pickles of Bradford did: exploit one's maximum nuisance value. But Pickles was not playing his equilibrium strategy. His diversion of the stream would have made no sense at all in the absence of the prospect of cooperation. The no-invitation argument implies that the community of Bradford should have rationally disposed itself to non-cooperation with farmer Pickles. Bradford should have refused to buy him off, and this in itself may seem to be a very strong claim.[8] As such however, that claim would support compliance with the natural distribution as an initial bargaining point, not with the Lockean proviso.

2.9 The Rationality of Compliance, 2:
Equal Concessions

In order to fully appreciate Gauthier's second argument for the rationality of complying with the Lockean proviso (provided such compliance would be compatible with advantage compared to the natural distribution), it is necessary to discuss some features of his theory of rational agreement in more detail. We explained that the principle of minimax relative concession (MRC) requires that contributions to the cooperative effort should relate to the benefits obtained in the same way for each person. In bargaining no rational person can be expected to make a larger concession than another rational person. So, if we have a point from which we can measure each person's benefit and each person's contribution, MRC will tell us how contributions and benefits ought to relate to each other with respect to that point. That point, the initial bargaining point, provides us with a measure of benefit and contribution, and with a measure of the concessions that are made in bargaining. Benefits, contributions, and concessions are defined relative to the initial bargaining point, but the position of that point itself may be anywhere. That is to be determined separately. MRC itself tells us nothing about the place of the rationally acceptable initial bargaining point. It only tells us how to proceed rationally relative to that point. In arguing for MRC Gauthier puts the position of the initial bargaining point between brackets, so to speak. The determination of the initial bargaining point is a matter of the so-called external rationality of bargaining, and once we have established such a point the determination of a Pareto optimal outcome is a matter of the internal rationality of bargaining.

Given the rational acceptability of the initial bargaining position rational cooperators will comply with MRC only. They are disposed to so-called "narrow compliance" and not to "broad compliance." The broadly compliant cooperator is ready and willing to cooperate on any terms as long as his position is somewhat improved compared to the initial bargaining point. But broad compliance, says Gauthier, cannot be rational. If it were rational to be prepared to make larger concessions in bargaining than the others do, it would be rational for the others to dispose themselves to being less than broadly compliant, and this is excluded by the assumption that they are equally rational. "[S]ince no person chooses to constrain his behavior for its own sake, no person finds it rational to be more compliant than his fellows. Equal rationality demands equal compliance. Since broad compliance is not rational for everyone, it is not rational for anyone" (Gauthier 1986: 178ff., 226).

Equal compliance can only be compliance with cooperative outcomes that reflect relative concessions as defined by MRC.

Let us now look at how Gauthier makes his second attempt to argue for the rationality of accepting the proviso point as the initial bargaining position. He again considers the fisher folk along the stream, one of whom is polluting the waters of the other, prior to a mutually advantageous trade between them. Suppose the polluter refuses to comply with the proviso, and goes on polluting, even though such compliance would be compatible with mutual advantage compared to the natural distribution. In that case, says Gauthier, "The particular interaction cannot then be defended by relating it to a practice that satisfies minimax relative concession. Hence it violates the requirement, fundamental to rational co-operation, of mutual benefit proportionate to contribution" (Gauthier 1986: 225). But there is an obvious fallacy in this move: if we bargain from the natural distribution, then, Gauthier says, MRC will be violated. Benefits will not relate to contributions for each in the same way. Those who are victimized by the natural distribution get disproportionate benefits from cooperation. But how can he say that? "Benefits" and "contributions" were to be measured relative to a yet-to-be-determined (rationally acceptable) initial bargaining point, and now these very concepts of benefit and contribution are used to determine the initial bargaining point itself. If we measure benefits and contributions relative to point x (say the natural distribution) and proceed to share them MRC-wise, then MRC will be violated. Surely this is no good. The principle of minimax relative concession leaves us helpless if we do not already have a fixed point relative to which we can define benefits and contributions. We cannot first put the initial bargaining point between brackets in order to define a rational method of proceeding, and then, miraculously, use the rational method of proceeding as a device in determining from where to proceed.

Gauthier conflates the external rationality and the internal rationality of bargaining, but he really thinks he is doing the trick. He repeatedly argues that compliance with the Lockean proviso is a matter of being narrowly compliant, of not making larger concessions than others, which is rational.

> [A] person disposed to narrow compliance expects others to adhere, and to consider it rational to adhere, to the proviso as a condition of co-operation. But then, given equal rationality, he must consider it rational to adhere himself to the proviso as a condition of co-operation. The disposition to narrow compliance thus includes the disposition to accept the proviso as constraining natural interaction, in so far as one has the

expectation of entering into society, into market and co-operative practices. (Gauthier 1986: 226)

But, again, the notion of narrow compliance itself, and of broad compliance too, makes no sense at all, if we do not already have an established point from which to measure how compliant the bargainers are in making concessions to each other. One is narrowly compliant if one accepts no less than MRC-proportionate divisions of benefits and contributions, and if one does not allow others the lion's share of the fruits of cooperation. Only MRC-proportionate divisions of the cooperative surplus are compatible with the assumption of mutual rationality. But the notion of narrow compliance cannot all by itself imply that benefits should be defined as benefits relative to the proviso point. Narrowly compliant persons would still not know what to do unless they were provided with an independently established, that is: independently argued for, initial bargaining point. Even if it may be true that it is rational to be narrowly compliant,[9] it has not been established that narrow compliance involves compliance with the proviso. Hence the rationality of compliance with the proviso has not been demonstrated.

2.10 Rationality and Moral Principle

Let there be no misunderstanding. Moral persons may have the strong intuition that the Lockean proviso is an obvious constraint on the outcomes of cooperative and market interactions, and they may well agree with Gauthier's repeated insistence that such a constraint would be impartial. A fine type of "cooperation" it would be which left you worse off than you would have been as a Robinson Crusoe. A nice type of "commonwealth-market" it would be, if its invisible hand invisibly threw you out of your fatherland, taking you away from your friends and relatives to start all over again in the state of nature of America (having paid for the trip yourself). Indeed, one would want to erect a system of individual rights, fixing endowments and bargaining strength for each in such a fashion that economic outcomes cannot reflect predatory and coercive activities, or even unintended nuisance. If, somehow, we are committed to a view of society as a "mutually advantageous" enterprise, then it is quite plausible to take "advantage" to mean "advantage compared to one's non-coerced and non-predated position." And if, on top of that, we have a notion of the fair sharing of advantage, then again, we must mean fairness in improving our positions while taking the absence of coercion for granted. Indeed, this book is dedicated to an effort to exploit the strength of this view and test it against some more or less recent proposals in the theory of distributive justice.

But such an intuitive status of the Lockean proviso would not be good enough for Gauthier. He is trying to build a road from Hobbes to Locke. He is trying to argue for the rationality of compliance with the Lockean proviso, and he cannot assume its moral force without arguing that rational utility maximizers would accept its constraint. "If the reader is tempted to object to some part of this view, on the ground that his moral intuitions are violated, then he should ask what weight such an objection can have, if morality is to fit within the domain of rational choice" (Gauthier 1986: 269).

In trying to argue for this "fit," Gauthier has defined "cooperation" in game theoretical terms as conditional adherence or commitment to a joint strategy, optimizing outcomes compared to the equilibrium outcomes of non-cooperative choices. But the idea of "solitary existence" relative to which he now wants to define rationally acceptable cooperative outcomes has itself no game theoretical interpretation. Nor are the expressions "coercion" or "predation" game theoretical qualifications for types of strategy. If we replace the sentence "he hit me on the head and I kicked his leg" with "he chose strategy A and I chose strategy B," and the sentence "I have a bloody nose, and he has a scratch on his knee" with "the distribution of utilities between us is (x, y)," then the replacements will not allow us to read the strategies as "mutually coercive" or the outcome as sub-proviso. Game theory relates outcomes to strategies in morally neutral terms, and under the assumption that the players are rational and know these outcomes, game theory allows one to read from the matrix how each will fare if they do not cooperate, and how each might fare if they manage to correlate on some joint strategy. But you cannot read from the matrix how each of the players would have fared without the other. The matrix only provides interdependent pay-offs. Perhaps this is the most fundamental problem in trying to argue for the rationality of compliance with the Lockean proviso. In order to do so, you cannot stick to a purely game theoretical analysis of interactive problems, you have to admit material from outside the matrix in a "thick" description of the problem and demonstrate the vital significance of that material for the rational actor. Demonstrating such significance is no easy task.

2.11 The Evanescence of Rights

I concluded section 2.7 with the observation that the Lockean proviso can only justify individual rights to scarce natural resources in the light of the bargaining or market power that such rights would allow agents to have against each other. The outcome of cooperative practices should coincide with the result of the principle of minimax relative concession when proceeding from the proviso distribution of utilities, even if the proviso distribution of utilities itself cannot actually be realized ex ante, which means: even if it is not possible to endow each with the enjoyment of everything she would have enjoyed in the absence of her cooperative partners. The scarce opportunities provided by the river as a waste dump and as a fishing ground were an illustration of the point. The right to use the river as one would have done in the absence of the other cannot be part of the endowment of both the upstreamer and the downstreamer. If the downstreamer is allotted such a right, then the upstreamer's bargaining position is worsened compared to his proviso position, and vice versa. So if it makes sense to speak about endowments at all, it appears that, in cases like these, endowments must consist in restricted and non-exclusive use rights, where the (mutual) restrictions reflect the other's bargaining interest. In other words: scarce resources ought to be shared. And they ought to be shared in such a fashion that the "balance of bargaining power" between the agents will be the same as it would have been in the absence of scarcity. And it follows immediately that the only morally relevant differences between agents, which the Lockean proviso will allow to determine the outcomes of cooperative and market interactions are differences in their persons. All speculation about private property in external resources, and the way that it should be established, is made redundant by the proviso. If we would agree with Robert Nozick (1974: 171) that "[t]he central core of the notion of a property right in X, relative to which other parts of the notion are to be explained, is the right to determine what shall be done with X," then there can only exist property rights to personal talents and capacities, and to the things that are directly produced through them, but not to any of the world's conveniences that have an existence independent of our own. Such things can never be part of the endowments with which we enter the market or cooperative interactions, and the right to use or exploit them, even if we exploit them in the market to the advantage of all, will always be subject to a (re)examination in light of the fairness of our bargaining position. The proviso establishes "self-ownership," but that is all. The familiar method of arguing from self-ownership to the ownership of things other than the self cannot be supported by the proviso—quite the contrary.

It is not obvious to me that Gauthier is always fully aware of these implications of the Lockean proviso. At times he appears to support the more or less classic "principle of original acquisition," which would best be described as "first come—first served", and indeed he believes that a system of exclusive property rights is in fact a prerequisite for mutually beneficial market relations.

The idea is that Eve, a member of a community of several individuals who are using a "commons," is the first "appropriator" of a part of that commons who claims it for her own exclusive use. Will she be violating the proviso? That depends. Although Eve may force (some of) the others who previously used her share to transact with her now, this need not worsen their position. Since she invests in her property, improves it by her "more intensive cultivation" and makes it more productive than it used to be, it may well be that the others, now trading with her, are at least as well off as they used be—per saldo. The exclusive ownership of her share guarantees that her investments will pay off. And only then can these investments be expected to pay off for the others as well. So, first appropriators who leave nobody worse off do not violate the proviso. And this is also true if Eve, as can be expected, will appropriate the best part of the former commons:

> Different persons will of course benefit differentially from the emergence of a system of exclusive rights. We may assume that Eve, who first takes land for her exclusive use, will take the best portion; nobody will then be able to make an equally advantageous appropriation. Eve does not leave her fellows "as good" to appropriate, although in taking for herself she leaves them as well off, and indeed better off, than before. . . . Advantage is thus not taken. (Gauthier 1986: 217)

But I think the analysis here is imprecise. First, it confuses the presumed wholesomeness of a system of property rights with the legitimacy of a particular distribution of property rights. Second, it conveniently assumes that the bargaining position of others is not worsened compared to Eve's absence, even though she appropriates the best part of the commons for her exclusive use, prior to mutually advantageous trade. That assumption seems unwarranted. Others besides Eve, say Adam, may be equally interested in the revenues from the more intensive cultivation of the fertile plot in the commons (say for the commercial production of yams). Yet Adam lost the running match and is now excluded from the supply side of the yams exchange. Instead he is stuck with a lousy plot, and his market power is considerably worse than it would have been in the absence of Eve. He is endowed with less than he would have been endowed with in rapid Eve's absence.

And then there is also this: suppose that Adam were a much more efficient producer of yams than Eve, or that he produced much better yams from the point of view of all yam consumers, so that, had he been the first to appropriate, consumers would have been much better served than they are now. If consumers had a say in it, they would prefer Adam rather than Eve to be the owner of the plot. Can we now maintain that Eve has not worsened the position of her clients while bettering her own in dealing with them? I do not think so. By being the first to appropriate, Eve has effectively eliminated a better (because preferred) competitor from the yams market, and thereby she has obstructed the yam consumers' access to cheap (or good) yams. They are worse off because of her. But she herself gains by her action. Without her clients, there would have been no point in her act of appropriation. Exploitation rights of scarce resources should be the endowment of those who turn these resources into consumer goods in the best, the cheapest, and the most efficient way. Otherwise producers will be exploiting their customers. Just as the service-market (not being dependent on property rights to scarce resources) allows us to pay for the singer, or the philosopher, or the plumber that we appreciate most, the commodity market ought to allow us to purchase what we want from the one we appreciate most as a producer, and not from the one who happens to control the relevant resources.

Again, consider the man who appropriates a large quantity of fish by blasting them out of the local pond with dynamite. He will certainly appropriate the fish before anyone else, but what he brings to the market is of considerably lower quality than what his competitors would have brought after scrupulously and slowly trying to catch the fish alive, using a net. But the net-fishers are going to lose out on the market for fish because they have lost the competition for the fish itself: there is little left to catch after the blast. This implies that the blaster is in fact exploiting his clients; he worsens their position compared to his absence. In other words: appropriating fish in this way simply means interfering with the productive capacities of others. In his absence other fisher folk would have produced better commodities, perhaps at a better price too—or at least they would have realized a better combination of price and quality. *Laissez-faire* in appropriation tends to violate the conditions for ideal competition: it will not eliminate inefficient producers. The normative prohibition against parasitism, however, will eliminate them, but it will require active and presumably political interference with the liberty of the blaster.

The only duty of an entrepreneur, it is sometimes claimed ironically, is to produce as efficiently as he can—the irony being that we may safely assume that even without moral incitement, entrepreneurs are sufficiently motivated to maximize profits. Irony or not, the claim is an understatement of the real duties of the entrepreneur. His duty is not just to produce as efficiently as he can, but to produce at least as efficiently as any of his competitors would have done in his position (as far as that position is defined by his control over resources). That implies that he may be required to produce more efficiently than he can. Where he fails to do so, he has no right to be in his position. Where he fails, factor endowments ought to be adjusted.

Despite the impression that Gauthier adheres to historical entitlements of "first arrivers" on the spot, there are also a few instances in *Morals by Agreement* that seem to imply that he is not really determined to escape the general conclusion that the Lockean proviso in fact does away with all speculation about "original" property rights to resources. In chapter 9, dealing with the relation between peoples and generations, Gauthier proves to be quite aware of the relativity of such rights to natural resources when he says that "in the state of nature, if not always in society, efficient use is a condition of rightful possession" (Gauthier 1986: 293). This statement is supported by two kinds of example. Gauthier considers whether or not Eve, being the original appropriator of a plot of land for agricultural purposes, will also be the owner of the oil that might be discovered underneath. And, second, he wonders whether or not the Europeans have somehow wronged the native peoples of America by claiming and cultivating stretches of their land. In both cases the answer is negative: Eve is not automatically the owner of the oil, and the Europeans, although they were "outsiders," *grosso modo* had a right to settle themselves in land that was already regarded as property by the Indians and Inuit. Why? The reason is that in both cases allowing others than the original holders to take and exploit the relevant resources would not worsen the position of anyone. If efficient oil drillers have their way instead of Eve, all will profit, and did not the Europeans bring vastly superior productive technologies to the American continent, thereby expanding the opportunities for everybody, including the natives? However, again the argument is imprecise. I will not comment on the fate of the American Indians and Inuit, and whether or not they regarded a life of toil wrestling yams from the greasy mud (I mean agriculture) as an attractive alternative to the glory of the successful hunter. But in the case of Eve and the discovery of oil underneath her property, it is obvious that there is at least one person who will not benefit from letting others expropriate her. Eve herself, if no one else, is going to be worse off if others appropriate "her" oil and exploit it. She would rather see her original property right respected so that, if she cannot exploit it herself, she might sell the exploitation rights. So the contention that all will be better off, or at least equally well off, if we switch the ownership rights in oil not-yet pumped-up from Eve to Mrs. Exxon or Mr. Shell, is simply not true. That Gauthier may nevertheless be right in insisting on such a switch is not due to the fact that all would actually profit from disowning Eve, but that Eve would be a parasite if we allowed her to regard the exploitation rights of the oil as merchandise.

Still these conclusions sit uneasily, at least to some extent, with other parts of Gauthier's doctrine. Chapter 4 of *Morals by Agreement*, dealing with the moral superiority of the competitive market, offers as a kind of knock-down argument against utilitarianism that it "undermines the fixity that rights must have." Utilitarianism, it is argued, although it can make some room for the right to engage in free market activity, must continually change the distribution of the (rights to) productive factors with which individuals enter the market in order to secure that the proper distribution of welfare is maintained.

> Once we recognize that to maintain the correct utilitarian relationship between factor endowments and the distribution of commodities we must continually adjust those endowments in the light of technological change, we must conclude that so-called rights in a dynamic utilitarian society must be evanescent. (Gauthier 1986: 108–9)

But this argument backfires. We have shown that Gauthier himself has in fact implied that in the light of technological change, such as, for instance, the emergence of oil drilling technology, factor endowments should also be redistributed—this time in order to avoid violation of the Lockean proviso, and so in order to maintain fair distributions of market power. In a "dynamic society" people's bargaining positions may change as a result of new technologies, new discoveries, new modes of production, but also as the result of changes on the demand side of the market. All these changes would warrant adjustment of entitlements. Gauthier's so-called rights to external resources are as evanescent as utilitarian rights are. Evanescent rights to resources are just the things that the Lockean proviso allows us to have.

We cannot at once have a security against parasitism and fixed rights in external resources.[10] Of course, that would not imply that we cannot at the same time employ the usual incentive-related considerations of stability for not letting productive resources change hands too often. But: when a person accepts a job in a factory he knows that the comparative quality of his performance will determine whether he will keep the job and for how long. He knows in advance that as soon as someone else comes along whom his employer believes will do better, he runs the risk of being fired. His "opportunity" to work (in that position) is as "evanescent" as would be a person's right to certain productive external resources under the strict application of the Lockean proviso; indeed, the evanescence of such opportunities is the very essence of how a competitive market works. Now, many believe that the evanescence of property rights in resources would be disastrous for productivity.[11] No one will work as a farmer this year, when she cannot be certain that she will also be working as a farmer next year. But why, then, are so many people working in employment relations this year, while they cannot be certain at all that they will be in the same position next year? The answer, presumably, is that resources require investments to make them productive while jobs do not. But obviously, it depends. People sometimes have to move to other places to get a certain job, or take additional training, and these are risky investments. But the existence of these investments does not move us to introduce some notion of a fixed right to one's job.

Or: when a retailer wants to set up shop in a certain neighborhood she knows in advance that the continuity of her success will simply depend on the quality (and number) of the competitors that might pop up in that same neighborhood. Yet, it is patently clear that it takes considerable investment to start a shop. Has this ever moved us to introduce a retailer's "fixed right" to a certain market share? Have we ever thought such a right necessary in order to reduce the risk involved in setting up shop? I do not think so.

Of course, we agree that wise employers should offer compensations for the investments of their employees when such investments carry a particularly unattractive risk, or, indeed, that they should offer contracts that guarantee a longer period of employment. When employees have to move to another town in order to get or keep their job, employers often offer compensation for the cost, and usually labor contracts exceed just a few days. Whatever way we look at it though, the point is that "holdings" in working opportunities or resources that require investments should just be stable enough to sufficiently invite these investments, not that they should be allocated once and for all, and certainly not that they can be appropriated in such a fashion that they may be sold at any price or passed on to one's heirs. Indeed, sometimes we even do introduce stabilizing devices that protect retailers from unbearable consequences of a possible misjudgment of the market, thus creating more favorable conditions for making investments. The idea of "bankruptcy" itself, and, more generally, the kind of legal arrangements that create a distinction between the liability of a person and the liability of her business, are, I believe, such stabilizing factors.

The economically desirable level of stability or evanescence of private control over productive opportunities is determined by efficiency considerations alone. As long as we remain committed to the Lockean proviso, there is no a priori argument for the fixity of property rights in external resources independent of economic outcomes, just as there is no such argument for the fixed ownership of jobs or market shares. Note, also, that as a matter of fact many resources such as minerals or oil or timber are exploited by economic agents who have no property rights in them; more often than not such resources are legally owned by states who give out concessions or franchises (for a limited period of time) to those agents who, they believe, will serve consumers best. When the performance of such companies is disappointing, they would lose the assignment. The system, as far as I know, has not hampered investment. On the contrary: since franchise systems introduce competition where it would have been excluded by fixed rights, the readiness to invest in competitiveness itself is maintained where resource owning agents might be tempted to lean back because of their secured and monopolized position. In fact it is amazing why the "stabilizing" monopoly that is sometimes sought through the formation of trusts or cartels should be criticized so vigorously on the grounds of efficiency, while this very same stability is called upon in an argument for the fixity of rights in external resources.

2.12 The Lockean Proviso and the Socialist Conception of Exploitation

I am not the first to observe that established private property rights in external resources pose a serious challenge to the justice of economic relations. Early revolutionaries like Thomas Paine, Utopian socialists like Fourier, Marxists like Marx, anarchists like Kropotkin, and even strong believers in the free market like Herbert Spencer are united in their suspicion of that institution. What is not always clear, however, is whether or not these political thinkers have also unambiguously detected the right grounds for such suspicion. Spencer, for instance, seems to have underpinned his antipathy by the idea that all established property in land had emerged from a long sequence of thefts and robberies. According to him the whole of human history had been "red in tooth and claw," and in order to undo the effect (in England) he feared the Normans would be required to give back the resources to the Danes, the Danes to the Norse and Frisians, and these to the Celts, until finally the "cavemen" would be restored in their original property rights. Spencer abandoned his initial charming idea that land ought to be publicly owned and leased out to the highest bidders (Spencer 1893: 440–44).[12] I say "charming," since an auction of resources would indeed put those resources in the hands of the people who can be expected to use them most productively—a result which, as we saw, is a desideratum following from the Lockean proviso. It is the efficient performers who can afford to bid most for resources. I shall not pursue Spencer's proposal here but in chapters 4 and 5 we will meet with a powerful variety of this idea: Ronald Dworkin's conception of "equality of resources," and we will see how the idea of a resource auction is used to support the introduction of a universal unconditional basic income. There I will point out some dangers inherent in the seductive charm of the auction proposal, dangers that ought to be avoided by those who want to oppose parasitic relations consistently.

From the point of view of the Lockean proviso the history of how present titles to land came into being—violent and illegal as they may have been—is not the most relevant thing to take into consideration. Of course, it is true that acts of violence in the past have often worsened the position of some in such a fashion that the violators may now collect benefits from them, but our point has been that any actual distribution of external factor endowments with which individuals enter the competitive market, however it came into being, should properly constrain the bargaining or market power of each in such a fashion as to be compatible with the Lockean proviso. The existence of tenure relations among the haves and the have-nots represents just an extreme case of unequal bargaining powers where resources have been concentrated in the hands of some who do not use them at all, and therefore lease them out to those who do use them productively: their tenants. History cannot provide one with a legitimate reason to be a parasite, even if one has never stolen what one presently holds. "Historical entitlement theories of justice" are as blind as a bat to the mischief of parasitism. Eve, being a good farmer but having no oil drilling skills, may be the legitimate holder of a plot of agricultural land just until oil is discovered underneath that plot. If at that moment Eve's customers decide that they rather would have the oil from that land than the yams it used to produce, Eve will have to go and skilled oil drillers will be brought in (Eve, of course, will be entitled to compensation for her investments). The point is not that stolen land ought to be given back to those who once legitimately owned it, not even if society at large is to be viewed as their offspring; the point is that the distribution of resources in itself ought to be a secure guarantee against parasitic relations.

There is an echo of Spencer's tooth-and-claw view of history in Marx where he considers the origin of the so-called "previous accumulation" of capital and describes (again for England) how the majority of small and relatively independent property owners (freeman, yeoman) with a protected status under late feudal law, were violently expropriated in the beginning of the modern era (Marx 1975: 1:741ff.). But there is an important difference in the conceptual role of this story. Marx uses the history of theft only to explain both the existence of accumulated capital and a propertyless proletariat in the industrial era, but not to justify the collective ownership of the means of production. The justification for collective ownership is provided by the actual effect of the institution of "fixed" private property itself, and not by the bloody history that passed on private property from one claw to the next. The effect of private property in the means of production, according to Marx, is that propertyless workers will be exploited and hence it seems there may be a close similarity between our considerations up to this point and Marx's analysis of exploitative economic relations.

Perhaps, then, this is the right place to point out certain fundamental differences between our Lockean conception of parasitism and the socialist conception of exploitation, and the consequences these conceptions ought to have for redistributive principles and legitimate politics. I will follow Jon Elster (1986: 121) where he gives the socialist definition of exploitation as it can be derived "from Marx' mature economic writings": "workers are exploited if they work longer hours than the number of labor hours embodied in the goods they consume."[13] The socialist conception of exploitation, then, concentrates fully on the inequalities of "embodied labor" that go into the exchange of goods, while the Lockean proviso defines parasitism in terms of how utility gains and losses from interactions relate to each other.

Clearly, there will be a substantial overlap in the practices that are condemned by these two notions. Indeed, when we consider the merchandizing of resources in its crudest and simplest form, as it exists between the feudal overlord and his tenants, we will see that this is the case. The tenant works the whole week but he has to pay, say, one-tenth of his production to his lord in return for being allowed to exploit the land. But the nobleman does not work. So, one-tenth of his production is what the tenant does not get back from his own labor effort. It has been appropriated by someone else. In the worst case the aristocrat's bargaining position may be so powerful that he will not just take one-tenth of the tenant's production, but all of it except what the tenant needs to stay alive, since that is what he needs to be able to work at all. In that case the owner takes all so-called surplus labor: all that exceeds the cost of labor itself. Had the tenant been the owner of the land, such "exploitation" would not have been possible. So, socialism condemns feudal privileges in land ownership. And so does the Lockean proviso. The tenant would rather have his lordship out of the way, giving himself costless access to the land he wants to use, and to the full and exclusive enjoyment of his own surplus labor, while the nobleman, who has made nothing available that would not have been equally available in his absence, would despair of getting any revenue without the existence of the tenant.

But now let me give just one simple example which will put the difference between the two notions of socialist exploitation and Lockean parasitism sharply into focus. Suppose that you and I are relatively well off individuals. We live as independent and self-supporting farmers in an area that provides us with abundant external resources, and we have never been in each other's way—let alone that we have predated on each other. Yet, our happiness still leaves something to be desired. We both have a good house to live in, but while I would like to have a summer residence on the borders of the nearby lake, you would like to have a small sailing boat. However, building a second house would take me six months of labor and building a boat would take you three months of labor. As it happens, this is too much work for both of us. Planning my activities I consider that I very much want to have a summer house but that I am only willing to work five months in order to get it. Likewise you find that two months of labor is the maximum that you are willing to invest in acquiring your boat. So, it seems, neither of us will have what he wants to have for the summer. Is that really so? Fortunately not. We may also cooperate. If I have to build my summer residence alone it will take six months, but if we would do so together it would take only two months. This is so because of the enormous gains in efficiency realized through the labor division between us: just consider how much easier it is for two persons to lift the heavy planks that are used in constructing a house. Likewise building your boat together would cost each of us only one month. Now, would it be a good idea if we agreed, and signed a contract, to build my house together first, and then build your boat together? It would not. If you are required to assist me for two months and then work for another month on your own boat, assisted by me, then you will have invested a sum total of three months of labor in the acquisition of your boat and we already stated as a fact that this was too much for you. In that case you might as well have built your own boat alone in three months, which you were not prepared to do. In short, on close inspection there is only one solution to our problem. You help me build my summer residence, which requires each of us to invest two months of labor. After that, and in return for your help, I build your boat alone in three months. Thus, we end up with what we want, since I have invested a sum total of five months in getting my house, which was my maximum, while you have invested two months in getting your boat, which was your maximum. Through our transaction, which is the only possible transaction, we both gain—as it were—one month of labor.

Of course, there is no remotely plausible way that this transaction between us can be called a parasitic violation of the Lockean proviso. You have not worsened my position and I have not worsened yours. On the contrary, we are both very pleased with each other's existence and actions; we have benefited from each other very much. Yet, the thing you now enjoy, the sailing boat, embodies three months of my labor, while the thing I now enjoy, the summer residence, embodies only two months of your labor. So from the socialist point of view you have exploited me; you have appropriated one month of my labor. But any attempt to force you to spend more labor on my behalf so that the (embodied) labor transfers would be more equal, would simply destroy the transaction opportunity itself. In that case, you would simply say: "then I prefer not to have the boat—thank you," which would mean that I would not have the house, unless, of course, if I somehow had the right to force you to work for me longer. If socialist society, then, is the kind of society that would be free of "exploitation," mutually beneficial transactions such as these would not be allowed.

So although socialism rightly rejects privileged ownership in resources such as land, and finds it exploitative, it seems that it does so for the wrong reasons. Unequal exchange of (embodied) labor by itself is no sign of unjust distributions of economic power. The inequality of the exchange may be entirely attributable to the differences in individual preferences of those involved in transaction.[14] I believe that this example, simple though it may be, reveals that there must be something wrong with the socialist conception of exploitation—given, of course, that we think of exploitation as something that ought not to happen and against which we have a moral right to legislate.

I also think that this flaw in the notion of exploitation indicates that the socialist project—a society without exploitation—may have unfortunate consequences. As we saw, a commitment to the Lockean proviso sustains the competitive market as far as it goes. It leaves intact the structure of (self-ownership) rights in internal resources, and individual preferences, in so far as they bring about mutually beneficial exchanges of services. Where rights in external resources violate proviso-relative equity in bargaining power, where they create (potentially rent-seeking) monopolies that are to the disadvantage of consumers and competitors alike, the proviso warrants robust collective action to bring about more efficient, and hence more just, distributions of external endowments—as long as stability considerations over time are taken into account. The proviso challenges the fixity of rights—however these rights are presently distributed and however they came into being in the past. And so the proviso may seem to justify something that looks much like what we call the "collective ownership" of external resources.

But nowhere does this type of collective ownership imply that the productive process itself ought to be collectivized as well. It does away, for instance, with tenure relations in farming, but it does not imply that land should be worked by a "cooperation" of farmers, nor that these farmers should be regarded as a kind of civil servants with a fixed salary irrespective of the market value of their productive output. Socialism, on the other hand, does turn the productive process into a public good, and "real existing socialism" seems to have suffered indeed from the inevitable tendency towards suboptimality that is inherent in the production of public goods.

In short: I believe that we cannot have a structure of economic relations that

1. is free of "exploitation" as defined by socialist theory;
2. is compatible with self-ownership, and hence free of parasitism, as defined by the Lockean proviso; and
3. secures Pareto efficiency in its outcomes.

Where the proviso requires us to interfere in the conditions of the market only, socialism will tend to interfere in the working of the market itself. The following quote from the socialist Bertolt Brecht in *The Caucasian Chalk Circle* (1961) seems a perfectly sound remedy against parasitic relations, but there is no reference to collective ownership.

> Take note what men of old concluded:
> That what there is shall go to those who are good for it,
> Thus: the children to the motherly, that they prosper
> The carts to good drivers, that they are driven well
> And the valley to the waterers, that it bring forth fruit.

The ancients were quite right in their noteworthy conclusion of a just distribution of belongings. It is ability and willingness (together constituting "being good") that justify rights in resources. This (except for rights in children) would be a prerequisite for just economic relations. It would be required by the Lockean proviso.

Appendix: Economic Progress and Social Disintegration

In section 2.8, I discussed the view that conflict and competition might be a feature of increased cooperative opportunities rather than a feature of life in the state-of-nature. Here I will give an example, in game theoretical terms, of the way in which the success of social interaction may undermine its own conditions, even if we do not assume solitude to be the starting point.

Let us think of two agents in the "state of nature" as having two options C and D. Pay-offs are interdependent. These two agents have an interactive problem. Let me stipulate further that their interaction has several subsequent rounds, and, what is important, that the eventual gains of a given round will determine the pay-offs of the next round. Pay-offs are accumulative.

Now, given that this is so, it could be true that the structure of the interactive problem will change after a number of rounds. Agents may accumulate wealth during a sequence of rounds in which non-cooperative equilibria are optimal and "mutually beneficial," but as both grow wealthier over time, suspicion and temptation, and the threat of suboptimality, may be introduced into their interaction.

Let us represent the positions of our two agents by the number of golden coins they have, or may gain through interaction with

Table 2.1. Iterated interaction with accumulative pay-offs

	D	C
d	50, 50	75, 75
c	75, 75	120, 120

Round 1: cooperation dominant

	D	C
d	70, 70	100, 90
c	90, 100	140, 140

Round 2

	D	C
d	90, 90	125, 105
c	105, 125	160, 160

Round 3

	D	C
d	110, 110	150, 120
c	120, 150	180, 180

Round 4

	D	C
d	130, 130	175, 135
c	135, 175	200, 200

Round 5

	D	C
d	150, 150	200, 150
c	150, 200	220, 220

Round 6

	D	C
d	170, 170	225, 165
c	165, 225	240, 240

Round 7: first Assurance Game

	D	C
d	190, 190	250, 180
c	180, 250	260, 260

Round 8

	D	C
d	210, 210	275, 195
c	195, 275	280, 280

Round 9

	D	C
d	230, 230	300, 210
c	210, 300	300, 300

Round 10

	D	C
d	250, 250	325, 225
c	225, 325	320, 320

Round 11: first Prisoners' Dilemma

	D	C
d	270, 270	325, 240
c	240, 325	340, 340

Round 12

the other. Let's say they both start with one hundred each. Now, choosing strategy D will involve an investment of fifty. If the other chooses D as well those fifty will be lost, for both of them. However, if the other does not choose D, then the return for the D-chooser will consist in a transfer of one-quarter of the wealth of the other. Otherwise, if both choose C, pay-offs will be an increase in wealth of twenty for both.

So given that x is the present state of wealth of one agent the pay-offs (in coins) for him in the next round will be as follows:

(C, C): $x + 20$
(D, D): $x - 50$
(C, D): $x - 1/4\,x$
(D, C): $x + 1/4\,x - 50$

Now observe from table 2.1 and figure 2.5 how the structure of the iterated interaction with accumulative pay-offs between these two

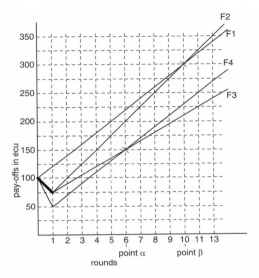

Figure 2.5. Iterated interaction with accumulative pay-offs

agents will develop, assuming that they always choose C (I give the pay-offs for 12 rounds, given that they enter the first round with 100 coins each). In figure 2.5, the pay-off (for each) of (C, C) is on F1, of (D, C) on F2, of (C, D) on F3, and of (D, D) on F4. As we can see: during the first rounds, C is the dominant strategy for both parties: whatever the other does, it is always more sensible for oneself not to invest 50 coins in a possible acquisition of a quarter of the other's wealth; this is so even if the other chooses otherwise.

This "socially" happy state of affairs lasts for some rounds, but in the seventh (point ∝) this latter feature of the interaction changes. Now it does pay off to respond to an "assault" on one's wealth with a similar strategy (mutual assault is better than being victimized). The interaction takes the shape of a so-called Assurance Game: one chooses C as long as one has good reason to expect the other to choose C. One wants to know the other's intentions.

Suppose our agents find a means to survive the threat of suboptimality inherent in Assurance Games (they find a means to check on each other's intentions). Then soon it turns out that suspicion has only preceded its own good reasons: in round eleven (point β) when the two agents have grown very rich they suddenly realize that it would pay off to catch the other off-guard, attack and take one-quarter of her wealth, and that one is liable to similar considerations by the other party. They are in a Prisoners' Dilemma. D has become the dominant strategy. So, driven by a mixture of greed and considerations of pre-emptive attack, they are now bound to realize suboptimal outcomes. Innocence Lost; Incipit Morality.

Thus, we see how economic progress and mutually beneficial interaction may undermine its own conditions, not only by producing scarcity and creating a problem of fair sharing, as Locke thought it would, but also by creating room for the predatory passions that were so pointless in the times when we were still living as "noble savages" without a need for constraint. (I leave it as a puzzle for the reader to find a realistic interpretation of D and C, and of the "rounds," in this game theoretic "history of mankind").

CHAPTER 3

THE BENEFIT OF ANOTHER'S
PAINS: ORIGINAL ACQUISITION
AND PARASITIC ACTION

> Among the Indians of North America, there is not
> any of those spectacles of human misery which pov-
> erty and want present to our eyes in all the towns and
> streets in Europe.... The life of an Indian is a con-
> tinual holiday, compared with the poor of Europe.
>
> Thomas Paine

3.1 Locke and Nozick: On the Proviso

In chapter 2, we saw how David Gauthier gave an account of what he called "the Lockean proviso." This account implied the prohibition of parasitic actions—actions that improve one's position through the worsening of the position of someone else. In this chapter, I will attempt to test the soundness of this principle as an interpretation of the intentions of John Locke himself. I will also discuss another interpretation of the proviso, that of Jeremy Waldron, which would imply that Gauthier's account of it is false. Waldron's contentions imply that the proviso does not prohibit parasitism. I will argue against Waldron's position and try to put Gauthier in the right on this point. If we read Locke as not prohibiting parasitism, then it is impossible to make any sense out of his doctrine of original acquisition.[1]

Finally, in the last sections of this chapter, I will consider Robert Nozick's effort to come to terms with some of the problems and ambiguities that are inherent in the Lockean proviso, and I will argue that he fails. But I will also show, on the basis of other elements of his theory, that Nozick is a consistent enemy of exploitation after all.

3.2 "As Good" as What?

The passage to which both Gauthier and Nozick appeal is in section 27 of chapter 5 (*Of Property*) in Locke's *Second Treatise of Government*, one of the most influential texts on politics ever written. In the following discussion, I will refer to Locke's text directly, following Peter Laslett's critical edition (based on the so-called Christ's copy) unless stated otherwise; so "27" will indicate "section 27 in chapter 5 of *The Second Treatise*."

In chapter 5, Locke explains that all natural resources have been given by God to mankind in common, that all have a common right to them, but that He has given them to mankind for their sustenance and to their advantage, and that therefore individuals have a right to take parts out of the common stock by labor. Labor entitles the laborer to private property, excluding others from the benefit of that part of the resources to which he joined his labor. This is the general normative doctrine to sustain the legitimacy of private property. As we shall see, however, there is an even more fundamental principle to account for the legitimacy of the acquisition of private property through labor.

There are also restrictions (generally called: provisos) on the process of acquiring property. The second is that people when they take parts of natural resources into their possession, even if they do so through labor, may not let something spoil. The first, which will concern us here, we find in 27 where it is said: "For this Labor being the unquestionable Property of the Laborer, no man but he can have a right to what that is once joyned to, *at least where there is enough, and as good left in common for others*" (italics added). Of course, this formulation leaves us with the problem of how to read the "as good." Where there is enough the laborer has to leave as good for the others. As good as what? I think two candidates suggest themselves for the comparison. One is ingenious and elegant but lacks textual evidence. The other creates all kinds of systematic problems in Locke's theory, which will concern us presently, but seems to be really his own intention. I begin with the wrong object of comparison for the "as good." It might be thought that "as good" is comparing what the laborer leaves for the others with what he took himself. He should leave something as good as the thing he took himself. There are some lines in *Of Property* that may mislead the reader into accepting this interpretation of the "as good." Both are in 34, where Locke says: "He that had as good left for his Improvement, as was already taken up, needed not complain." And where Locke talks about: "the Ground . . . whereof there was as good left, as that already possessed." The thing "as good" left here is said to be "as good as that already appropriated," but the last quote is immediately followed by: "and more than he knew what to do with, or his Industry could reach to." And this suggests another reading of the "as good," which I think is in fact the right one. It is abundantly clear from

Locke's text that he intends "as good" to mean "*as good as what there used to be*—before the appropriation." I will give a few instances where this is unambiguously so:

> [T]here was still enough, and as good left; and more than the yet unprovided could use. So that in effect, there was never the less left for others (33)

> [H]is Neighbour, who would still have room, for as good, and as large a Possession (after the other had taken out his) as before it was appropriated. (36)

> Men had a Right to appropriate, by their Labor, each one to himself, as much of the things of Nature, as he could use: Yet this would not be much, nor to the Prejudice of others, where the same plenty was still left, to those who would use the same Industry. (37)

Obviously, Locke thought that in the beginning natural resources were so abundant that in fact there was enough for any individual appropriator not only to leave for the others something as good as what he took himself but also enough for him to leave for the others something as good as there used to be before he appropriated. So I suggest that we read the passage in 27 as follows:

> For this Labor being the unquestionable Property of the Laborer, no man but he can have a right to what that is once joyned to, *at least where there is enough, and as good left in common for others as there used to be.*

3.3 More Grammar: "At Least Where"

A difficulty has been made about the meaning of the words "at least where" in the passage under consideration. The problem, raised by Jeremy Waldron, is the following: traditionally the clause starting with "at least where" has been taken to imply a restriction on the legitimacy of the natural process of acquiring private property. "*At least where* there is enough, and as good left in common for others" has been taken to imply that where there is not enough, and not as good left in common for others, other men than the original laborer would maintain a (common) right to what the laborer joined his labor to. Waldron, however, wants to "argue that the traditional interpretation is strained and artificial, that Locke did *not* intend the clause to be taken as a restriction or a necessary condition on appropriation" (Waldron 1979: 320).[2] For this attack on orthodox exegesis, he offers several arguments having mainly to do with the implied inconsistency of the traditional interpretation with Locke's conception of legitimate politics. We will return to these considerations. But first let us examine a rather remarkable argument that is also employed. Waldron claims that the "most natural reading" of the "rather ambiguous" logical connective "at least where" is to take it as a connective introducing a sufficient condition. He thinks that

> [O]n the most natural reading of the passage in question, Locke is saying something like this: For this Labour being the unquestionable Property of the Labourer, no Man but he can have a right to what that is once joyned to, *certainly* in circumstances where there is enough and as good left in common for others, and perhaps even if there is *not* enough and as good left in common for others. This, I think, is the interpretation that would be given to the passage in question by somebody coming fresh to it, unbiased by the traditional view. (Waldron 1979: 321)

But would it really? Suppose that Waldron, in a generous mood, says to you: "Of course, you may borrow my car, at least if you take care to tell me." Would you now feel obliged to tell Waldron that you were about to borrow his car, or would you also feel free to drive off without saying a word? I think it is beyond reasonable doubt that the latter reading of Waldron's words would be quite ridiculous, if not positively malicious, and certainly it would not be the "most natural" reading of these words for someone coming fresh to them, without bias.

Of course, Waldron is quite right that "at least where" (or "at least when" or "at least if") is ambiguous if he wants to say that, depending on the context, it can either introduce a sufficient or a necessary condition on what has preceded. "P at least where Q" in some cases only means "Q implies P," but in some cases it means as much as "not-Q implies not-P," and it is hard to find a comprehensible system that determines the shift between these cases. Compare, for instance:

(a) Of course she can be made happy, at least when you play
     Beethoven to her as you did last time.

and:

(b) Of course she can be made happy, at least when you do not pester
     her constantly as you did last time.

No doubt it is our general knowledge about the respective effects that playing other music than Beethoven's and pestering may have on a person's happiness, that makes us quite certain that "at least when" introduces a sufficient condition in (a) and a necessary condition in (b); playing Bach or Brahms might do as well as Beethoven—who knows?—but pestering will not do as well as not-pestering. Pragmatic considerations, then, can determine quite decisively what is the "most natural" reading of "at least when."

Waldron's claim, however, goes much further. His claim implies that there are also cases where the respective contents of P and Q fail to specify a context that sufficiently determines the meaning of "at least where," and in this he may be right. Then he concludes that in those cases we should stick to the most natural reading. But what is the most natural reading if there are both clear-cut cases that force a restrictive reading on us and clear-cut cases that force a nonrestrictive reading on us? The most natural reading, it seems to me, is a fiction, and it is not very helpful to suggest that it is biased to read "at least where" as introducing a restriction on the natural right to appropriate. There is no simple argument from pure grammar.

3.4 Textual Evidence

The most natural thing to do for a traditionalist, or his critic, is to look for direct support for, or refutation of, the restrictive reading of "at least where" in the remainder of Locke's text on the legitimacy of original appropriation through labor. Where such materials may prove to be indecisive, and perhaps contradictory, one may try to include further considerations of general consistency in one's interpretation.

Waldron, in his later book on the right to private property where he resumes his argument from naturally spoken English in favor of the nonrestrictive reading,[3] admits that there is one passage where Locke seems to be saying what the traditionalists say he is saying (Waldron 1988: 209–18). In 35 Locke argues that no one may enclose a part of the land that is called "common" in England or any other country, and he gives two reasons for that prohibition. The first is that it is left common by the law of the country, and I will return to the implications of that remark presently. But then he adds: "Besides, the remainder, after such inclosure, would not be as good to the rest of the Commoners as the whole was, when they could all make use of the whole: whereas in the beginning and first peopling of the great Common of the World, it was quite otherwise."[4] According to Waldron, then, there is "some tension" between this passage and the nonrestrictive interpretation of the proviso in 27, and he also says that this is the passage where Locke "comes closest to explicit recognition" of the restrictive reading. Some tension? Surely he means "blatant contradiction"! And, of course, this is the passage where Locke "comes closest" to explicit recognition of the restrictive reading. Neither he, nor anybody else, could have come any closer because it is an explicit statement that where not as good is left the natural right to appropriate is restricted. At least it would be such a statement to someone coming fresh to these words.

In 36, we read that in the state of nature "No Mans Labor could subdue, or appropriate all: nor could his Enjoyment consume more than a small part; so that it was impossible for any Man, this way, to intrench upon the right of another, or acquire, to himself, a Property, to the Prejudice of his Neighbour." Note that it is said that, under these conditions of plenty, it was impossible to entrench upon the right of another, not only that it was impossible to do something harmful to another—through making an appropriation. Again it seems to me that the implication is clear: where conditions of plenty give way to those of scarcity, it is possible to violate another's natural right through taking possession of something. Waldron, who also quotes this passage, thinks that Locke merely describes the happy situation in the state of nature without wanting to imply normative restrictions. That there is as good left in common for others, says Waldron (1979: 322), is only presented "as *a fact about* acquisition in the early ages of man." Yes, but that natural rights are not violated through acquisitions is presented as a fact about acquisitions in the *early* ages of man.

There is another passage that provides direct support for the restrictive reading. It is not discussed by Waldron. In 45, Locke describes what has happened "in some parts of the world, where the increase of people and stock, with the use of money, had made land scarce and so of some value":

> [T]he Leagues that have been made between several States and King-doms, either expressly or tacitly disowning all Claim and Right to the land in the others Possession, have, by common Consent given up their Pretences to their natural common Right, which originally they had to those Countries, and so have, by *positive agreement, settled a Property* amongst themselves.

This passage unambiguously shows that, under conditions of scarcity, when one country has taken land into its possession there still remains another country's natural (common) right to that land, a right which, evidently, may (perhaps tacitly) be given up—as presumably will happen if reciprocated by the other. Hence, the Law of Nature does not imply that I lose my right to x when you take x into your possession without leaving for me something as good as there used to be. If the nonrestrictive reading of the original proviso in 27 had been right, this statement of Locke would have been quite puzzling because in that case the other state would automatically have lost its natural common right to the already "possessed" land—as it does in fact under conditions of plenty—and there would have been no occasion for giving up something, and making agreements.

So I believe that there are at least three passages where Locke's text allows but one conclusion: in 35 he tells us that we cannot appropriate any part without the consent of others, where the remainder would not be as good; in 36 he describes the state of nature as a state without rights violation; and in 45 he says that, under conditions of scarcity, we keep our rights to the things of which others have taken possession. The only plausible conclusion of these passages supports the restrictive reading of the first proviso in 27: where there is not enough, and not as good left for others, these others do not lose their natural right to something that we mixed our labor with.

This textual support for the restrictive reading of the first proviso, together with the observation that the grammar of that clause in 27 does not force the nonrestrictive reading on us, should at least convince us that the restrictive reading is not simply an unhappy mistake or a biased violation of Locke's text. Nor is there any suggestion that "Locke includes the proviso almost as an afterthought" as another author wants us to believe (Wolf 1995: 795). On the contrary: there is good reason to believe that a restriction is in fact what Locke had in mind, at least when he wrote this part of his book, and perhaps also when he wrote the rest, perhaps not.

Yet, there is no denying that the restrictive reading brings its own problem, for the proviso obviously leaves the content of the Law of Nature less than fully determined: we are allowed to take whatever we want in the state of nature, where our appropriations do not violate the rights of others, but how should we proceed when resources are scarce so that the takings of one person will reduce the possibilities to take for the others? It seems that the Law of Nature is silent on that question.

A few "solutions" are suggested by a number of passages within chapter 5 and elsewhere, e.g. that the land should remain "common" by compact as in 35, or that we should (tacitly or positively) agree to give up our natural rights to those things that others have mixed their labor with, on a reciprocal basis, as in 45, but there are also those passages that suggest that positive institutions, civil laws, should speak where the Law of Nature is silent, as, for instance, in chapter 11, section 139, where we learn that "the prince or senate," though they may not take to themselves "the whole, or any part of the subjects' property," they nevertheless "may have power to make Laws for the regulating of *Property* between the Subjects one amongst another." But whatever type of solution we favor, I think that Locke never made it his systematic concern to answer our question, for I believe that it is also true that he never recognized the magnitude of the problem that is implied by his first proviso in 27. On the contrary: there is overwhelming evidence in the remainder of Locke's *Second Treatise* that the very idea that the Law of Nature can be silent, and that we need politics to tell us what our rights are, is radically at odds with his view on (the limits of) political authority. This evidence is amply pointed out by Den Hartogh (1990) in his argument against Tully: politics is there in order to maintain and guard our natural rights in a more effective way than we can do ourselves; it is not there in order to create our rights. In fact, all our rights are natural rights and remain to be so even if we do live in political institutions. What we have given up by "tacitly consenting" to the establishment of political authority is not some part of our natural rights (e.g. to private property) but only our natural power to punish trespassers of the Law of Nature. Also, since the introduction of scarcity is bound to increase the number of cases of controversy over the correct application of the Law of Nature—men are biased towards their own advantage, we need an unbiased "Umpire" or arbitrator to settle our conflicts.[5] This too is a specific and privileged function of political power that we could do without in the state of nature when it was obvious to see for everybody what belonged to whom. So, it is the interpretation and the execution of the Law of Nature that properly belongs to the state, but the state has no business making laws other than the Law of Nature.

The systematic problem, then, is serious and dilemmatic. On the one hand, we have the well-supported view that the state cannot be the source of property rights, only their guardian; on the other hand, we have the first proviso, which implies that the Law of Nature does not fully determine a solution for the controversy that might arise under conditions of scarcity. And Locke scholars generally, assuming rather than showing consistency in their subject, have tended to downgrade or ignore the (textual) evidence in support of the existence of either of the two horns of the dilemma.

Den Hartogh takes Locke's view of the legitimacy of political power as established and, considering the problem of unequal original appropriations under conditions of scarcity, he concludes that "there is no need for the civil law to correct injustice, for there is no injustice" (Den Hartogh 1990: 665). In the same vein Waldron observes that "where the imputation of inconsistency is based on a strained reading of the text, and where a more natural reading avoids the inconsistency, then the strained reading should be dropped" (Waldron 1988: 213).

On the other hand, it seems that Tully moves in the opposite direction by putting all the emphasis on the importance of the first proviso as a restriction (and on some other passages that I have not been concerned with) and then proceeds to give an interpretation of Locke's view of politics that fits rather uneasily with the evidence, as it is displayed by Den Hartogh.[6] The result appears to be that we now have roughly two kinds of Locke, both more or less consistent in their own right, but the consistency is gained at the expense of giving all evidence its proper weight.

3.5 "Without Injury"

My own idea is that Locke himself was ambivalent between the two positions that are now attributed to him. In this section, I will argue that he may not have been fully aware of the problems raised by the political implications of his first proviso, but that there are also signs that he has not been unaware of a flaw in his argument in chapter 5. Furthermore, I will do two things in this section: I will point out that the systematic problem, and the threat of inconsistency, is even more serious than we may have suspected until now, and I will point out a fundamental confusion, which may well have been the origin of Locke's ambivalence, and which may still be present in the minds of his interpreters (of whatever conviction). It deserves some analysis because it will bring into sharper focus what the moral problems involved in the controversy over the two readings of the clause in 27 actually are.

The penultimate section 50 in *Of Property* is sometimes referred to as conclusive evidence for the nonrestrictive reading of the enough-and-as-good clause in 27, for instance by Den Hartogh (1990: 664), since there it seems that Locke unambiguously and approvingly says that the introduction of money has warranted divisions of property that do not fit with the idea that nobody should be allowed to be a hindrance to others. I give the passage at length from Laslett's critical edition (Locke 1970, 302):

> [I]t is plain, that Men have agreed to disproportionate and unequal Pos-
> session of the Earth, they having by tacit and voluntary consent found
> out a way, how a man may fairly possess more land than he himself can
> use the product of, by receiving in exchange for the overplus, Gold
> and Silver, which may be hoarded up without injury to any one, these
> metalls not spoileing or decaying in the hands of the possessor. This
> partage of things, in an inequality of private possessions, man have made
> practicable out of the bounds of Societie, and without compact, only
> by putting a value on gold and silver and tacitly agreeing in the use of
> Money. For in Governments the Laws regulate the right of property, and
> the possession of land is determined by positive constitutions.

Of course, in itself, the passage is quite perplexing because it is difficult
to see why men would consent to governments regulating the right
of property when they already have consented having it regulated by
money, but this is not my main point. The main point to be concerned
with is that Locke admits that disproportionate and unequal divisions
of private property do not constitute an injury to anybody, since money
can be hoarded up without being an injury to anybody.

Unfortunately, this passage can be shown to be one of the few places
where Locke seems to have had real difficulties in formulating what he
wanted to say. This is the single passage where Laslett decided to divert
from his master-text, the hand-corrected text of the Christ's copy of
the third edition, and to seek authority in the fourth edition, because
the Christ's copy was not sufficiently clear.[7] And indeed, the corresponding passage in the earlier editions reads quite differently. I quote
from Carpenter's text (Locke 1924, 140–41), based on the first edition:

> [I]t is plain that the consent of men have agreed to a disproportionate
> and unequal possession of the Earth—I mean out of the bounds of soci-
> ety and compact; for in governments the laws regulate it; they having,
> by consent, found out and agreed in a way how a man may, rightfully
> and without injury, possess more than he himself can make use of by
> receiving gold and silver, which may continue a long time in a man's
> possession without decaying for the overplus, and agreeing those metals
> should have a value.

Note how, subtly, the thing that can be done "without injury" is
changed. In the earlier text it is taking possession of more than can be
made use of which is said to be noninjurious, while in the later text it
is hording up of gold and silver which is said to be noninjurious.

Why has Locke gone through such trouble to reconstruct this
passage? I think that he really was uneasy about what he wanted to
say because, in using the words "without injury," he introduced an

ambiguity, which he felt, but could not locate. It is this ambiguity that I want to detect and explain. I will give one example in order to make the point, and I will situate it in the real circumstances of our own day. I will situate it on that no longer great but still "remaining common of mankind," the ocean, which recently saw actual military hostilities over rights of original acquisition. The Spanish, with their enormous commercial fishing fleet, were about to exhaust the fishing grounds that the Canadians traditionally depend on for their own fishing industry—or at least this is what the Spanish were accused of by the Canadians. The Canadian navy arrested a Spanish trawler at high sea, the Spanish were outraged, and the European Community, despite its usual lack of firm unity,[8] threatened to launch a wholesale commercial boycott of Canada. Some representatives cautiously tried to negotiate their way out the controversy, but charges were also brought at the international court in The Hague. In other words: it was a fine mess from the Lockean point of view.

Let us put ourselves on the seat of the Judge of Nature for a moment and try this case. The Canadians as well as the Spanish are fishing largely for commercial purposes. Undoubtedly, they consume a small part of their catch themselves, but the bulk is brought to the market where other nations buy their fish. Let us assume for a moment that these other nations are not themselves active in the fishing business: they demand fish because they want to consume fish, but for some reason it does not pay off for them to engage in fishing themselves.[9] They prefer to buy. So, obviously, the problem between the Spanish and the Canadians has its origin in the existence of this external market; it is because they both want to sell fish that they both want to catch fish in such quantities that they now are competitors. In this sense, Canada and Spain have left the state of nature between each other in a way that perfectly matches Locke's description of that process. Had these nations not been able to receive "gold and silver" in return for the overplus of their catch, they would only have bothered to catch a small part of what they now want. In that case no controversy would ever have arisen between them, for Spain could have caught whatever it wanted for its own consumption, while leaving as good for the Canadians. Let us greatly reduce the real numbers and say that both Spain and Canada only want five fish for their own consumption, and that there are twenty fish in the Atlantic Ocean, so that, in the state of nature, everybody—including ten fish—would lead happy lives without being disadvantaged by the activities of others. This does not mean, of course, that everybody may do as he or she likes in the state of nature. It is still forbidden to steal the fish that the other has caught. Locke's doctrine that labor gives exclusive property right excludes that fish already caught can be reappropriated through theft or robbery—at least in the state of nature.

Through the introduction of money both the Spanish and Canadian "appetite" for fish is greatly increased because both of them not only like fish but also like to hoard up gold and silver, and this is what they can get in return for fish that they do not eat themselves. Of course, stealing is still prohibited, as much as it was in the state of nature. But the interesting thing about the new situation is that disadvantage can now also be produced without stealing. Let us first look at what the position of each would have been if the other had not existed at all or if one of the countries had not been interested in fishing at all. In that case the best result for the remaining party would be to catch fifteen fish, eat five, and sell ten to the other two consumer nations. So, as long as Spain manages to catch fifteen fish, it will neither suffer nor benefit from Canada's activities. In that case Canada would be as well off as it would have been in the state of nature, and it will not benefit from the existence of a market for fish. The benefits thereof have all been "appropriated" by Spain. This situation would be reversed if Canada manages to catch fifteen, leaving five for Spain. On the other hand, as long as they catch more than five fish each, their activities will be to the disadvantage of each other—reciprocally. Any catch of less than fifteen fish will be a disadvantage compared to the situation in which the other would be absent or not active, but, of course, any catch of more than five fish will be advantageous compared to the state of nature when money (or markets) had not yet been introduced. So there is a range of "disproportionate and unequal partages of things," which will nevertheless leave both parties better off than they would have been in the state of nature, thanks to the presence of the external market. As I pointed out before, in chapter 2, the market introduces competition as well as increased wealth. Competitors on the market, as opposed to suppliers and demanders, cannot be assumed to work to each other's advantage. They would rather have each other out of the way.

Now, suppose we took the requirement to leave "as good" for the others to imply that Spain's or Canada's appropriations may not be such that the position of the other would thereby be worsened compared to the absence of the appropriator, then obviously neither would be allowed to catch more fish than he would have caught in the state of nature. Doing so would worsen the position of his competitor. Neither would then be able to improve on his state of nature position, despite the fact that the introduction of gold and silver, in itself, has provided increased opportunities for gain. This, indeed, would seem to be a perfectly perverse consequence of the proviso, and one radically at odds with Locke's idea that people have consented to put value on gold and silver. So, if there is a "natural" way of reading Locke's words, one would be inclined to believe that he did not intend to say that any appropriations of more than five fish, in the Spanish-Canadian example, should count as illegitimate.

If Locke had a restriction in mind with the formulation of his proviso, it would probably not have been his purpose to obstruct the gains of cooperation and transaction. Competitors, by their very nature, necessarily constitute an "injury" to each other because they cannot leave something "as good" for each other, but these are the injuries inherent in the working of the market itself. What you catch to sell, another cannot catch to sell. The supporter of the nonrestrictive reading of the proviso would be right to point out that "leaving the state of nature" cannot be consistent with a prohibition on appropriations that fail to leave as good an opportunity for others.

But can we conclude from these findings that no restriction at all should follow from the proviso? Can we get a consistent Locke by simply pointing out that no commercial fisherman can be as well off as he would have been without competitors, that is as a monopolist, catching all there is and setting prices all by himself?

Let us turn to our two fishing nations again. As I pointed out, there is a range of catch-distributions between them such that both will be worse off than each of them would have been as a monopolist, but that will also leave them at least as well off as they would have been without the existence of an external market. But suppose now that the Spanish manage to catch more than fifteen fish. They eat five of those themselves, and sell ten to the other two consumer nations, but what shall they do with the remainder? Well, since the Canadians can now catch less fish than they want to consume themselves, they are demanding fish on the market. If Spain catches sixteen, seventeen, eighteen, nineteen, or twenty fish, Canada will be forced to buy all or some of the fish that it wants for its consumption and that it would have caught in the state of nature. Since buying is more expensive than catching, these transactions will represent a loss to it compared to the state of nature. The Canadians will not only be worse off than they would have been in the absence of the Spanish, they are also worse off than they would have been in the absence of gold and silver. The Spanish, on the other hand, are now not only better off than they would have been in the

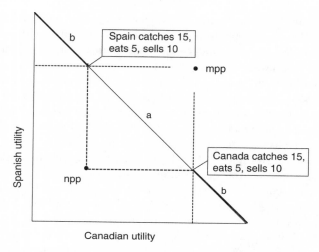

Figure 3.1. Injury for Spain and Canada

state of nature, they are also better off than they would have been in the absence of Canada. The relation between Spain and Canada is now parasitic. The Canadians are exploited.

In figure 3.1 we can see how utility distributions between Spain and Canada would relate to the distribution of the catch between them. The "natural proviso point" (npp) represents the position of each as it would have been in the absence of the possibility of receiving gold and silver: they both catch and eat five fish. Of course, if Spain or Canada would try to steal the fish the other has caught, and a fight emerges, then one of them, or both, might be doing worse in the state of nature than they would have done without the other. The "market proviso point" (mpp) between Canada and Spain represents the position of each as it would have been within an external market but without the existence of the other. As we can see, mpp is outside the outcome space: extra-Paretan, so to speak. They cannot both be doing as well as they would have done without the other. Utility distributions on the (thin) line, marked (a) are mutually "injurious" compared to the absence of the other, but advantageous for both compared to the absence of gold and silver; distributions on the lines marked (b), however, are parasitic: one of them is doing worse, the other better, than he would have done in the state of nature, or in the state of money without the other.

The main question now is: just how disproportionate and unequal may the partage of fish be, according to Locke? If no restrictions are placed on the right to appropriate through labor, then the labor principle of original acquisition allows, indeed may even invite, parasitic actions. If the introduction of money sets us free to grab anything we can lay our hands on without restrictions whatsoever, then we are also free to rush ahead, take what another wants, and sell it to him or her. It would imply that even Gauthier's "Lockean proviso" would be wrongly attributed to Locke himself. Can we arrive at that position by simply ignoring the two or three passages where Locke is grammatically saying otherwise? Can we get a consistent Locke in this way? I think not. If we want to read Locke as allowing parasitism, we should ignore much more than just a few passages. In fact, we should ignore the very foundation of Locke's doctrine that only labor gives property rights, and that foundation is his "labor theory of value."

3.6 The Foundational Principle

Let us return to the state of nature! Why does Locke think that labor rather than some other process establishes an exclusive private property right in a previously commonly owned thing? Why, for instance, should the public utterance "I intend to use x" not be sufficient to establish such a property in x? Why may we not take what another has already mixed his labor with, whereas we may take any x even if someone has announced his intention to use x? The reason why it is labor and not some other procedure that gives a title, is, I believe, quite obvious from Locke's text. In fact he has put it very well in 34: "He that has as good left for his Improvement, as was already taken up, needed not complain, ought not to meddle with what was already improved by another's labor: if he did, 'tis plain he desired the benefit of another's Pains, which he had no right to."

So there are two features of labor that together make it the obvious process to establish property: on the one hand, things are assumed to be improved through labor, and, on the other hand, labor itself is considered to be a cost, or a pain. If we steal, we take the benefit of another's costs, and that is in fact what we have no right to do. Labor adds value to natural resources, and, where unimproved resources are plentiful, it is clear that the thief or robber seeks that added value, and not the resources to which the value has been added. If I harvest from land that you ploughed, I seek to spare myself the pain of ploughing while I deny you the benefit of it. If I steal the fish that you have caught, I spare myself the trouble of catching. This, at least, is obvious where there is still land to be ploughed, or fish to be caught. It is this unilateral transfer of value that is in fact morally objectionable, and the foundational reason for connecting exclusive rights to the things that are improved through labor is to prevent a practice of parasitism. So much should be clear. Locke's labor principle of original acquisition is not just a "first come, first served" principle. It is only because, in the state of nature under conditions of plenty, "coming first to x" means "adding value to x" that we ought not to meddle with x when others already did so.

And this puts our interpretational problem of Locke in the sharpest focus. If the labor principle of original acquisition is sustained by a moral objection to parasitism, then it is most implausible that this very same principle could be extended in such a fashion as to sustain, sanction, and invite relations that are in fact parasitic. Such an extension, however, is exactly what is implied by the nonrestrictive reading of the first proviso, as advocated by Waldron. To put it bluntly: if the labor principle would warrant such relations, it is no longer comprehensible why there is something wrong with the desire for the benefit of another's pains, and if it is not comprehensible why there is something wrong with that, then neither is it comprehensible why there would be something wrong with theft and robbery—whether in the state of nature or in the state of money.

To resume, we cannot make Locke a consistent moral philosopher on the issue of private property by ignoring a few troublesome passages as the result of an "afterthought." His texts may be ridden with ambiguities, but on some things he has been clear enough. He has overlooked, perhaps, that access to the market, by which I mean access to the opportunity to engage in mutually beneficial (trade) relations with third parties, is itself a scarce good, and that the "as good" clause in 27, if taken literally, would simply put too strong a constraint on appropriation. But the idea that the doctrine of private-property-through-labor would warrant exploitative and parasitic actions, where the objection to such actions is explicitly given as the reason to establish such a thing as private property in the first place, is beyond the most lenient conception of consistency.

We shall have to do with a Locke who, as a matter of moral principle, rejects parasitism, whether in the state of nature through theft and robbery or in the state of money through original snatchings that put others in the position of a coerced buyer. Of course, there is another question whether or not Locke thought that this principle was actually violated in his own age. His notorious remark that a day laborer in England is better off than an (Indian) king of a large and fruitful territory in America strongly suggests that he did not think so. But these are empirical claims[10] that do not really touch on the conceptual structure of his moral theory: people may not seek to exploit their fellow men. The principle of original acquisition falls within the scope of this constraint. This, at least, is the minimal significance we ought to attribute to the first Lockean proviso. Gauthier is right.

3.7 Use and Appropriation

To provide a last example of a political philosopher who seems to be entangled in the web of ambiguous Lockean notions of justice in original acquisition, scarcity, and parasitic action, I will devote this section to a discussion of the "historical entitlement theory of justice" that is defended by Robert Nozick, the author of *Anarchy, State, and Utopia* (1974), who is often appreciated as the most eloquent spokesman for a free market society.

The main methodological problem in dealing with Nozick's doctrine of justice, at least with the features that concern us most, is that the relevant parts of it are in different sections of his book, and that they are discussed in heterogeneous contexts. On the one hand (in section 7) we have a doctrine of justice in original acquisition, including a "Lockean proviso," which prohibits original appropriators of previously unowned resources to deny others the opportunity to use these resources, and on the other hand (in section 4) we have a piece of reasoning about justice in transaction, which boils down to a prohibition of so-called (partially) unproductive exchanges. As I will point out, these two prohibitions have an overlap. Both prohibit certain types of action. Yet, as a prohibition, the latter is more stringent than the former. The requirement not to force unproductive exchanges on others rules out parasitic actions per se, while the Lockean proviso (as taken by Nozick) only rules out certain types of parasitic action.

Nozick is a professed "Lockean" and it seems that he is ready to acknowledge the prohibition of parasitic (trans)actions through original acquisitions of "previously unowned things." He takes what he calls "the Lockean proviso" to prohibit a person to worsen another person's position by appropriating something. He gives an example of the standard case in which this proviso would have to be effective.

> Once it is known that someone's ownership runs afoul of the Lockean proviso, there are stringent limits on what he may do with (what it is difficult unreservedly to call) "his property". Thus a person may not appropriate the only water hole in a desert and charge what he will. Nor may he charge what he will if he possesses one, and unfortunately it happens that all the water holes in the desert dry up, except for his. (Nozick 1974: 180)

However Nozick feels that Locke's clause in 27 should be taken to fix every person's "base line position" (compared to which he may not be made worse off by the acquisitions of others) in some kind of pre-economic state of nature. The proviso is not meant to provide every person with some share of access to the market or with some share of access to the kinds of resources that can be used in order to produce things with which to enter the market. If a person's position is worsened through the acquisitions of others, he should be compensated, but the level of compensation (his base line position) is determined by the use he could have made of the goods that are appropriated by others, not by the market value of their appropriations. The original appropriator gains the right to sell, but he may not sell to those who would otherwise have used the goods he has appropriated.

> Fourier held that since the process of civilization had deprived the members of society of certain liberties (to gather, pasture, engage in the chase), a socially guaranteed minimum provision for persons was justified as compensation for the loss. . . . But this puts the point too strongly. This compensation would be due those persons, if any, for whom the process of civilization was a *net loss*, for whom the benefits of civilization did not counterbalance being deprived of these particular liberties. (Nozick 178–79 n.)

Hence (to return to the example in the section on Locke): if five fish is what you would have caught in the state of nature for your own consumption, there should be no complaint if someone else appropriates all the rest with the purpose of selling to third parties what he cannot eat himself. The distinction between using an x and appropriating an x is given its decisive meaning as follows:

> Someone may be made worse off by another's appropriation in two ways: first, by losing the opportunity to improve his situation by a particular appropriation or any one; and second, by no longer being able to use freely (without appropriation) what he previously could. A *stringent* requirement that another not be made worse off by an appropriation would exclude the first way if nothing else counterbalances the diminution of the opportunity, as well as the second. A *weaker* requirement would exclude the second way, though not the first. (Nozick 1974: 176)

And then he proceeds to say he assumes that "any adequate theory of justice in acquisition will contain a proviso similar to the weaker of the ones we have attributed to Locke."

Of course, this way of putting things leaves us with the colossal problem of what to do when my using a thing worsens your ability "to use freely what you previously could" (e.g. when, counter to Locke's convenient stipulations, there is scarcity in the state of nature). Indeed, there is something deeply puzzling about the notion of "using without appropriating," since all plausible ways of using a thing involve some kind of labor, and labor is supposed to give a property right. Here, however, I will bypass these questions and simply point out why Nozick's distinction between "use" and "appropriation" does not actually do what it purports to do: it does not exclude all exploitative action.

Let us concentrate on his example of the appropriator of the only water hole in an isolated area. And let us think of this area as an island with a certain limited population.[11] We may not appropriate the only water hole on a desert island in such a way that others can no longer drink what they want to drink. We may not charge them for drinking out of "our" water hole. But, it seems, as long as we allow others to drink freely from our water hole, we have not wronged them by appropriating that water hole. They are still as free to use what they previously could.

But what if there is a second group of people who cannot reach the water hole on our desert island—they are on some other island they cannot leave—but who are willing to give some of the things they have on their island, say, home grown yams, in exchange for some of the water from the hole in our area (suppose that such exchanges were possible through a system of remote-controlled toy cargo ships)? To whom should those, very desirable, yams go? To the first "appropriator" of the water hole? Or to all inhabitants of our island? Nozick's interpretation of the Lockean proviso implies that the benefits stemming from exchanging the water may go all to the first appropriator, since exchanging water for yams is not using water. So, the original appropriator may not exclude others from drinking the water from his well, but he may forbid them to take water if they want to sell that water to others in exchange for yams, or he may charge them if they want to do so. We may fail to see the rationale behind this distinction between using water to drink and using water to sell, but this is simply what is implied by the libertarian view of justice in original acquisition. It may seem that what counts is that I, not being the original appropriator, am no longer allowed to enter a beneficial market with the outsider third party on my own conditions (for either I will be excluded from that market entirely by the original appropriator, or he will charge me for entering that market). It may seem that what counts is that my position is worsened, compared to what it would have been in the absence of the original appropriator, but then we would be trying to measure the legitimacy of original appropriations by the stringent variety of the proviso and not the weaker one that Nozick distinguished. Note also that if I had been the original appropriator, I might have been ready and capable to sell to the outsiders at a lower price (e.g. because I am a more efficient and less costly operator of toy cargo ships), and that this makes no difference. The actions of the original appropriator may be to my disadvantage as well as to the disadvantage of his clients.

But let us face a more complicated and also more serious situation. Provided that he allows others to use his appropriation for their consumptive purposes as they previously could, the original appropriator is the only one who may enjoy commercial benefits from the thing he has appropriated. And if others seek such benefits the original appropriator can legitimately demand a share of such benefits as payment. He may hire it out. Suppose now that the outsider third party is not so much interested in exchanging her yams for water, but that she rather wants apples in return for her yams. You, being the original appropriator of the water hole, see a wonderful opportunity to improve your situation. You use your water to irrigate a plot of land where you work hard to grow apples, which you ship to the islanders who ship back enormous quantities of yams for you to eat. However, demand for apples "over there" is not yet exhausted: they want more, and they are willing to provide more yams in return. But your apple growing capacity is exhausted: you are not able, or not willing, to work still longer hours in the apple yard for additional yams. Fortunately, some of your compatriots are eager for yams too, and they are quite willing to start an apple yard of their own for the purpose of entering into transactions with the other islanders, and they want your water for their irrigation systems. Again you sense a wonderful opportunity to improve your position. Of course, you had felt obliged all along to allow these compatriots to drink from your well, and to take an occasional shower, and you even would have allowed them the use of the water if they had wanted it to produce apples for their own consumption, but now that they are seeking commercial benefits for which they want your water, you feel entitled to charge them. So you allow them the use of your originally appropriated well but you ask them to turn in part of the yams they earn with their activities. Thus, you gain an extra quantity of yams on top of your own earnings.

Have you done anything you should not have done according to Nozick? Have you worsened anybody's position by not allowing her the free use of the well? You have not. On the contrary: the people who buy your water are even better off than they would have been if they had only used the well for private consumptive purposes, since now they may acquire some delicious yams on top of their free drinks. How universally beneficial your appropriation has been! Nobody has suffered, nobody is below the base line position, everybody benefits. Actually, this is one of those many occasions calling for three cheers for the spirit of free enterprise.

I assume this is how Nozick would allow original appropriators to reason if we are to make any sense of his distinction between use and appropriation. As we saw, he thinks that anybody who has not suffered a net loss by the "process of civilization" (by which he presumably means the development of market relations between formerly unconnected individuals) cannot have a ground for complaint, whatever the distribution of the benefits of that process and whatever the contribution each has made to that process.

But surely, your charges would be as blatantly exploitative as charging for drinking the water would be, since through your control of the water hole you would get free access to the benefits of my hard apple growing labor—my pains, so to speak. True, if I water the apples I want to sell to others, I do not use the water for my own consumption, but charging me for the water would be exploitative nevertheless.

Again, in figure 3.2 we can see the consequences of Nozick's distinction between using an x and appropriating an x, and how the proviso works out in practice. Let npp represent both our utility levels if we both only use the water hole for private consumptive purposes, such as drinking, taking a shower, and, perhaps, irrigating plots of desert from which we take fruits that we eat ourselves. Let mpp be the point representing our respective utility levels when we both use the water in order to irrigate land on which we grow apples that we exchange for yams with the outsider third party, while I do not charge you for the commercial use of that water and neither do you charge me (mpp is not necessarily in the middle of the Pareto line, nor is npp). Now, let us suppose that you are the original appropriator. What would the Nozickian proviso prohibit you to do to me? Well, in the absence and in the presence of the outsider third party, you may not charge me for the consumptive use of the water, so distributions on the lines marked (B) (Pareto efficient without the third party) and the lines marked (b) (Pareto efficient with the third party) are morally impossible. However, distributions on the

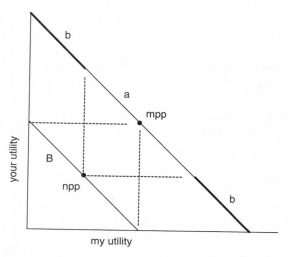

Figure 3.2. Use and appropriation

line marked (a) are perfectly permissible. In that case you have charged me for the commercial use, though not the consumptive use, of your water. As we can see, these positions are worse for me than I might have expected to be in your absence, and better for you than you might have expected to be in my absence. No wonder: they can only be reached if, in fact, I work for you without pay.

3.8 Extortion and the Concept of "Productive Exchange"

Let us turn to the other half of Nozick's theory to see if we can find more plausible principles there. The context, this time, is Nozick's defense of the legitimacy of the so-called "minimal state"—that is, the state that has monopolized jurisdiction and the right to punish violations of justice—against the position of the ultra-right anarchist, who holds that the right to (prepare for) self-defense should always remain effective, even within political communities. Nozick's quarrel with the political anarchist over the right to self-defense is not my main concern here. What interests me is Nozick's underlying analysis of what he calls "productive" and "unproductive exchanges." I will pursue that analysis and try to show its inconsistency with his doctrine of appropriation through original acquisition. I will try to show how the idea of "productive exchanges" warrants a general moral objection to parasitic action, including parasitic original appropriations, where the Nozickian proviso, as we saw, does not. Along the way we will come across a criticism of Nozick's concept of productive exchange by Eric Mack, which I shall try to parry on my own account, and on Nozick's behalf.

In general, Nozick says, transactions between persons will be to the benefit of both parties. The one sells, the other buys, and both prefer their position after the exchange to their position before the exchange. That is why they exchange. Generally, it is also true that both parties, after the exchange, are better off than they would have been without the other or if the other had had nothing to do with them. They are both glad that the other is there. However, there are particular transactions that are not mutually beneficial in this latter sense. Sometimes purchasers (have to) buy something, and they will be better off with their purchase than they would have been without it, but they are not better off than they would have been without (the existence of) the other person (in their neighborhood). Typically, this is the case when the other is hindering us, and when we pay him to stop doing that.

Yet, there is a third kind of exchange. In the two cases we discussed, both parties profited from the fact that there was a possibility to transact at all. Whether we purchase a "bonus" or a "non-malus" from the other does not matter, we are better off purchasing it than not. But in the third type of transaction this is no longer true, for here the fact that the possibility of transaction exists explains the existence of the "malus" to one of the parties: the activity that hinders us would not have been there in the first place, if there had been no possibility to sell the abstention. Typically, this is so when we have to deal with an extortionist. He is the person who will (or threatens to) do harm to us, but only because he knows that we are ready to pay him for not doing so.

The first two types of transaction Nozick calls "productive exchanges," the third type he calls an "unproductive exchange." Unproductive exchanges are characterized by the fact that one of the parties would have been better off if either the transaction were impossible or prohibited, or if the other party did not exist.

> If your next door neighbor plans to erect a certain structure on his land, which he has a right to do, you might be better off if he didn't exist at all. . . . Yet purchasing his abstention from proceeding with his plans will be a productive exchange. Suppose, however, that the neighbor has no desire to erect the structure on the land; he formulates his plan and informs you of it solely in order to sell you his abstention from it. Such

an exchange would not be a productive one; it merely gives you relief from something that would not threaten if not for the possibility of an exchange to get relief from it. (Nozick 1974: 85)

Surely, our "next door neighbor" must remind us of Mr. Pickles from Bradford (whom we met in chapter 1), who changed the course of a stream just in order to let the community of Bradford buy their relief from being cut off from their water supply. Obviously, unproductive exchanges are parasitic and exploitative, and Nozick, unlike the House of Lords in England, is ready to prohibit them. And he goes even further than that. He is also ready to put restrictions on productive exchanges of the second type—buying abstention from a harm—when the seller of the abstention would profit from that exchange in such a way as to make him in fact better off than he would have been without the other party. Suppose your next door neighbor is independently interested in building his "structure" and that receiving a certain amount of money would leave him indifferent, then he should not receive more than that amount in selling his abstention to you. Receiving more would allow him to actually better his position at your cost; it would allow him the benefit of your pains, so such a transaction would be, as Nozick calls it: partially unproductive.

Consider two persons, A and B, and suppose we ask each of them two questions:

1. Given that the other exists, is it a good thing for you that there is a possibility of transaction with him?
2. Given that there will be a possibility of transaction with the other (if he exists), is it a good thing for you that the other exists?

Then the combinations of sets of answers from A and B will shift between the cases of productive, partially productive, and unproductive

Table 3.1. Existence and exchange: benefit and burden

	Productive exchange		Partially productive exchange		Unproductive exchange	
	A	B	A	B	A	B
Question 1	Yes	Yes	Yes	Yes	No	Yes
Question 2	Yes	Yes	No	Yes	No	Yes

exchanges (table 3.1). These combinations of sets of answers to our two questions are not exhaustive. In the present context there are two interesting alternatives. First, there are those situations in which both would be a "spontaneous" hindrance to the other, but where the possibility of transaction gives both an opportunity to better their position; they can exchange abstentions: I will not build the structure on my land that I find beautiful and you find ugly, if you stop playing your trumpet during the night, which you like to do but I do not like you to do. This would result in the case shown in table 3.2.

And, second, there are those situations where one of the parties threatens to inflict a harm in order to prevent that a harm will be done to himself: I threaten to build a structure on my land which (I know) you will hate and that I do not particularly like myself, but you can buy relief from that by stopping to play your trumpet during the night. This would result in the case shown in table 3.3.

3.9 Eric Mack on Boycott

The possibility of the fifth case has been presented as a serious objection to Nozick's prohibition of (partially) unproductive exchanges. As Eric Mack (1981) construes Nozick's argument, there are two conditions a transaction should satisfy in order to be called (partially) unproductive:

1. One of the parties would be better off if the other party did not exist or had nothing to do with him at all.
2. One of the parties would be better off if exchanges were prohibited or impossible, or if exchanges involving a transfer of value higher than the value that would leave the recipient indifferent were prohibited or impossible. (The would-be seller of an abstention from a harmful activity is not allowed to sell at all, or, if he has independent motives for that activity, he should only receive a price that would leave him indifferent.)

Table 3.2. A fourth case

	A	B
Question 1	Yes	Yes
Question 2	No	No

Table 3.3. A fifth case

	A	B
Question 1	Yes	No
Question 2	No	No

Then Mack proceeds to argue that the second condition is typical for all standard market transactions as well. As he puts it:

> Characteristically, the seller gets more than some price *m* which would have motivated him to sell had exchange for more than *m* been forbidden or impossible.... If exchange at above *m* were forbidden or impossible the buyer would be better off....
>
> We can also see that in typical free market exchanges the activity of the buyer also satisfies, in the same partial way, the second condition for unproductivity. For "buyers" are just sellers of money and "sellers" are just buyers of money. (Mack 1981: 178–79)

Prices in standard market transactions tend to exceed the so-called "reservation price" of both sellers and buyers. And hence, it seems, the first condition—would one of the parties be better off without the other?—will in fact determine the productive or unproductive character of an exchange. But if that is the case, Mack says, it is no longer clear what is objectionable in unproductive exchanges.

In order to show why certain forms of exchange that satisfy both conditions are morally unproblematic he gives an example of what he calls a "peaceful boycott." A group of people no longer wishes to do business, or so they say, with a "wicked retailer who racially discriminates in hiring." By threatening a boycott they hope to convince the retailer to stop his wicked practice. What they in fact do is offer him the abstention from the harmful boycott, in return for a change in his own conduct. Is the second condition for unproductivity satisfied? It is, Mack says, because the boycott would not threaten if not for the possibility to sell the lifting of it. Is the first condition also satisfied? It is, says Mack again: without the presence of his would-be boycotters the retailer would have been better off because he would have invested his energies at another site (presumably where his customers would be less morally sensitive to racial discrimination).[12] So peaceful boycotts satisfy both conditions for unproductivity and may be prohibited. In fact, it seems, the lifting of a boycott is a fully and not only a partially unproductive activity, since there would be no threat of a boycott if not for the possibility of selling the lifting of it. And what objection can there be to peaceful boycotts against racists!?

What has been overlooked in Mack's argument is that the wicked retailer's activities must be taken as being harmful to the people who now threaten the boycott, and that in selling the lifting of the boycott they do not better themselves compared to his absence. The best they will possibly do for themselves is restore the position they would have been in, if the wicked retailer had not existed or had resided somewhere else (assuming a non-wicked retailer taking his place), but probably they will even suffer a (small) loss compared to that position, since they will have to invest in the credibility of their threat (petitioning in the neighborhood, organize meetings etc.)[13]

Mack believes that boycotts are interesting because "they are evidence that there is no significant borderline between hard market bargaining and blackmail," but they are no such evidence at all. The blackmailer[14] is a parasite; he wants to improve his position beyond what it would have been without the existence of the person he now threatens to harm; and, of course, there is no reason to change his name when his ends happen to be political ones. But the boycotter, as he emerges from Mack's description, is not a parasite; he merely seeks to protect himself from a setback to his ends—political or otherwise—that others (are going to) bring about. Boycotters would be better off if the racists were out of the way to begin with, but blackmailers and extortionists would be worse off without their victims. That, it seems to me, is a very significant borderline between the hard bargain that boycotters drive and the crime that blackmailers commit.

Mack's first condition to what Nozick has called partial unproductivity is not correct. It leaves out an essential element, for what Nozick is obviously trying to rule out is the possibility of transaction which makes one of the parties worse off than he would have been without the existence of the other, precisely because it makes the other better off than he would have been without the existence of the first. Possibilities of transaction that do not satisfy Nozick's condition for partial unproductivity, including boycotts, may indeed allow or even invite tough bargaining but they do not allow or invite parasitic action.

Let us see how the welfare of two parties, A and B, involved in exchanges, will develop under three different conditions. In situation 1 they are alone, the other does not exist or has nothing to do with them. In situation 2 they are not alone; the other exists, but they have no possibility to transact. In situation 3 the other exists and there is a possibility to transact. In figure 3.3, giving the utility developments over these three situations, we can see how the five types of transaction we have distinguished differ from each other, and we can see how the two cases of fully unproductive exchanges and partially unproductive exchanges contain a problem that is absent in the other three. Unproductive exchanges, and partially unproductive exchanges in so far as they are unproductive, may be prohibited without compensation being due to those whose liberties are constrained by such a prohibition. Hence, it appears that Nozick is willing to prohibit parasitism through the possibility of transaction; indeed he sees the justice of it and wants to go all the way.[15]

Now, if we regard "appropriating" things as an activity (and how else should we regard it?), and as a potentially harmful activity, then it must be evident that the prohibition against (partially) unproductive exchanges should fully apply to the situations that arise from the original appropriating process. Rushing ahead and appropriating all the water there is, and then selling it to people who want to use that water but not in ways that are detrimental to your own interest is just the same as forcing the others into an unproductive exchange. And even if they are going to use it in ways that are harmful to you, you may demand that you will be compensated in return for letting them have the water, but you may not use your bargaining advantage in such a way as to actually benefit from their being deprived of free access to the water. There should be no way that you are to benefit from their activities if they do not benefit from yours in the same way.

Appendix: Notes on Some Editorial Peculiarities of John Locke's *Second Treatise of Government*

> The problems of political theory will never be solved by worrying about the positions of commas.
>
> Peter Laslett

1 Punctuation and the Proviso

There is a remarkable development in the editorial history of the central passage we have discussed in the sections on Locke's theory. I believe it has not been pointed out before. The student of Locke who wants to find out what the master himself has actually

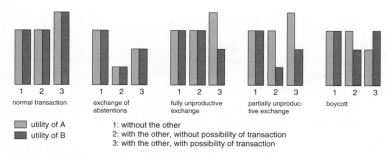

Figure 3.3. Utility development over three situations, five types

written, and who is aware that the *Second Treatise* has known several subsequent editions during Locke's lifetime, and also several thereafter in which corrections by his own hand have been incorporated, may hope to find an authoritative text by consulting a few modern editions. But this proves to be a rather perplexing exercise. Let us consider the two places where the enough-and-as-good formulation of the first proviso is used; the first is in 27, where the sentence starts:

> For this *Labor* being the unquestionable Property of the Laborer, no Man but he can have a right to what that is once joyned to, . . .

And the second occurrence in 33 begins:

> Nor was this *appropriation* of any parcel of *Land*, by improving it, any prejudice to any other Man, . . .

Then the modern editions continue the clause as follows:

Carpenter's edition (1924), based "on the first state of the first edition of 1690" (Locke 1924: fly leaf):

> 27: . . . , at least where there is enough, and as good left in common for others.
> 33: . . . , since there was enough and as good left;

Laslett's edition (last reprint with amendments: 1970), based (mainly) on a copy of the third edition of 1698 (the so-called Christ's copy) "with its errata list and the very extensive corrections in Locke's own hand and in Coste's" (Locke 1970: 127):

> 27: . . . , at least where there is enough, and as good left in common for others.
> 33: . . . , since there was still enough, and as good left;

Macpherson's edition (1980), based on the sixth edition of 1764, "the first edition to take full account of all Locke's changes" (Locke 1980: 1):

> 27: ..., at least where there is enough, and as good, left in common for others.
>
> 33: ..., since there was still enough, and as good left;

Gough's edition (1966), also based on the sixth edition of 1764; however, "the *punctuation* and the spelling have been modernized" (Locke 1946: xliv [44]):

> 27: ..., at least where there is enough and as good left in common for others.
>
> 33: ..., since there was still enough and as good left;

Since all these editors claim some degree of authenticity for their texts—and there is no reason why we should not take their word for that—it seems that Locke has been through quite some difficulties making up his mind about where exactly he wanted to have the commas. The first edition had one in 27 and none in 33; the third, corrected, edition had one in 27 and one in 33; and the sixth edition had two in 27 and one in 33. Who knows what an autopsy on the second, fourth, and fifth editions might reveal? Perhaps Locke might have even applauded, at some time in his life, the luminous idea of getting rid of these itchy little things altogether, as Gough the modernizer decided to do.

But no, John Locke was a serious man, and there are no other twelve or so pages in the history of political philosophy—with the exception, perhaps, of chapter 13 of the *Leviathan*—that have been as profoundly influential as this small chapter on property. It is here, after all, that we find the intellectual nucleus of both libertarianism and socialism. It is here that we find the first instance of the labor theory of value, and the insight that the possibility of accumulated capital is as radical a change in the course of human history as Original Sin. But it is also here that the defenders of the free market, and even anarcho-capitalists, sometimes seek refuge. In short, these pages have an intellectual gravity from which no effort in political theory can escape. We have all the reason in the world to be concerned when commas suddenly start multiplying in a text like that.

Of the four editions considered, one stands out because it forces an interpretation on us that is not implied by the other three, although it is not completely excluded by the other three either. That edition is Macpherson's. If we say that there "is enough, and as good, left in common for others," then we can only mean that there is enough left for the others and that there is as good left for the others. When we say, however, that there "is enough, and as good left in common for others" we may also, and more plausibly, mean that there is enough and that there is as good left in common for others. In the latter reading the "as good" qualifies what is left, while the "enough" qualifies what was there before something was left. In the former, Macpherson-implied, reading "as good" and "enough" doubly qualify what is left. Now, is the laborer entitled to:

1. what he joined his labor to, where there is enough left and as good left in common for the others,

or is he entitled to:

2. what he joined his labor to, where there is enough and where there is as good left in common for the others?

As I said, the Macpherson edition forces (1) on us, and, indeed, many Locke scholars (Den Hartogh, Waldron) tend to take the passage in this way. I myself tend to favor the other reading (and regard the second comma in 27 as a mistake) because I find the "double qualification of the left over" grammatically weird. How could the "enough" and the "as good" qualify the same thing (what is left over for the others) without these two expressions being either contradictory, or one of them redundant?[16] Rather, one would expect Locke to want to say something like this: each may take for keeps whatever she likes where there is enough (for everybody) and where (by consequence) something as good as there used to be is left for the others.

2 Thomas Hollis, Editor of Punctuation

In the end I felt compelled to check on the sixth edition—Macpherson's master text—myself. That edition was published in 1764 by Thomas Hollis, a scholarly gentleman and art lover. The library of the University of Leiden has a copy of it. There I found, of course, that the second comma in 27 was not an invention or error of Macpherson; it was really there. Then I decided to check on the fourth edition of the *Two Treatises*, published in 1713, reprinted in the first collected edition of Locke's works in 1714, as such reprinted in 1722, in 1727, and in 1740. Leiden has a copy of that collected edition of 1740 as well (Locke 1970). The second comma is not there. What can we conclude from these findings? I am afraid that we should conclude that Hollis's second comma in 27 is suspect. But in order to understand why, one must know how the several editions came into being.

The "To the Reader" of the collected edition quotes from Locke's "last will and testament":

> ...; *I do hereby further give to the publick library of the University of Oxford, these following books; that is to say,* Three Letters concerning Toleration: Two Treatises of Government, (*whereof Mr. Churchill has published several editions, but all very incorrect*):....

Also from the "To the Reader":

> As to this edition of all his works together, I have this to advertise the reader, that most of them are printed from copies corrected and enlarged under Mr. *Locke*'s own hand; and in particular, that the two Treatises of Government were never, till now, published from a copy, corrected by himself.

So, there is evidence that Locke legated a corrected copy of the *Two Treatises* to Oxford University, and that the fourth edition is based on that text. According to the editor's note, Hollis's sixth edition

> ...has not only been collated with the first three Editions, which were published during the Author's Life, but also has the Advantage of his last Corrections and Improvements, from a Copy delivered by him to Mr. Peter Coste, communicated to the Editor, and now lodged in Christ College, Cambridge.

Hollis had acquired this copy in "his private walks," and it was he himself who donated it to the library of Christ's College (Locke 1970: 11). It is this so-called "Christ's copy" on which Laslett's critical edition is based too.

So, what we now have is Laslett's edition based on the Christ's copy with one comma in 27, and no indication of textual variations in the "collation"; Hollis's edition with two commas in 27, also said to be based on the Christ's copy; and the fourth edition with one comma in 27, allegedly based on a second master-copy with Locke's corrections. (This second master-copy has never been recovered.) Hence, there is reason for suspecting that Hollis's edition is unreliable on this point. It would seem that he modernized the second comma into 27, or that it stems from the process of collating the Christ's copy with (one of) the first three editions—but these, as we know, were all very incorrect.

So, indeed, in the spirit of Mr. Gough I propose to modernize the second comma away.

3 *Thomas Hollis, Lover of Liberty*

Meanwhile, during my search for the origin of the wild comma in 27, my curiosity was raised by something else, and I hope that the reader will forgive me a still further prolongation of this nonphilosophical intermezzo. I noticed that the fly leaf of the Leiden copy of Hollis's edition carried a hand-written dedication:

> *An Englishman, a lover of Liberty, Citizen of the World, is Desirous of having the honor to present this book to the public Library of the University of Leyden. A. MDCCLXV*

Who was this gallant Englishman who had anonymously made such a precious gift of Locke's work, and only one year after its publication? Further excavations from the library archives brought me nothing, except that, indeed, the *Catalogue of Books brought into the Library, from the year 1754 onwards* has an entry in its "Juridici" division in 1765: *Locke on Governement* [*sic*]. *Lond. 1764 Oct. 3 G.* But (with the generous help of Mrs. Silvia Vermetten of the University Library of Leiden) I managed to trace the anonymous benefactor after all. He had been identified on several other occasions. In 1759 he had donated the Collected Works of Milton, and in 1761 he had sent thirteen "effigies of eminent British writers, modelled in wax" (among them Milton and Locke), all accompanied by similarly worded dedications. He turned out to be no one else than Thomas Hollis, the editor and publisher, himself.[17] Finally, I noticed what I had overlooked before: Laslett (Locke 1870: 154) quotes the letter that accompanied Hollis's donation of Locke's corrected copy of the *Two Treatises* to Christ's College:

> *An Englishman, A Lover of Liberty, Citizen of the World, is desirous of having the honor to deposite This Book in the Library of Christ College Cambridge.*

Thomas Hollis's edition of Locke's work may not be entirely reliable, but he certainly cared a lot for the spread of Locke's ideas.

4 *Translation of the Fifth French Edition*

Here is another peculiarity in the history of editions. As we saw, one of the strongest supporting passages for the restrictive reading of the clause in 27 was in 35 where Locke says that nobody may enclose part of a "commons": "Besides, the remainder, after such inclosure, would not be as good to the Commoners as the whole was, when they could all make use of the whole." For some reason, the French edition (Locke 1755) allegedly based on the fifth English edition of 1728, translates this passage as follows:

> Au reste, on peut ajouter à la raison tirée des Loix du Païs, cette autre *qui est d'un grand poids* [italics added], savoir, que si on venoit à fermer

de certaines bornes & à s'aproprier quelque portion de la terre *commune*, que nous suposons; ce qui en resteroit ne seroit aussi utile & aussi avantageux aux membres de la Communauté, que lorsqu'elle étoit toute entiére.

Evidently, the translator thought that this argument was of such "great weight" that he decided to say so on his own account—in Locke's text. And this is the second instance in the history of only twelve pages to show that editing was a rather adventurous business in the eighteenth century, and not only because of its potential liability to political persecution.

5 Le Chevalier Rousset de Missy

The editor of this French text, whose initials on the title page read L.C.R.D.M.A.D.P., is listed as unidentified by Laslett (Locke 1970: 126), but a paper recently inserted (by whom?) in the copy of the University Library of Amsterdam says that he is *Le Chevalier Rousset de Missy Academie du Plessis.* The authors' catalogue of this library straightforwardly gives the initials as a "name variation" of Jean Rousset de Missy (1686–1762). He was a political journalist, residing in the Netherlands. Several other editions of French translations of English texts have been attributed to him.

CHAPTER 4

CLAMSHELL RENT? USE, USURPATION, AND USURY

[A]nd we know that parasites, when they become
too numerous, are pests.

T. S. Eliot

4.1 Dworkin and Van Parijs: Equality of Resources and Basic Income

In the last two chapters, we encountered several instances of how certain principles of justice in original acquisition will, under certain conditions, seriously violate the Lockean proviso as interpreted by Gauthier, and hence will institute parasitic relations. Gauthier, Locke, and Nozick all have their own problems in spelling out a theory of justice that can be consistent with their own moral objection against parasitism. Gauthier cannot be true to that objection and keep his commitment to a concept of "fixed" rights in external resources. Locke, who thinks that we have no right to the benefit of another's pains, cannot at the same time claim that the introduction of gold and silver will set people free to call themselves the owners of anything they were the first to mix their labor with. And Nozick's distinction between consumptive and commercial use of resources does not really do the trick he wants it to do. His objection against "unproductive exchanges," however, is helpful.

In this chapter and the next, I will shift my attention to theories of justice of an altogether different type. Where our first three authors seem to set out from a doctrine of justice in original acquisition that does not at all reflect the various interests that individuals may have in their property rights (and therefore run into trouble with parasitism), I will now discuss a theory of justice in original acquisition in which the interests of all those involved in, and affected by, the initial distribution of resources play a very significant determining role. I will discuss Ronald Dworkin's theory of justice that is known as "equality of resources." Will his approach avoid the clash with our moral objection against parasitic relations? In the course of the second half of this book, I conclude that it will not. But my journey towards that conclusion will be rather roundabout. The roundabout way is via Philippe Van Parijs and his advocacy of a radical reconstruction of the welfare state.

More or less recently, at least in the European arena of political philosophy, an old proposal has gained renewed attention and, indeed, approval. The idea that every person is unconditionally entitled to a so-called "basic income," a monetary grant to be given to each regardless of one's willingness to work or regardless of one's other sources of income and financed through an income tax, has found new intellectual grounds to foster it. The idea of a basic income originates as far back as Thomas Paine's *Agrarian Justice* (1796), and it has been advocated by several authors since (including Léon Walras), but in our days, as is observed with some satisfaction by its adherents, it is no longer just an academic issue for philosophers of justice and political economists. Although "there are no signs yet of a stampede" (Manza 1995: 888), it is really on the agenda of at least some political movements in Europe and the United States (notably BIEN and USBIG), and it is increasingly discussed in circles of party politicians and policy makers. The most eloquent, vigorous, and consistent spokesman for a basic income is, I believe, Philippe Van Parijs. In a series of articles, some written together with Robert J. van der Veen, and in an elaborate monograph—*Real Freedom for All: What (if Anything) Can Justify Capitalism?* (1995b)[1]—Van Parijs has put forward his arguments.

The recent appeal of the universal grant may not be difficult to understand. The European welfare states, committed as they are to the idea that the involuntarily unemployed are entitled to support, have increasingly been inclined to develop more and more sophisticated criteria and instruments to assort the various groups of potential beneficiaries of the welfare system. Are these beneficiaries involuntarily unemployed in the first place? Do they lack other means of support? Have they done their best to find a suitable job? What is a "suitable job," anyway? Are they not involved in the black labor market? Are they married? Are they divorced? To what extent should run-or-chased-away partners be held responsible for the support of the other and their children? Are some entitled to special compensations? How old are they? What employment history do they have, if any? Should they be allowed to pursue a study? Should we finance their study? And then: should all support be in cash, or should shares of it be provided in kind? And, of course, there is the almost perpetual discussion about incentives and whether or not the system should be a safety net, a hammock, or a springboard. All these and similar worries are found to be relevant to the type and level of welfare support a person may or may not be entitled to under the present system. And indeed, a huge and quite costly machinery of civil servants, controllers, job centers, career advisors, and the like has developed to counter abuse of the system and, more generally, to keep the volume of expenditure under control.

The present system requires that we know so much about people, it is so presumptuous. A basic income would do away with this cumbersome business in one single stroke. Every person, with or without a job, married or not, divorced or not, pensioner or not, student or not, or whatever, would simply receive a basic sum of money, preferably sufficient to cover the costs of subsistence, and that is it. Indeed, some, such as Robert Goodin (1992), explicitly argue for a basic income because it is "minimally presumptuous." A basic income for every person would simply be more "target effective," even if our target actually is to support those who deserve support, for whatever reason.[2] The only question that remains to be answered is whether the basic grant is economically viable. But it seems that in this respect calculations have been encouraging.

Obviously, Van Parijs is aware of the practical attraction of abolishing the present complicated welfare system, with its reliance on, at best, very questionable methods to find out the truth about individual cases, and its tendency to intrude in areas we like to think of as private matters. But this attractiveness is not his basic argument for the basic grant. His argument is more fundamental. What he says is not that a basic income should be introduced because it would come in handy to save us the trouble of having to separate the deserving from the nondeserving (or less deserving) of support, or because it nicely circumvents our skepsis with regard to the methods that we use in that sorting process. He argues that all of us are entitled to a basic grant regardless of all the fine distinctions and considerations that are thought to be important under the present welfare system. These distinctions, if at all feasible in practice, are not just troublesome and costly, they are irrelevant. We are entitled to a basic income, we have a right to it, because we exist, not because it is so difficult to single us out from the ones who deserve support. We have a right to it as "individuals rather than households; irrespective of any income from other sources; and without requiring any present or past work performance, or the willingness to accept a job if offered" (Van Parijs: 1992: 3). It is a philosopher's argument about basic human entitlements, not a politician's argument about the efficient realization of a pre-set goal, however lofty.

We may also put it thus: there may be several more or less plausible arguments to the effect that, given our limited epistemic capacities and given the costs of implementing a highly refined system of justice, a basic income for all must be considered as the best proxy for justice. There is only one argument, however, not that a basic income is a good proxy for justice, but that it is justice itself. That is Philippe Van Parijs's argument, and that is the argument with which I will be concerned here.

As a philosophical argument about basic human entitlements Van Parijs's justification of a basic income is vitally dependent on Ronald Dworkin's doctrine of equality of resources. I will give a rudimentary description of that doctrine, and of some considerations that led to its adoption; I will be rather crude in my paraphrases and omit various details that are not immediately relevant to the doubts I want to raise. I will show how Van Parijs argues from equality of resources to the basic income. And I will, of course, subject the relevant outcomes to the test that has concerned me all along: will there be parasitism, and if so, have we found any plausible justification for that?

4.2 Equality of Resources

Dworkin proposes to distribute external resources to persons on the model of a "Walrasian auction" at which persons are allowed to purchase their share starting with an equal amount of token money. He asks us to imagine a small population, washed ashore on an island after a shipwreck and facing the problem of how to share the resources they find. How should they proceed given that they have agreed to distribute resources equally among them? According to Dworkin, they should appoint a "divider" who

> hands each of the immigrants an equal and large amount of clamshells, which are sufficiently numerous and in themselves valued by no one, to use as counters in a market of the following sort. Each distinct item on the island (not including the immigrants themselves) is listed as a lot to be sold, unless someone notifies the auctioneer (as the divider has now become) of his or her desire to bid for some part of the item, including part, for example, of some piece of land, in which case that part becomes itself a distinct lot. (Dworkin 1981b: 286)[3]

The resulting distribution of resources will be equal because it will satisfy the so-called "non-envy test": no one will envy the bundle of resources someone else has purchased, no one will prefer someone else's bundle to his own, since, by assumption, he could have used his equal amount of clamshells to purchase that bundle instead of his own. If I am outbid on item A, and purchase item B instead of A, it must mean that I preferred B plus some other item to A, that I would rather spend my clamshells on B plus something else than on A. Of course, the auction is only a piece of drama to help us picture what an equal distribution of resources would actually look like, but it is fundamental that such a distribution would satisfy the non-envy test.

However, there are serious problems with Dworkin's proposal as it now stands. One problem is the following: the intended use a person may have for a certain item he is bidding for may not be anticipated by the others and nevertheless that use may be so bothersome to them, that had they suspected such use, they would have taken care to outbid the present purchaser—possibly in coalition with his other "victims." Dworkin mentions a person bidding for a plot of land for the purpose of building a glass box on it, while all others who are unaware of his distasteful plans intend it to be a Georgian square. They never bothered to outbid him, expecting the space to remain empty, yet now they suffer for their lack of foresight while the present distribution of resources does not genuinely reflect the value each attaches to every single item (or plot). Such a situation, which raises the problem of externalities, calls for a "principle of correction." The distribution and subsequent use of resources should genuinely reflect the importance that different individuals attach to controlling them, and the auctioneer, who by now has become the Auctioneer, clairvoyantly knowing about external effects that various kinds of use of resources may have on unsuspecting others, may restrict the liberties on the use of some items, or see to it that compensation will be obtainable. "Equality of resources aims that each person have an equal share of resources measured by the cost of the choices he makes, reflecting his own plans and preferences, to the plans and projects of others" (Dworkin 1987: 27). Dworkin admits that he is "haphazardly racing" over the problem of externalities, but I believe that his intentions are nevertheless very clear. The distribution of resources, and their use as made possible by some antecedently instituted "basic system of liberties and constraints" ought to satisfy the general requirement that all true opportunity costs are internalized. So we may gather that two distinct requirements should govern the distribution of resources. The distribution of resources ought to satisfy the non-envy test, given that the basic system of constraints and liberties secures that no costs will be displaced by the subsequent use that persons make of their acquisitions.

The fundamental reason for wanting the original distribution of external resources to satisfy the non-envy test is that this is the only way to bring about a distribution in which each is held responsible for his or her preferences, but not for his or her circumstances. The envy-free distribution, then, is offered as an implementation of the fundamental liberal idea that justice in distribution ought to be neutral with regard to the various preferences, or life plans, or "ambitions" that individuals may entertain. We do not give more resources to a person because the satisfaction of her ambitions requires more resources than the ambitions of other persons. If someone wants to purchase an item through the auction that some of the others also find important, the purchaser will be forced to spend many of his clamshells in outbidding the others, leaving her with less clamshells to spend on other things. So be it. Neutrality with regard to individual ambitions requires that we make people responsible for the consequences of their own expensive preferences. The bundle of goods a person ends up with, then, will reflect how her priorities relate to the priorities of others, but it will not reflect any other differences between them. Since all of them start with an equal amount of token money their circumstances are the same in the relevant respect. The content of people's bundle of external resources cannot be determined by any other feature than their equal purchasing power. Equality of resources negates the relevance of the fact that some may be fast runners and could therefore be the first to arrive at a popular resource and the ones to take hold of it.

Dworkin has a second distributional concern. The clamshell auction attributes responsibility for the consequences of individual preferences and not for individual circumstances as far as people's control over external resources and opportunities is concerned. But what about the distribution of internal resources, considered in themselves? Some of us are strong, some weak, some talented, some not, some have "disabilities," some have not, some are more sensitive to illness than others, and surely this distribution of internal resources has nothing to do with how people's priorities over things in life relate to each other, and does not satisfy the non-envy test, far from it. It is here that Dworkin proposes a radicalization of the distinction between preferences and circumstances, and introduces, what we may call, a "thin veil of ignorance." We are to imagine ourselves stripped of all our distinctive features except that we do know our own preferences. Personal qualities, talents, handicaps, diseases, and all other things that seriously affect our lives besides the external resources we control are now to be thought of as risks against which we can insure, this time starting from an initial position of equal control of resources. The general idea is, of course, that we will now get a distribution of insurance policies that will reflect our priorities over "internal circumstances," just as the distribution of external resources through the auction reflects our preferences for those resources. Some inconveniences will seriously affect some people but not others, depending on what they want in life. The variety in their policies will reflect these differences, and compensations will be a function of the number of persons with sufficiently similar policies against similar inconveniences, and, of course, also a function of the frequency of the occurrence of the inconvenience insured against. Policies against missing left little finger tips will be popular among those who would like to be active as musicians, volleyball players, or typists, but not among would-be philosophers who will tend to give priority to a policy against headaches.

The conceptual problems with Dworkin's "insurance auction" are tremendous. Several questions immediately spring to mind. Should people be allowed to seek compensation for inconveniences by means of it, or just reparations? And related to this: do we insure against the fact that our qualities may not be in demand on the (labor) market and hence against purely economic setbacks, or do we also insure against not being able to engage in a certain hobby? Should we be compensated for being unpopular on the marriage market? Furthermore: how does the auction handle the fact that risks in actual life are often a function of lifestyles, and hence of preferences, and not of "brute luck"? How, on the other hand, does it handle the fact that in actual life preferences in their turn are often determined by internal circumstances: how can I want to be a philosopher if I have not the slightest grasp of what a "philosophical problem" would be? The mental act involved in "stripping ourselves from our internal resources" may be just too demanding to give any reliable information about the motivational state we would be in without our actual talents—even in principle.

Many of these and similar problems are spelled out and discussed in Philippe Van Parijs's book, and he develops an altogether different approach to inequality of talent. It would go too far for my present purposes, however, to enter into that discussion. My main interest in this chapter is to question the plausibility of Dworkin's distributive principle of external resources, the non-envy test, and the way this principle is put to use by Van Parijs in defense of basic income. We may or may not agree with Van Parijs when he argues that "If the wealth stocked on top of a cupboard is to be shared among all, it makes no sense to restrict it to those who are tall enough to reach it" (Van Parijs 1995b: 123). However, the main thrust of *Real Freedom for All* is that if the wealth stocked on top of a cupboard is to be shared among all, it also makes no sense to exclude those who are too indolent to reach for it—even if they are tall enough.

It is this implication that I want to question. Therefore, I shall make a radical abstraction here. In order to circumvent the special problems related to the unequal distribution of talents, handicaps, body length, and the like, I will simply consider the distributive problems of a population of which I assume that the members are equally talented. They do not differ in any respect except in the priorities they have over the various external resources that they find on their island. Thus, we introduce an artificial, and far from trivial, condition that enables us to put the spotlight on the heart of the matter: is the non-envy test plausible? Thus, too, I must admit, I hope to drag Van Parijs into the arena where I believe his arguments are weakest.[4]

4.3 From Equality of Resources to Basic Income

How then is the universal unconditional basic income justified given that we start with a population of identically talented persons who all hold an equal share of resources, distributed following Dworkin's clamshell auction? What, especially, is the justification for income transfers from those who like to work hard, the "Crazies" as Van Parijs calls them, to those who do not like to work hard, the "Lazies," as they are called? Suppose we imagine both a Lazy and a Crazy in the possession of an equal plot of land, then this is what the justification, in its simplest version, looks like:

> Crazy may be desperate to use more than her plot of land, while Lazy would not mind being deprived of some or even all of his in exchange for part of what Crazy would produce with it. This directly yields the following suggestion. There is a non-arbitrary and generally positive legitimate level of basic income that is determined by the per capita value of society's external assets and must be entirely financed by those who appropriate those assets. If Lazy gives up the whole of his plot of land, he is entitled to an unconditional grant at a level that corresponds to the value of that plot. Crazy, on the other hand, can be viewed as receiving this same grant, but as owing twice its amount because of

appropriating both Lazy's share of land and her own. Thus, in our society of Crazies and Lazies, the legitimate level of basic income is just the endogenously determined value of their equal tradable right to land. (Van Parijs 1995b: 99)[5]

Through the auction each of us acquires an equal share in the natural resources of the world, and if others, despite the full ownership of their own equal share, are more eager to work on our share than we ourselves are, then there is no reason why we should not sell or lease out our share to them if that suits us. Those who prefer a reduced income from renting their equal share of resources to a higher income from working that share themselves should be allowed to pursue their leisure-loving lifestyle. Of course, the rents they take will have to be paid by those who wish to increase their income above what their own initial shares will allow them. The redistributive net income transfer as realized by a basic income in a world in which control over natural resources is unequally distributed is justified as the ex post equivalent of the price involved in resource/income transfers as they would have emerged from initial equality. There is a universal and unconditional right of every individual to a share in what we might call "resource rent." In a further development of his argument in favor of the unconditional basic income, to which we shall return in the next chapter, Van Parijs goes on to establish a right to "employment rent" in a similar fashion. Jobs, like natural resources, are essentially external opportunities and everyone is entitled to an equal share in them. Those who are more eager than others for such opportunities should be willing to pay for a larger share in them than their initial equal share. Again, the beneficiaries of this "pay" will be those who are willing to give up (a part of) the share in the opportunities that they are initially entitled to. They are the ones to benefit from a basic income.

Note, however, that an essential feature of the argument depends on the assumption that the right to sell or lease out resources to others will be contained in the "base line system of constraints and liberties," which was to secure that envy-freeness would be a proper guarantee against displacements of opportunity costs. Obviously, resources that carry the right to sell them can attract other bids than resources that may only be put to private use. Obviously, too, the envy-free distribution of resources when they are marketable may differ from the envy-free distribution of the very same resources when they are not marketable. In other words, the right to sell or lease out resources may to a large extent determine which distribution of resources will be the one that is envy-free. And hence the absence or presence of such a right is going to determine what an equal distribution is. But that means that we cannot simply say, as Van Parijs seems to do: Lazy and Crazy are to share the land in a mathematically equal fashion, and now we are going to give them the right to enter a market with their shares. We cannot simply say that because it is not clear beforehand that a mathematically equal distribution would result from the auction whether or not there is the pre-set liberty to lease out resources under all circumstances.

So the question seems to be: how will the right to sell or lease out resources, as part of the base line system of constraints and liberties, affect distributions of resources? I will try to work out this problem in more detail and see how it relates to the argument for a basic income. There are three questions that will especially concern me: given the presence or absence of the right to lease out resources in the base line system of constraints and liberties:

1. Which distribution(s) will be free of envy?
2. Which distributions will allow parasitic relations (as defined by Gauthier)?

And I will add one further consideration:

3. Which distributions will be Pareto optimal?

4.4 Basic Income to Highest Sustainable Basic Income

There is another serious complexity in Van Parijs's argument that deserves special attention. His "primitive" argument is that the value of all resources ought to be equalized and that this means that a tax and redistribution system will have to be adopted that will produce a net transfer of income from the hard-working people, who occupy large shares of resources, to the not so hard-working people, who occupy relatively small shares of resources, or, perhaps, no resources at all. Truly equalizing the value of external resources would in fact imply taxing their value at 100% and then redistributing the proceeds equally. But it is well known that taxes, and certainly high taxes, may provide individuals with negative incentives; they may discourage people in their ambitions to work, since they reduce the returns that people get from their labor investments. And if people work less hard because they are taxed at a certain rate, then the objective amount of money raised by these taxes will steadily decline until an equilibrium is reached such that people will still find their work rewarding. That objective amount may be lower than if a different rate of taxation had been chosen, as may be expected if the rate is 100%. In other words, given the incentive effects, the total tax yield will vary with the rate at which people are taxed.

It is easy to see that if the sum total tax yield is used to bring about a net transfer from the high incomes to the low incomes, those with low incomes have an interest in a tax yield that is as high as possible. The higher the tax yield, the higher the net transfer. That does not mean, however, that they also have an interest in a tax rate as high as possible, since high rates may produce low yields and vice versa. Think of the person who would be entirely dependent on the transfer. The only money she will get, having no access to other sources of income, is her share of the money that is raised by taxing everybody and that is redistributed equally to all as a basic income. She will be dependent on her basic income. And clearly she would want her basic income to be as high as possible.

And Philippe Van Parijs wants it to be as high as possible too. He is not just arguing for some basic income, he is arguing for the highest sustainable basic income, by which he means that the tax rate should not be such that the incentive effects will—in the long run—reduce the basic income to a level that is lower than it might have been with a different tax rate. Why does Van Parijs favor the highest sustainable basic income?

It is here that I will have to anticipate a discussion of the concept of "real freedom" that will occupy us in chapter 6. A truly just society, says Van Parijs, is a society in which real freedom is equalized. And real freedom is the freedom to do whatever one might want to do. The fact that the value of resources is to be distributed equally in the manner that would result from Dworkin's auction is, in fact, motivated by Van Parijs's contention that resources are the principal carriers of real freedom. Resources provide us with the opportunities to realize various kinds of life, and if they are distributed in such a way that opportunity costs are equalized, then, indeed, everybody will be provided with the same measure of real freedom. As we saw, from an equal distribution a market could emerge that would provide some with their fair share of the value of the resources in the form of income in return for giving up their share of the resources themselves. The result of this market ought to be mimicked by a tax and redistribution scheme. But why, ought that scheme to be such that the basic income would be the highest sustainable? That ought to be so, Van Parijs argues, because it is obvious that the higher one's income is, the higher one's real freedom;

more money means more options to choose whatever one might wish to choose. And since those who have a basic income only are the ones with the lowest income, the ideal of equality of real freedom warrants that their income will be as high as possible. We may allow diversions from strict equality but only if they work to the advantage of those who are worst off.

> [I]nstead of the rate that equalizes the external resources, let us choose the rate that maximizes the tax yield and so the level of the basic income, while we take account of the influence that a full anticipation of the taxation has on economic behavior. Justice need not necessarily be taken as simplistic egalitarianism. One can also take account of the (anticipated) effect of the distribution itself on the sum that is to be distributed, without justice betraying itself. This leads us to the adoption of a maximin-criterium, which means the maximization of the minimal grant in the form of external resources. (Van Parijs 1995a: 68–69; my translation from the Flemish)

So it seems that we have two aspects of one argument. The first is that ideally resources are to be shared equally, resources being the embodiment of real freedom. The second is that by the redistributive actions we take in the real world, we should try to approximate the natural market outcome of equality of resources by maximizing a basic income provision, which means: at the highest sustainable level.

4.5 Legend and Explanations

In order to answer the questions at the end of section 4.3, and in order to evaluate the relation of these answers to the argument for a basic income, I shall proceed in a straightforward manner. To make my points I shall first confine myself to examples of very simple types of situations (which will prove to be complicated enough) involving only two persons and only one resource: let us think of land that can be used to produce a certain crop[6] (say: yams). In the later sections of this chapter, I shall argue for more generalized conclusions.

I believe there are three relevantly different situations when we ask how the respective interests of two persons may relate to the total amount of yam-specific fertile land that is available; all these situations answer to the idea that one of the two persons dislikes work more than the other. Following Van Parijs I shall call these two: Lazy and Crazy.[7] Moreover, as promised, I shall assume that their productive talents are identical, thereby circumventing (for argument's sake) the effects of the inequality of internal resources. Lazy dislikes work more than Crazy does, but if he works he will produce as many yams as Crazy does, in the same time, on an equally large plot of land. Now, imagine a piece of land consisting of four identical plots, all equally fertile and smooth to work on, and each of them requiring one day of equally strenuous farming labor (plowing, sowing, harvesting, etc.) in order to make it produce a certain amount of yams, no matter who does the work. The three situations are illustrated in figure 4.1. I will call these three situations: constellations (of interest). In the following sections each of these constellations will be treated separately. In constellation A, Lazy's trade off between yams and leisure time is such that, in the absence of Crazy, he would want (and take) only one-quarter of the land to work upon, while Crazy's preferences are such that, in the absence of Lazy, she would want one-half of all the land to work on. Ergo: there is one-quarter of the land neither wants to work on. I will call these shares of land that they would want and take in the absence of the other their "independent interests."

Similarly, in constellation B, Lazy wants to work on just one-quarter of the land, while Crazy wants to occupy three-quarters. Between them they would divide the available land, if the distribution coincided with their independent interests. There would be no superfluous rest.

In constellation C, Lazy wants to work half the land and Crazy wants to work three-quarters of the land. Since they cannot both have their way, we must consider one-quarter of the land as contested between them. (See fig. 4.1.) Now let us look at how the liberty or prohibition to lease out land, as part of the basic system, would affect the three questions about envy-freeness, freedom from parasitism, and Pareto optimality. The distributions in each case that I will consider are:

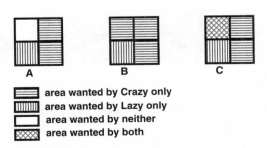

Figure 4.1. Resource-related preferences for work

1. a mathematically equal distribution and
2. a distribution in which Lazy gets one-quarter of the Land and Crazy three-quarters.

The reason for this latter selection will soon become clear.

So in all three constellations of interests we get four possible "regimes":

1. Lazy and Crazy both get half the land, and land is tradable.
2. Lazy and Crazy both get half the land, and land is not tradable.
3. Lazy gets one-quarter, Crazy gets three-quarters, and land is tradable.
4. Lazy gets one-quarter, Crazy gets three-quarters, and land is not tradable.

Of course, there are more possible regimes (Lazy gets nothing, Crazy gets all, etc.), but I shall ignore those because the four just mentioned will suffice to capture the general idea of how regimes work out in practice. Graphically, I will represent the four regimes as in figure 4.2 (for the example of the **A**-type constellation of interests).

Some explanations: if Lazy's land is surrounded by a white border, it means that both he and Crazy are allowed (and technically able) to sell (shares of) their land. It means that if they would want to sell or lease out land there will be no external (practical or) legal impediments to doing so—provided, of course, that the other is interested. If, on the other hand, Lazy's land is surrounded by a black border, it means that neither he nor Crazy will be allowed to sell or lease out land even if they would both be interested in a transfer.

Picture it this way: if we (or the Auctioneer or Justice Personified) allow a person to be the rightful owner of a piece of tradable land, we

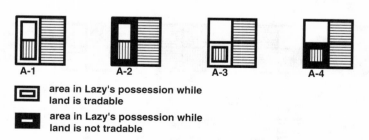

Area in Lazy's possession while land is tradable

Area in Lazy's possession while land is not tradable

Figure 4.2. A-type constellations under four regimes (graphics to be read as before)

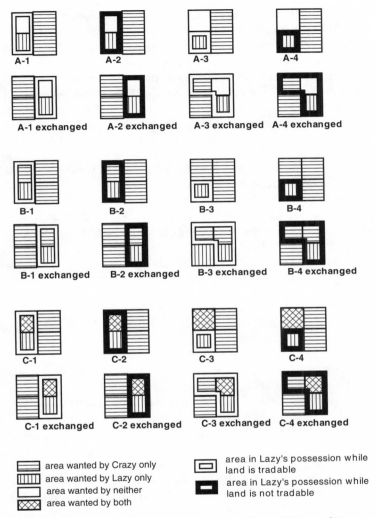

Figure 4.3. Overview of all regimes applied to all constellations of interest and their exchanges

(or He or She) will put that person on that land and then build a huge wall around it, which cannot be passed except through a gate of which the owner has the key. If he owns a non-tradable piece of land he will likewise be enclosed on his own property, but this time there will be no gate and no key. Ownership of non-tradable land simply means that others do not have access to that land and cannot be given access either. A certain regime allows parasitic relations if, given the constellation of independent interests, Crazy would be better off without Lazy, while Lazy would be worse off without Crazy (or vice versa).

A regime is Pareto inferior if, given the constellation of independent interests, both the positions of Lazy and Crazy can be improved by switching to another regime, or if the position of one of them can be improved without worsening that of the other by such a switch.

A certain regime satisfies the *non-envy test* if, given the constellation of independent interests, the situation is such that neither Lazy nor Crazy would prefer to have what the other has. So we check on the envy-freeness of a regime by letting the parties reverse their shares and then mapping their independent interests on those.

I give an overview of all four regimes applied to all three constellations of interests, and their exchanged counterparts, so that we may now check which distributions satisfy envy-freeness, freedom from parasitism, and Pareto optimality (see fig. 4.3).

4.6 A-Type Constellations: Unconditionality and Maximal Sustainability

Let us proceed with the check. In A-1 Lazy owns half the land and he is allowed to trade (part of) it, but since Crazy possesses all the land she wants to work on, she will have no interest in any possession of Lazy at all. So Lazy, though permitted to, will not be able to extract any benefits from Crazy. And this is also true vice versa. Parasitic relations cannot emerge from A-1, since neither will be able to improve his or her position compared to the absence of the other.

Will the non-envy test be satisfied? It will. Since they both hold exactly the same parcels of land nothing would change in their situation if they switched shares, which is obvious if we compare with A-1 exchanged. Could anybody's position be improved by switching from A-1 to one of the other three regimes? We can reduce Lazy's share and/or remove the liberty to sell land, and it will not affect the position of either. So A-1 is also Pareto optimal.

These conclusions also hold for A-2: there is no reason for Lazy and Crazy to envy one another if they hold exactly similar pieces of land, and there can be no parasitic transactions if trades are forbidden. Moreover a switch in regime would improve the position of neither.

But things change in A-3. In A-3 Lazy is allowed to trade his land but like before he will not be able to do so, since he owns nothing that Crazy finds interesting enough, so he will not be in a position to receive benefits at the cost of Crazy. There can be no parasitism. Nor would a switch of regimes improve anybody's position. But is the non-envy test satisfied? This time it is not. For if Lazy and Crazy would now reverse their shares, so that Lazy would have three-quarters and Crazy only one-quarter, then Lazy would be able to extract benefits from Crazy, given that he is allowed to lease out the part of his property he does not want to work on himself. Since Lazy owns more than he wants to work on himself while Crazy is interested in that surplus he can trade with Crazy in A-3 exchanged. That is Lazy's reason to envy Crazy in A-3.

Let us turn to A-4 type regimes. As before, Lazy owns only one-quarter of the land, which is precisely the amount he wants to work on, Crazy owns the rest which is one-quarter more than she wants to work on. But since neither is allowed to sell anything he or she owns, it does not matter to Lazy whether or not he possesses anything more than the plot he wants to work on himself. So he does not envy Crazy. Crazy, of course, prefers her own bundle to Lazy's bundle, since otherwise, in A-4 exchanged, she would have less than she is independently interested in. A-4 also satisfies Pareto optimality: the other regimes would not be preferred by either of them.

Of the four regimes we searched in A-type constellations of independent interests only one fails one of the tests. That regime is A-3, which violates the non-envy test. A-1, A-2, and A-4 are all "normatively" equal distributions in Dworkin's sense, since they all satisfy the non-envy test, and they are all parasitism-proof and Pareto optimal on top of that.

Of course, we know that Van Parijs would opt for A-1 as the equal distribution, but it is interesting to note that although the distribution is mathematically equal, and although the parties are granted the right to lease out shares of their original property, and although Crazy is using a larger share of the resources than Lazy is, A-1 situations cannot provide us with an argument for an unconditional basic income. Obviously, no yams-to-land exchanges would emerge from A-1, since although Lazy may be oversupplied, Crazy is not undersupplied and she will simply not be interested in the purchase of any additional land to her own. No market price will emerge and so there seems to be no justification for any system of taxation and redistribution that will result in a net transfer of yams from Crazy to Lazy. And Van Parijs must be in agreement with this. He is. "Crazy wants a higher income and is therefore prepared to work more. If for this purpose she uses no more than an equal share of society's scarce resources—say, land—she should not be taxed one penny to help feed Lazy" (Van Parijs 1995b: 90). Yet, this simple observation must already be sobering to the basic income enthusiasts: the unconditionality of a right to a basic income has its limits and does not have the robustness it seemed to have in the beginning.

It may be offered as a rejoinder that there is some significance to the difference between having no right to a basic income and having a right to a basic income that is zero. Having an unconditional right to a basic income that is zero is still an unconditional right. Perhaps. But it is worthwhile to note that this distinction does not seem to do its work when Philippe Van Parijs argues against Senator Yee of Hawaii that he was being unfair to the Hawaiian "welfare hippies" (or to those who spend their days surfing off Malibu) when he wanted to deny them the right to a welfare grant (Van Parijs 1991: 101). Perhaps Senator Yee never paused to ask whether or not there were still unoccupied fertile resources on Hawaii (did not the hippies have a legal right to pick their own coconuts?), but, to my knowledge, neither did Philippe Van Parijs when he came to the rescue of the hippies' entitlement to full-time leisure. Yet, the unfairness or fairness of Yee's attitude vitally depends on that question even on Van Parijs's own terms. As we will see in the next chapter, this is not even the only relevant question: he should also have asked whether there were still (perhaps well-paid) jobs available in "paradise."

But there is a more serious ambiguity in Van Parijs's argument. In section 4.4, I observed that the justification for a basic income has in fact two aspects. There is the justification for having a basic income at all, which relies on the analysis of the market effect of equality of resources, and there is the justification for the highest sustainable basic income, which relies on the analysis of the incentive effects on the tax yield. From A-1 situations, we can learn that there is an inconsistency in these two arguments. For we find that there is no relation between market transfers from ideal equality and the highest sustainability of a basic income in reality. In A-1, the competitive value of the land is zero so that there is no case for a net transfer at all, but it does not follow that there is no tax scheme that would allow a stable net transfer of income from Crazy to Lazy. On the contrary, the odds are that there is a tax rate that would allow a stable basic income and a net transfer from Crazy to Lazy. There is no reason at all to assume that a taxation and redistribution that would result in a basic income of only one yam will eventually lower productivity in such a fashion that a basic income of only one yam cannot be sustained. In fact it may be much higher than that. In other words, a basic income that can be sustained is not in itself a basic income that can be justified. Or, more generally, the highest sustainable basic income can be much higher than the maximally justifiable basic income in "Dworkinian" terms. The maximally justifiable level of basic income is determined by the market value of resources that would emerge from equality. The highest sustainable level of basic income is determined by the incentive effects of taxation in actual fact. A-1 shows that there is no intrinsic relation between these two levels. And that in itself, I believe, suggests that there is something misleading in the idea of an unconditional right to a basic income that is as high as can be sustained. Whatever way we look at it, there can be no right of that kind, even if there may be some right to a basic income.

4.7 B-Type Constellations: Usurpation

Clearly B-1 might allow Lazy to make use of his share of land in a way that would be parasitic (see fig. 4.4 for B-type regimes). He owns a plot which is of no independent interest at all to him, but which he can sell to Crazy because she has less in her possession than she wants to work on. Nevertheless, the non-envy test is passed, since exchanging their share would not alter the situation at all. Also, B-1 is Pareto optimal: we cannot change regimes without worsening the position of at least one of the parties.

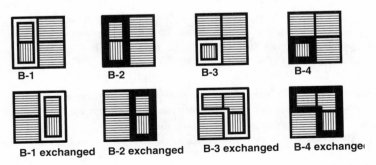

Figure 4.4. B-type regimes and their exchanges (graphics to be read as in previous figures)

In B-2, Lazy may not exploit Crazy in a similar way as in B-1, since now he is not allowed to sell the superfluous part of his property. The non-envy test is met because reversing shares does not change the situation. But B-2 is not Pareto optimal: both Lazy's and Crazy's position will be improved if we switch from B-2 to B-1. Crazy prefers being exploited, given that she controls a mathematically equal share. In this case introducing the right to have exchanges would be welcomed by both of them.

In B-3, Lazy is allowed to trade (part of) his share, but since Crazy is fully satisfied with her own three-quarters of the land, Lazy has nothing to trade with. However, the non-envy test is not passed, since if Lazy possessed three-quarters of the land and Crazy only one-quarter, he would have had something to trade with: two-thirds of his property, as will be apparent from a comparison with B-3 exchanged. B-3 is Pareto optimal nevertheless.

In B-4, no trades are possible so costs cannot be displaced, and the non-envy test will be passed, since the superfluous two-thirds of the land in the possession of Lazy in B-4 exchanged will then not be tradable either. B-4 is Pareto optimal; any change of regime would leave Crazy worse off or both unaffected.

So in B-type situations, there are two regimes that pass the non-envy test and prove to be free of parasitic opportunities. Those are B-2 and B-4, which happen to be the two regimes that do not allow land to be tradable. Only B-4, however, is Pareto optimal as well. So if envy-freeness, insensitivity to parasitism, and Pareto optimality were to be thought of as three independently desirable features of a distribution, then, in the B-type constellation of interests, a mathematically unequal distribution of non-tradable land would certainly stand out as superior to all other possibilities. We may also generalize this result over A- and B-types of constellations of interests. A-4 like B-4 satisfies all tests.

Unfortunately, Van Parijs does not share these desiderata that can be reconciled so neatly. It is clear that he believes, as before, that mathematical equality plus the liberty to sell is the relevantly equal distribution: B-1. But as we observed, B-1 blatantly violates the objection against parasitism. It would enable Lazy to take shares of land into his possession for which he has no independent interest whatsoever, not even a little, while Crazy would very much like to use that share in a productive way. Crazy is forced to work as a tenant for Lazy because Lazy has the right to own what he cannot use. As I will say: Lazy is allowed to be a usurper of land. Why should he be allowed to be that? Why should we believe that there is any distributive problem in

B-types of situations? After all, if interests relate to land in the manner of A- and B-types, there is in fact no scarcity of land, so why do we not just allow Lazy and Crazy to use the shares they want to use? Why, in other words, would there be a case for distributing exclusive property rights to land? Why would it not suffice, in this case, to distribute access rights or rights of usufruct? Why bother issuing clamshells, having auctions, post-auction markets, and redistributive tax strategies? Just tell people not to rob each other of the fruits of their labor and each can do as he likes without being in the others' way.

Again, there seems to be a tricky ambiguity in Van Parijs's text. This time it concerns the definition of scarcity. Discussing how the value of land will be influenced by the ratio of supply and demand he says: "True, the fewer people are interested in some asset and the less keen they are to acquire it, the lower its value. In particular, if those interested in it are fully satiated with less than the total amount available, that is if there is no scarcity, the value of the asset would be zero" (Van Parijs 1995b: 105). But this is simply not true. In the B-type constellation of interests in land, Lazy and Crazy are fully satiated by the total amount available if we let each of them have just what he would also have taken without the other. There is no scarcity as long as we do not interfere with the shares that they would spontaneously have chosen to work on, each following their own trade-off between work and leisure. But it certainly does not follow that land will not acquire market value when, for some reason or other, we decide that each of them should have half of the resources available, and that superfluous shares may be sold. In fact we introduce scarcity of market supply by letting them share equally an asset that is not in scarce natural supply.

What seems to be happening here is that the rigid egalitarian concerns underlying Dworkin's (and Van Parijs's) distributive principle enforce an equal sharing of the land's commercial value, while that commercial value itself would not have existed in the first place without the egalitarianism. There is a suggestion of circularity: of course, Lazy will want an equal share once it is stipulated that he may sell what he cannot use—that is why B-3 fails the non-envy test. And, of course, both Lazy and Crazy will want to have the liberty to sell and buy, once it is stipulated that they shall have an equal share—that is why B-2 fails the Pareto optimality test. If the land is scarce, then both should have half; and if both have half, then the land is scarce. So is scarcity of natural supply a condition for a justifiable basic income or is it not?

It is not! In order to see why, we have to return to the foundations of Van Parijs's egalitarianism. What he wants is equality of real freedom, and having real freedom is having the freedom to do whatever one might want to do, not just the freedom to do what one happens to want to do. Resources are the carriers of real freedom. Equality of resources means equality of real freedom. We should not give Lazy fewer resources because he actually wants fewer. He might have wanted to work harder, and if we give him less than half of the land we have not given him an equal share of the freedom to work as hard as he might have wanted to. So here we have the true villain in the story that says that it is all right to exploit your fellow men: it is the concept of real freedom. It is the idea that you are entitled to the exclusive and unconditional control of options for which you have no actual use. Basic income is justified by the market value of those options. Crazy is allowed to use Lazy's spare options, but Lazy will want yams in return. According to the doctrine of justice under scrutiny here, he shall have them. But that means that absence of scarcity in the natural supply of resources, and the fact of full satiation of all by what there is, cannot be a condition for a basic income. It implies that even the practice of pure speculation may be justified as a way of swelling the basic income: even if the natural supply of resources abundantly exceeds the amount that would satiate all, equality of real freedom will still allow (parasitic) transfers of the fruits of Crazy's labor to Lazy. Compare the variation in figure 4.5 of the B-type constellation of interests and note that it will respond to the three tests in the same fashion as the original.

In order for Lazy to be able to make his parasitic profits out of the share in his possession that is wanted by Crazy, he must maintain a firm grasp on an area that is wanted by neither. He must not only usurp land that he does not want, he must also usurp land that nobody wants. There is land that nobody is using, but Crazy will have to be Lazy's tenant nevertheless.[8] And that is justified because Lazy is to be as real-

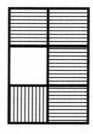

Figure 4.5. A variation of the B-type constellation

free as Crazy is. There is no scarcity, indeed there is abundance, but that does not change the right of the parasite. It is hard to see how these observations relate to the statement quoted above.

4.7.1 Fish Ponds and Green Acres

If land is the only resource both Lazy and Crazy shall have half of it, and the fact that Lazy happens to want less for his own use is irrelevant. Would this argument retain whatever plausibility it may seem to have, if there are more and different kinds of resources involved in which Lazy and Crazy have various interests for various reasons? I will give an example that is somewhat more complicated than the simple sharing of land. Let us say that there are two resources; there is some land that will only produce yams, and there is a fish pond from which a certain amount of fish can be caught. Let us assume the following: both Lazy and Crazy like yams tremendously and neither is particularly fond of fish, but—although both are still equally talented—Lazy, unlike Crazy, thoroughly detests the hard agricultural work that the production of yams requires. He hates it so much that, had he been alone without Crazy, he simply would have preferred to sit angling alongside the fish pond all day. True, he prefers yams but nevertheless he will settle for fish if that spares him the trouble of wrestling with the greasy mud. Crazy, on the contrary, would not have cared for the fish pond, had she been alone without Lazy. In fact she even dislikes fish somewhat more than Lazy does and she certainly would have invested her labor in the land. Let us say that she would have used about all the fertile acres there are—there are not very many—for her own productive use when she would have been alone. Again, then, it seems that the small island with the fish pond and the green acres supplies such resources that each of the two shipwrecked persons can do exactly what he or she would have done had they been the sole survivor. There is no scarcity. Lazy can take the fish pond and sit in the sun all day, Crazy can work the acres, each according to their individual trade-offs among yams/agricultural work/fish/angling.

But would the clamshell auction produce that distribution if the freedom to sell resources were part of the base line system? I do not think so. What is much more likely is that the auction would make both end up with half the land. Why? Well, Lazy is fond of yams, he just dislikes to work to get them, but now he is in the position to acquire a share of yams without doing the work. If he acquires half the land, he can lease out all of his share to Crazy in return for a quite substantial amount of yams. And if he prefers that amount of yams to the fish he would have caught otherwise, he will choose a bidding strategy that will make him end up with half the land indeed. The liberty to sell or lease out his share of resources does not only give him an interest in more resources than he is independently interested in, it also gives him an interest in other resources than he is independently interested in. And Philippe Van Parijs must agree with this outcome, since according to his definitions real freedom is equalized only if the competitive value of the resources is equalized, and that is only the case when the clamshell auction clears. So, here is a fish pond that does not count as a resource, since nobody is bidding for it, but that would have been quite exhausted by Lazy had he been alone, and here is Crazy working as a tenant because she is not alone.

If we generalize these proceedings to a situation of more people and more kinds of resources, we can see how the Lazies may "boost" their basic income. They can turn usurpation into a systematic bidding strategy. At the auction they should simply try to follow the toilers in bidding for whatever opportunities they are bidding for. Do you know a person to be crazy, hold your own bid until she bids for something. Then you will know where to invest your clamshells most effectively. Go after the things the others are after, and let them buy you off.

But what have you in fact done? You have sought and taken clamshell rent! Your bidding power for resources is the same as everybody else's, but for some reason (you are Lazy) you value what other persons can give you over what the best feasible bundle of resources, considered in itself, can give you. Hence, you secure for yourself (part of) the resources of which you know that others want them very much, and then use those assets in transaction with them. You might as well have traded your clamshells directly with the others, demanding in return from them the same service (a certain amount of yams), in advance, before the auction even started.[9] Where my interests in the resources are created by your interest in them, my interests must be in you.

The apparent attraction of Dworkin's original idea of the auction was that its distributive result would reflect every person's priorities over the various resources under auction. It now turns out that if we allow for the marketability of these resources, we will make the actual distributive result reflect everybody's priorities over the various resources and over things that were explicitly excluded from the auction: other people's labor and services.

4.7.2 Gin and Juice

It might appear from the examples used so far that the possibility of parasitism inherent in equality of resources is vitally dependent on the fact that some are given free access to the labor of others. And although it is certainly true that the possibility of exploiting labor is the most significant implication of equality of resources, given the present discussion of basic income, it is not true that its exploitative consequences depend on a special status of labor. The important distinction is not between labor and other goods. Parasitism may also occur when labor is not at all involved in post-auction transactions.

Consider two persons, Long and Strong (named after their preferences for drinks). They are both inexhaustibly fond of so-called Bloody Mary's, mixes of tomato juice and gin, but their preferences for the ratios of gin and juice they want in their glasses are different:[10] Long finds any diversion from three parts juice to one part gin positively appalling, while Strong will not care for a single sip in any other ratio than one part juice to two parts gin. Think of Long and Strong as castaways on an island and as both being presently in the possession of 300 bottles of gin and 300 bottles of juice. It can be shown that the unique market clearing price of beverages emerging from this distribution of property will be three bottles of gin for every bottle of tomato juice so that the outcome of transactions between Long and Strong (in bottles) will be as follows:

Long: 360 juice, 120 gin   Strong: 240 juice, 480 gin

Can we object to this outcome? It would appear not. Their initial holdings of bottles of juice and gin are exactly equal and envy-free. The market outcome is efficient, and it is fully determined by the different tastes of Long and Strong for Bloody Mary mixes. So what can possibly be wrong with the outcome?

I maintain that the "initial" situation is not sufficiently described. By only referring to the fact that the initial circumstances of Long and Strong—defined by their bottle holdings—are equal, we hide an essential and morally relevant feature from our perception. That feature is brought out by the question: where do the bottles come from? Have they all been found on the island, or have some of them perhaps been brought by Long or Strong? I will sketch two scenarios preceding the same equal initial distribution.

In scenario A, they find 600 bottles of juice and 600 bottles of gin on the island. It is all they find, and it is all they have. They decide that both will have half of each stock. In scenario B, they only find 600 bottles of gin on the island while each of them separately brings (on a private raft) 300 bottles of juice. They share the gin equally. (They decide that since they have brought juice in equal quantities neither of them is entitled to some sort of compensation prior to the envy-free allocation of the bottles of gin they find.)

In both cases they start trading with the described allocative result of consumption goods. Let us now compare how each of them would have fared without the other, in either scenario. In scenario A, Long would have had 600 bottles of juice and 600 bottles of gin, and with a preferred ratio of 3:1, he would then have prepared his preferred mix from 600 juice and 200 gin. Strong, with the preferred ratio of 1:2, would have mixed her drinks from 300 juice and 600 gin. In scenario B, Long, bringing only 300 bottles of juice when alone, would have mixed those 300 juice with only 100 gin, while Strong, when alone, bringing 300 bottles of juice, would have mixed those 300 juice with 600 gin (as before). After exchanges at market clearing prices, Long consumes 360 juice and 120 gin, which is less than he would have had in scenario A, when alone, but more (of both goods!) than he would have consumed in scenario B, when alone. Strong, on the other hand, is worse off compared to solitude, in either scenario. She actually ends up with 240 juice and 480 gin, while she would have had 300 juice and 600 gin, when alone.

So equality of resources violates the proviso in scenario B while it does not in scenario A. In A, both are worse off compared to solitude—it seems they have (competitively) shared the burden of company—but in B, Long is a parasite who benefits from the juice that Strong brings, while Strong suffers from the fact that Long is allowed to hold an equal share of the gin they find. In B, Long's presence is a burden to Strong, while Strong's presence is a benefit to Long. As we may say: in scenario B the envy-free distribution allows Long to usurp 200 bottles of the gin they have found on the island. When alone he would not have touched these 200 bottles; they have no independent interest for him and now he only wants them because they have value as merchandize; they allow him to exploit Strong.[11] (See table 4.1 for a representation of the two scenarios.)

Why is this parallel to the equal sharing of land interesting? Because it brings out, more clearly perhaps, how from the point of view of the Lockean proviso the essential distinction is between what the castaways find on the island and what they bring to the island—even if they bring the very same amount of the very same thing—while the requirement of envy-freeness is wholly insensitive to this distinction.

Table 4.1. Bloody Mary consumption in two scenarios

| | By Long | | | | By Long | | | |
| | Alone | | Together | | Alone | | Together | |
Bottles consumed	Juice	Gin	Juice	Gin	Juice	Gin	Juice	Gin
In scenario A	600	200	360	120	300	600	240	480
In scenario B	300	100	360	120	300	600	240	480

In the basic income approach to the distribution of the two goods, yams and leisure, each of which, like juice or gin, is only worthwhile in some combination with the other, these goods are treated as if they are both found in certain quantities on the island. The castaways are then conceptualized as if they command an equal amount of both these goods, having brought nothing themselves, and start trading the one for the other: Crazy can have more yams if she prefers a different yams/leisure ratio than her equal share allows her to have, but then she will have to turn in some leisure to the benefit of Lazy—and work for him—just as if she were trading gin for juice in scenario A. But this modeling of the Crazy/Lazy problem would be misleading. The thing they find on the island is land, or more generally, resources, and this thing can only have value if they mix it with something else: labor. But labor is not what they have found on the island, it is something that they bring separately, and in equal quantities.

4.7.3 *"Roemerian Exploitation" and "Lockean Parasitism"*

In chapter 2, I offered some considerations on the difference between the socialist conception of exploitation and the Lockean conception of parasitism. There I argued that the socialist definition of exploitative relations as relations that are characterized by an "unequal exchange of (embodied) labor" would morally condemn perfectly innocent trans- actions between persons who would benefit greatly from each other's existence and actions. I also argued that the socialist definition simply ignores the output of interactions in terms of utility gains or losses that are so vital to the moral assessment of relations in the light of the Lockean proviso. As a response to counter-examples of unequal yet morally unproblematic exchanges of labor,[12] John Roemer has tried to give a more plausible (but still "socialist") definition of exploitation.

Roemer's initial deviation from the "classical" Marxist concept was as follows: "A group of people S is exploited by its complement S in a society with private ownership of the means of production if S would benefit, and S would suffer, by a redistribution of ownership in the means of production in which each owned his own per capita share" (Roemer 1989: 90). This Roemer called the property relations definition of exploitation (PR). We should immediately note the great similarity between Roemer's approach to justice and that of Philippe Van Parijs—the similarity in the stress on asset equality being recognized by the latter (Van Parijs 1995b: 178ff.). And, obviously, the possibility of usurpation as an evil that we detected in the heart of the argument for a basic income must now be part and parcel of Roemer's ideal of non-(PR)-exploitation too. It is, and it is noted by Roemer. In the B-type constellation of interests (and assuming that the "groups" S and S may contain only one person each: Lazy and Crazy), it is obvious that a prohibition of PR exploitation would require a mathematically equal distribution of the land and hence that it would imply parasitism in the Lockean sense. In the B-type case we either have "Roemerian exploitation" or "Lockean parasitism." In Roemer's definition of exploitation, then, the unequal distribution of land between Lazy and Crazy would imply that Lazy is exploited by Crazy instead of the other way around! But this proves to be too much, even for Roemer himself. His own troublesome example ("delicate issue") of the B-type is the following:

> Maggie owns a big machine and Ron a small one.... Their preferences differ. Ron wants to take leisure, and is willing to consume just a small amount of the consumption good in order to do so. Maggie wants a lot of consumption good, and is willing to work very hard in order to maximize her consumption of it. Preferences have been autonomously formed. Maggie uses her own machine to capacity, but wants still more consumption, and so sells her labor power to Ron, who pays her a small wage to operate his machine, taking the profits therefrom for his consumption. (Roemer 1989: 95)

Next, Roemer consistently observes that PR would imply that Ron is exploited (because he would be able to extract even more "machine rent" out of Maggie if he were to have half of both machines, and hence he would be better off by an equal redistribution of the assets). As I said, this proves too much to digest and therefore Roemer decides to deviate from his own initial deviation, and to give in somewhat to the original socialist definition of exploitation as the unequal exchange of (embodied) labor, which results in the following hybrid: "an agent is exploited in the Marxist sense, or capitalistically exploited, *if and only if PR holds and the exploiter gains by virtue of the labor of the exploited* (that is, the exploiter would be worse off if the exploited ceased working)" (Roemer 1989: 96). So that now we may conveniently conclude that neither Ron nor Maggie is exploited in the example above. These caprioles in the definition of exploitation, however, do not prevent Roemer from holding on to the claim that the distribution of machines, though no longer defined as exploitative, is still unjust: each should have half of them. I tend to agree that the distribution is unjust, but the reason for that is that it does allow Ron to exploit Maggie, not vice versa. And giving Ron more than he owns now would be even more unjust because it would allow him to be an even greater usurper and hence an even greater parasite. In fact, he should have less.

4.7.4 Usurpation and the Exploitation of Non-Transacting Parties

Test your intuitions concerning usurpation! The possibility to deliberately exploit a system that is designed to provide access to a valuable good in a fair and efficient way is not especially dependent on the use or abuse of vouchers such as clamshells. Usurpation may also occur, for instance, in an arrangement that divides access according to a civilized version of the principle that those who arrive first shall be served first.

Here is just one realistic, and recent, example of a usurpatory practice in economic life. Both in the United States and in the European Community so-called trade marks (and also company logos) are protected. That protection serves consumers as well as producers. When a successful company delivers high-quality goods under a certain name, then that name will serve as a quality guarantee for consumers, but only, of course, when other companies are not allowed to use the same name for the same kind of goods the quality of which may be inferior to the original. However, there is an international problem. Companies who have deposited their trade mark in the United States will not automatically enjoy legal protection of their name in Europe. Would they want to enter, for instance, the Benelux market they would have to officially deposit their name again in that region. And, of course, successful American entrepreneurs, considering expansion of their business to Europe, will want to operate under their already established and reputed American trade mark name. Will they be able to do so? There seems to be no great problem. They just register their name in the Benelux as they did in the United States. But not so! A London-based small enterprise, called Mayfair Projects, has specialized in depositing trade mark names in the Benelux of companies from America (and elsewhere) that are expected to want to expand to Europe in the near future. When the real bearer of the name now seeks entrance to the Benelux market, he finds Mayfair in his way. Mayfair is the legal owner of the name that the Americans want to use. Now what can Mayfair want to do with such a name? Precisely. Sell it! This is what happened, for instance, to "Ben & Jerry's Homemade Inc.," the highly reputed producer of ice cream in the United States. When they wanted to open up ice cream parlors in the Benelux, they found that Mayfair had already deposited "Ben & Jerry" for ice cream, and they had to buy back their own name. The same had happened before to "Arby's" (a fast food chain) and they paid thousands of dollars for a transfer of the trade mark registration. Fortunately, Ben & Jerry's did not. Instead they sued Mayfair and were put in the right by the judge who considered that Mayfair was guilty of—indeed, what else—abuse of rights.[13]

Just think for a moment that we would allow usurpers like Mayfair to go ahead. Here is some free advice to college students who want to earn some easy money on top of their poor grants, which I hope will illuminate the point. Go to the Main Post Office of your town of residence; go there about one hour before closing time, and do not forget to bring your books. You will find that the office is particularly busy, since many people will want to send parcels, buy stamps, or whatever, on their way home. You will also find that they have to wait for their turn by drawing a number from a machine and sit until their number shows up on a sign. Sometimes the waiting time can be as long as twenty minutes. Now, you take a few numbers from the machine and sit down with your books. After approximately 15 minutes, start to be attentive. When your numbers almost show on the sign get up and offer them to the highest bidder. My guarantee is that you will make some profit: the customers who have arrived last will gain a lot of time for their bids, but the ones who came in earlier will be so irritated by the long delay that they will be ready to spend good money to gain just a few minutes. And, of course, you can try to repeat this procedure several times, and you can do it every day, and if the management will let you (which I doubt) you may develop a flourishing commercial queue-jumping enterprise with branches in banks, supermarkets, railway stations, in short: in all places and institutions where people have to wait long, and where they will be crazy enough to want your place more than you want it yourself. And how about hospitals?! Now

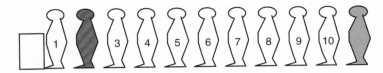

Figure 4.6. A queue

here is a gold mine. You should put yourself, like a real vulture, on the
waiting list for cardiac treatment, and for a liver transplant as well, and
sell your place in due time to one of those many workaholic managers
who failed to properly manage their own health. And never mind the
protests of the doctor. Your motives for wanting to be on the list are not
his business, are they? Is it not just your right to be on that list? After
all, you might have had a heart attack, and you might have needed a
new liver. Moreover, you need not be afraid of competition, since you
are the original finder of a "hole in the market" and that entitles you to
the benefits thereof—at least for some time. In fact, you should ask for
an international patent. (But take good care to deposit your trade mark
in time; usurpers may be on the lookout.)

There is an interesting observation that we can draw from the
commercial activities of Vultura Queue Jumping Enterprises Inc.:
the people who are exploited (in the Lockean sense) need not be
the people who are in fact involved in transactions with the usurper.
Consider the far-fetched example of the queue again. Suppose I am
the person who arrives last and suppose that before me there are ten
other persons. The first of those is now being helped at the desk; the
second is you, and you are a usurper in the sense described above.
You are only there in order to sell your place; you have no independent interest in your place in the queue. Suppose also that I have to
wait two minutes for every person who is in the queue before me.
And suppose that I am the one who buys your place, since I bid most
for it. (See fig. 4.6.)

How will all those who are involved in the queue relate to each
other in the light of the proviso, if this transaction in fact takes place?
As follows:

1. You will be better off because of me. You gain some money
   that you would not have had without me, the others all bidding less than I do.
2. I am better off because of you. I gain 16 minutes, which I
   can only gain because of your usurpatory activity. Of course,

I have to pay you for those 16 minutes, but from the fact that
I do so we must conclude that these 16 minutes are more precious to me than my money is.

3. You are better off than you would have been without all the
others (numbers 3, 4, 5, 6, 7, 8, 9, 10) because without them
(in the queue before me) I would not have wanted to pay you
such a good price.

4. I am still worse off because of the others (standing between
you and me) because without them I would not have had any
reason to spend the money I now have to pay you.

5. The others are worse off because of me. Without me they
might have jumped the queue, since then their price would
have been best. And even if they were not prepared to do
so—if I am the only one who is willing to pay at all—then my
presence motivates you to take a place, which I will take from
you. I end up before the others, so that thanks to me they have
to wait for two minutes longer.

6. The others are worse off because of you. Without you, each of
them would have gained two minutes, since then you would
not have usurped a place and sold it to me.

To summarize, you and I are better off because of each other, and
the others and I are worse off because of each other, but the relation
between you and the others is parasitic: you gain because of their existence, they lose because of your existence. In other words, although you
transact with me in a way that is mutually advantageous to both of us,
your pecuniary advantage in that transaction is in fact paid for by each
of the others with a loss of two minutes of waiting time. You exploit
(some of) the non-transacting parties. Without them you would have
done worse, but without you they would have done better.

Non-waiting time is scarce. During peak hours queues distribute
waiting minutes more or less equally among those who have an independent interest in waiting as shortly as they can. Usurpers from Vultura
Inc. add to the pressure of the scarcity of time on others, although they
themselves have no independent interest in it, and they capitalize on
the increased scarcity. As we may put it: they exploit scarcity itself. They
would do worse for themselves had there been no scarcity at all, and by
seeking private control over supply, they will create more intense scarcity than the scarcity that arises from the limited natural supply.

I think the point can be generalized to equality of resources. In
principle, it is conceivable that with larger numbers of people involved

at the auction, who have widely divergent preferences over work and leisure, the transactions between the Lazies and the Crazies would not be parasitic on the Crazies themselves, but on some of the non-transacting parties. Indeed, if all parties are sufficiently shrewd and foresighted in their bidding strategies we might even expect bidding coalitions to develop between the extreme Lazies and the extreme Crazies, where the Crazies would invite the Lazies as "phantom purchasers" to combine with them in outbidding those whose preferences are in-between those of the Lazies and the Crazies. These in-betweens would be exploited by such an arrangement. They would do better without the Lazies; the Lazies would do worse without them.

An interesting parallel suggests itself:[14] the democratic process on the basis of one person, one vote. Why, and to whom, is it generally considered to be unfair if we allow the buying and selling of votes? Suppose there is a plot of land that nobody wants for herself but that could serve some collective purpose: it can be turned into a Georgian square (alternative A) or a glass box can be built on it (alternative B). If neither is done, the land will be reclaimed by mother nature and slowly turn into a jungle, which most, but not all, people find a horrific prospect. It so happens that there are two parties in this political community each commanding a roughly equal, and fairly large, amount of local support. Party A wants to realize alternative A in the empty space, while B favors alternative B, but all agree that justice requires that each shall have an equal share of political influence, a so-called vote, and that the majority shall have its way. A small minority, however, is completely indifferent whether the contested spot shall be turned into a Georgian square, or whether a glass box shall be built on it, or whether it shall be left to evolve into a jungle. The persons in that minority have no interest in their votes per se because they do not care what will happen to the empty spot. Yet, the supporters of alternative A (being the more conservative and old-fashioned members of society, which also explains their preference) happen to be somewhat richer than the supporters of alternative B, and they do have an interest in the votes of those who are not themselves interested; and this enables the A supporters to buy some of the votes of those who are disinterested, just enough so to tip the balance of the ballot in their favor. Would it be sufficient to point out that both transacting parties, the indifferent sellers and the A supporting buyers, have gained from the transaction compared to the situation in which transactions would have been forbidden? Of course not. The fate of the B supporters ought to be considered as well, and it is obvious that their position is worsened by allowing votes to be sold. Their pro capita share of political influence is lower than it would have been, had the disinterested parties been prohibited to turn their votes into merchandize or had their lack of interest debarred them from holding votes in the first place. This is the crux of the argument: have the disinterested parties also gained something from the presence of the B supporters? They have! It is only the fact that B supporters exist (in such numbers as they do) that makes the votes of the disinterested parties desirable for the A supporters. The cash obtained by the disinterested persons is paid for with a loss of political influence by the B supporters. This turns the disinterested sellers into parasites, not of those with whom they transact, but of the others. If people have no use for their votes in this particular matter, except a usurpatory one, it would seem that there is no point in giving them votes in the first place.[15] And if our egalitarian concerns force upon us that all shall have one vote, we may still try to counter usurpatory parasitism by prohibiting that votes are turned into merchandize.

Note that such a prohibition on vote sales would not produce a Pareto inefficient distribution of political influence. Those who are not independently interested in their votes and are also not allowed to sell them just stay at home during the elections. Their absence proportionally increases the per capita weight of all the other votes. An equal share of political influence left unused by one person is not "wasted"; it is automatically distributed over all the others and used by them.

4.8 C-Type Constellations: Usury

Next, let us see what we can find out about the various regimes in C-type constellations of interests (see fig. 4.7).

If transactions, involving land, between Lazy and Crazy could be reached in C-1, they would imply a violation of the non-parasitism requirement, despite the fact that the contested quarter of the land, which is in Lazy's possession, is of some use to himself. It will all depend on Lazy's and Crazy's respective trade-off functions between (additional) yams and (additional) working hours. Yet any transaction of the above kind would mean that Crazy is exploited by Lazy. She suffers losses compared to the situation in which she worked and possessed three-quarters of all the land (as would have been the case in Lazy's absence) while Lazy receives benefits compared to the situation in which he possessed and worked two-quarters of all the land (as would have been the case in Crazy's absence). C-1 is no guarantee

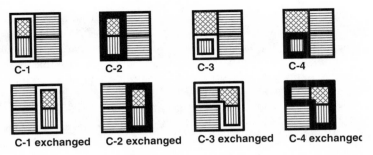

Figure 4.7. C-type regimes and their exchanges (graphics to be read as in previous figures)

against parasitic relations. It satisfies the non-envy test and is Pareto optimal nevertheless.

C-2, on the other hand, lacks Pareto optimality, since both would prefer a switch to C-1, enabling both to do better even though Crazy would be taken advantage of in that case. The non-envy test is satisfied, as before in all cases of mathematically equal distributions. Since trades are ruled out in C-2 parasitic benefits are impossible.

C-3 is comparable to C-1, because now Crazy might be in the position to extract parasitic rents from Lazy, depending on their yam/work trade-off functions. Anyhow, C-3 is ruled out by the non-envy test (compare C-3 exchanged). C-3 would be Pareto optimal, however.

C-4 does not allow parasitism, since trades are impossible, but it fails the non-envy test, since Lazy will prefer C-4 exchanged to C-4 itself. Neither will it guarantee Pareto optimality, since Lazy and Crazy might want to do (parasitic) business with each other and are not allowed to do so.

So C-type constellations of interests seem to force a disturbing conclusion on us: none of the regimes, however attractive their consequences for A-type and B-type constellations of interests might be, will satisfy all our tests in C-type constellations of interests. Earlier we concluded that unequal distributions of non-tradable land would do very well for both A-type and B-type constellations, but now we find that such a regime, as we can read from C-4, cannot be free of envy nor Pareto optimal in a generalized fashion.

As before, Philippe Van Parijs would favor C-1. And as before, in B-type constellations of interests, that regime would not be free of parasitism. But there is also an important difference compared to B-1. As we noted, the regime of equal distributions of tradable land will allow Lazy to take land in his possession for which he has no independent interest, and which he would not have used if he had been alone. Under appropriate circumstances, involving more resources of various kinds, Lazy's liberty to do so would even invite him to employ a bidding strategy by which he could seek possession of those goods that are of interest to Crazy but not to himself. Lazy could try to get possession of green acres, although he would never have touched them when alone, since by doing so he would get free access to a share of the yams Crazy produces. The intention to exploit others, and only that intention, would then explain Lazy's strategy of appropriation. This is what I called usurpation.

In the present case, C-1, the origin of Lazy's parasitic opportunity proves to be of a different kind, because now it is not true that Lazy has land in his possession for which he has no independent interest. Had he been the sole survivor of the shipwreck he would have worked on the two plots of land that are now assigned to him under equality of resources. The possibility to exploit others is not what moves him to take what he cannot independently use. That he is enabled to take parasitic rents nevertheless is explained by the fact that shares of the land in his possession may be of higher value to Crazy than they are to Lazy himself, but it is not explained by some practice of usurpation.

By contrast to usurpation I will call the parasitic rents that Lazy may take in C-1 "usurious." Usury is practiced by persons who better themselves at the cost of others through the selling or leasing out of shares of resources for which they do have an independent interest. Usurpers are those who take advantage of others by selling or leasing out resources for which they do not have an independent interest. When we return for a moment to Robert Nozick's terminology as analyzed in chapter 3, we can also explain the difference between usurpation and usury as follows: usurpers force fully unproductive exchanges on their victims while usurers only force partially unproductive exchanges on their victims. If it were not for the possibility of selling abstentions from a harmful activity—in this case the appropriation of a scarce good, the activity of the usurper would not have threatened at all. This is not true for usury. The harmful activity of the usurer would also have existed "spontaneously," without the possibility of selling abstention from it.

Is it possible to have a distribution of resources that is free of parasitism and Pareto optimal at the same time? It would seem not, if we look at the overview of the test results from the previous sections (table 4.2).

It seems that we can read from this overview that the choice between Pareto optimal and non-parasitic distributions is forced upon us. There is

Table 4.2. Overview of test results for all regimes under all conditions

	satisfies non-envy test	is parasitism-proof	is Pareto optimal
A-1	x	x	x
A-2	x	x	x
A-3	o	x	x
A-4	x	x	x
B-1	x	o	x
B-2	x	x	o
B-3	o	x	x
B-4	x	x	x
C-1	x	o	x
C-2	x	x	o
C-3	o	o	x
C-4	o	x	o

x: satisfies; o: fails

no single distribution plus basic system satisfying the non-envy test and the no-parasitism test that is also Pareto optimal for all constellations of interests. There is a distribution plus basic system that satisfies the non-envy test and no-parasitism test, but it violates Pareto optimality: equal distributions of non-tradable land violate Pareto optimality in B- and C-type situations. There is also a distribution that satisfies the non-envy test and is Pareto optimal in all situations, but it violates the no-parasitism test: equal distributions of tradable land allow parasitism in B- and C-type situations. But there is no regime that satisfies Pareto optimality and freedom from parasitism at the same time under all conditions.

Envy-freeness, Pareto optimality, and a guarantee against parasitism—as features of an initial distribution of resources—do not go together very well, so much is clear. If all three characteristics figure on a list of desiderata, that list is bound to be inconsistent. Is this inevitable? If so, what should have priority?

As we have seen, these questions are at the heart of an important controversy in the theory of distributive justice, the urgency of which is highlighted now that the idea of a universal right to an unconditional basic income is gaining political respectability. Obviously, philosophers like Philippe Van Parijs and, perhaps, Ronald Dworkin, give a high priority to the envy-freeness of the initial distribution, and they may be inclined to play down the significance of our moral objection to parasitism.

For now, I will postpone a further discussion of the difficulties we have encountered until chapter 6. There I will attempt to demonstrate that Pareto optimality and the objection against exploitation can be reconciled by a distributive principle that will not respect envy-free-ness in the strict sense, but that does reflect a robust egalitarian concern for the values that are meant to be protected by people's real freedom.

In the remainder of this chapter, I want to do two things. First, I will discuss a proposal that specifically addresses the question of how distributive justice should proceed in case a particular resource could not be shared but has to be assigned to one of the contestants in its entirety. I will reject that proposal.

Second, I want to demonstrate, to prevent misunderstandings, that sometimes redistributive tax policies can be Pareto optimizing without establishing parasitic relations between the suppliers and the receivers of the transfer.

4.9   Resources That Cannot Be Shared

Hillel Steiner and Jonathan Wolff (2003: 188–89) have proposed "a general framework for resolving disputed land claims," which they hope will be attractive, but they consider the special case in which the land cannot be shared in the usual sense, as neither party will accept a split. The land will have to go to one of the parties in its entirety.

The conflict-resolving method is as follows. When two persons or peoples have laid claim on a particular parcel of land that cannot be shared between them (and if they do not want to resort to war), the land should be auctioned. It will then go to the party who bids most for it but the proceeds of the auction, the amount of money that wins the bid, will go to the party who loses the land. As the authors envisage for a characteristic two-party case, the contestants will have different indifference points between

a. accepting the sum N and forfeit all claims to the land, and
b. bidding $N + M$ for the land.

These indifference points will determine a range of possible outcomes for the auction, such that one of the parties prefers to cash in the bid of the other instead of bidding higher in order acquire the land, while the other prefers to receive the land in return for her bid. To settle on one such outcome constitutes, according to Steiner and Wolff, a bargaining problem "with a twist."

I will return to the twist. But first I want to demonstrate that, under certain conditions, the auction may have outcomes that are objectionable for the very same reasons we already pointed out in relation of Van Parijs's proposal and the Dworkinian foundation of it. Consider the party L(ow) whose indifference point is the lower of the two. And let us assume that by cashing in some sum of money Q, higher than L's indifference level N_L, L would not only be doing better (by his own lights) than if he were to receive the land in return for N_L but also better than if he were to receive the land without paying a penny for it. In other words, if he were the exclusive owner of it L would sell the land for Q. Now, possibly, Q may well be well below the indifference point of the other party, call her H(igh), so that the transfer of Q from H to L is one of the conceivable outcomes of the auction.

Suppose the transfer of Q, or an even higher figure, were the actual result of the auction. This means that L will consider himself to be better off than he would have been with an exclusive and unencumbered right to use the land. So Q contains an element that constitutes a net benefit for L compared to the situation in which there had been no competition for the land to begin with, in the absence of the other claimant. The auction allows L to take a net gain from the land's scarcity. Now let us look at the fate of the second party. Not only must H pay the amount that is needed to fully compensate L for the loss of the land, but the auction also forces H to pay that extra sum that will improve L's position beyond what it would have been in conditions of noncompetition. H herself, however, is considerably worse off than she would have been without competition for the land, in the absence of the other claimant. So the auction enforces a purely parasitic transfer of benefits from H to L for which there is no justification with a reference to the fact that they are competing for the land. In fact, they need not even be competing for the land in the usual sense to achieve this unattractive result because, after all, L's level of full compensation might well be at zero. L might not care for the land at all and he might simply sustain a claim to it in order to enter the auction with the sole purpose to exploit H's intense desire for it, in fact to exploit H herself. In that special case L would be in the position of a usurper, since he would have no independent interest in the land; otherwise his parasitic benefits would be that of a usurer. But anyhow, nothing in the nature of the auction itself can set a minimum to the level of positive interest the contestants actually have for the land.

Now for the "twist" of this bargaining problem. Can L make sure that the auction will indeed grant him some exploitative gain above his own level of full compensation? If he is going to bid higher than his own indifference level, N_L, in order to compel H to follow, is he not at risk that H will fail to follow so that L will be stuck with the land for a price that it is not worth to him? Steiner and Wolff say that he is, and that even if L knows H's indifference point, his greed will still be held in check by his fear of H's acting spitefully. H may be disposed to punish L for driving up the price too far, rather self-destructively taking a loss for both by not following L's excessive bids. L will not await this to happen, and this is why the authors expect that the final sum to be transferred will be somewhere in between L's and H's indifference levels, as a quasi-bargaining result. But, of course, this "somewhere in between" may involve transfers at the exploitative level of Q, or higher; it just depends.

Yet there is a more disturbing possibility. The game L and H are playing, as modeled by Steiner and Wolff, is relevantly similar to a sequential ultimatum game: one player proposing a split of certain sum of money, the other accepting the split or refusing it, leaving both with nothing.[16] As long as H's own indifference level is not reached a refusal of H to outbid whatever L's bid is, would be irrational. L can therefore only be compelled not to bid up all the way up to H's indifference level if he may assume that H is irrational. In other words, with fully rational agents (going for the so-called subgame-perfect Nash equilibrium), the auction can be predicted not only to give some exploitative net gain to L but in fact the maximum: all of the difference between L's level of full compensation and H's indifference point.[17]

Of course, this makes the auction result even harder to accept. However, the essence of my objection to Steiner and Wolff's proposal does not depend on the incoherence of their predictions with rational choice. Whatever way we expect the level of the transfer to be reached, with or without spiteful motives at work, I see no justification at all for an arrangement that not only fails to firmly secure that the burden of scarcity will be shared on a reciprocal basis, but on occasions actually turns scarcity into a benefit to some while others are required to take on the cost of that.

Steiner and Wolff claim that their proposal "treats the disputed land as if it were the joint property of the two parties," but under certain conditions it is rather as if they give the disputed land in its entirety to the party who attaches least value to it and then allow him to sell it to the other for a negotiable price. The outcome of that procedure would be quite similar, and as unjust, as the auction result.

4.10 Non-Parasitic Transfers

I end this section by giving an example from the practice of policy making to show that the objection to exploitation may still allow significant transactions between persons with varying preferences over the available opportunities. I will consider "resources" other than land, and the context is not that of an initial distribution of productive opportunities in a quasi state of nature, but the distribution of the options that people have to travel from their homes to work and back, in the modern world where many people have to live a long distance from their place of work. For many years now, the public road system in central areas of Holland is overburdened. During peak hours people have to wait a long time in queues, safety is diminished, and the air is polluted. The Dutch government has tried to counteract this situation in a variety of ways, one of them being to tax petrol in order to subsidize the public transport systems, notably the railway corporation. Could such a tax and subsidy system ever be justified given what we have said about exploitation and usury, and given that we think that people are to be held responsible for their own choices? I believe it can, given certain assumptions that are not too far-fetched to match reality. Let us assume that traffic jams are the joint work of roughly two kinds of people. There are those who, for some reason or other, will stay in their cars, whatever the price of a train ticket, and whatever the length of the tailbacks. They greatly value that they are "on their own," and they are willing to get up an hour earlier, and be home an hour later, in order to secure their privacy, though of course they would prefer to have it without investing all this time. There are also those who would much prefer to go by train if only the tickets were not so expensive. They appreciate that traveling by train allows one to read or have conversations with one's colleagues. Obviously, the car lovers would greatly benefit if the train lovers could be moved to actually use the train, for that would solve the traffic jams and save time. And obviously, the train lovers would benefit if the price of a train ticket were reduced significantly. If we now assume the possibility of a market-like bargaining system between the car lovers and the train lovers, it is quite conceivable that the car lovers would be ready to transfer money to the train lovers in order to move them off the road and into the train. Such transfers would result in everybody being happier than they presently are in the traffic jams, and hence these transfers would realize a Pareto optimal outcome, compared to the present situation. Such transfers, that could have resulted spontaneously from negotiations between the two groups had there been no transaction costs, are now realized de facto by the government's tax and subsidy policy. It works in everybody's interest, although "honestly earned" money is taken away from some and given to others.

But why would such transfers of money between the two groups not be exploitative? After all, the car lovers only pay money in order to stop the others from being in their way. Why do we not just demand that people who prefer to travel by train pay for their own tickets in full? Are we not allowing the train lovers to benefit from the fact that they are a nuisance to others? The point is, however, that the train lovers who are now in their cars have not usurped their share of scarce access to the road system. They do not take something for which they have no use. Given the current price of train tickets, being in traffic jams is simply the best available option for them. What they say is not simply "I have a right to be here, and if you want me out of the way, then pay." What they say is "I have an independent interest in being here and *therefore* I have a right to be here, and if you want me out of the way, my interest should be secure, so pay!" The tax and subsidy system only secures that independent interest.

Yet, the objection against usury—exploitation not based on usurpation—does suggest a restriction on such a tax and subsidy system. Although we cannot be sure how much money would be transferred from the car lovers to the train lovers in a real negotiation process, justice would certainly require that there is an upper limit to that figure. What may not happen is that the train lovers end up better off than they would have been without the competition of the car lovers, and this suggests that the reduction of the price of train tickets that is financed by the car lovers should be just enough to move the train lovers out of the way, not more than that. Any amount of reduction exceeding the amount that would minimally move the train lover to actually use the train would in fact allow him a financial gain on top of his train ticket, a gain which would be entirely unproductive for the car lover, and hence exploitative. In a generalizing way, we should conclude that petrol taxes (to this purpose) should be just high enough to make the train just cheap enough to attract just enough travelers to just sufficiently relieve the road system.

Nonexploitative transaction arrangements can be mimicked by take and give policies. Where the market fails because it would be too expensive or too cumbersome to organize bargains, and where the possibility of Pareto efficient transactions might therefore escape all, democratic politics may take over. As in the example: a tax and subsidy arrangement solving traffic jams, reducing the rate of air pollution, increasing safety on the road, and thereby improving the position of both car lovers and train lovers should attract the warm approval, and the votes, of all involved.[18]

CHAPTER 5

S(H)ELLING LABOR: THE
RIGHT TO WORK

I am Brahman. But we're stuck without a maid.

J. A. dèr Mouw (Adwaita)

5.1 Van Parijs: Resources to Employment

In a response to the idea of a universal unconditional basic income, Jon
Elster has argued that such an institution, besides being very difficult to
implement in actual societies, would violate many people's intuitions
about justice, including, it seems, his own. He argues that any proposal
for a guaranteed, substantial, and unconditional income for everybody
"would fail because it would be perceived as unfair, indeed as exploitative" (Elster 1989: 215).

In the last chapter, I argued that, regardless of people's perceptions,
a basic income financed through a tax on the productive use of natural
resources would be exploitative indeed, if by "exploitative" we mean
parasitic in the Lockean sense.

As I observed in the beginning of that chapter, the proposal for
a basic income, or citizen's income, or demogrant, is not brand new.
Thomas Paine is generally acknowledged as the founding father of the
idea that such a labor-free income should be financed by taxing all
land rent and distributing the proceeds equally. But Philippe Van Parijs's
proposal is especially innovative, more radical, and more significant
than its predecessors because he extends the argument from resource
rent to so-called "employment rent." The first half of this chapter will
be devoted to a discussion of this special argument, and I will criticize it: if there is a parallel between jobs and natural resources, then
there is a parallel between the arguments against giving equal access

to them unconditionally, and without taking account of people's independent interest. Subsequently, I will argue that the idea of fair access
to employment would be better served by a policy of sharing jobs and
reducing labor time. Finally, and after a short historical detour through
the city of Amsterdam in the seventeenth century, I will offer some
considerations with respect to the quality of employment, and how it
should affect its just distribution.

Philippe Van Parijs (1995b: 102) thinks that a basic income financed
exclusively through a taxation of natural resources would be "pathetically low," if not "frankly negligible," but that is not a reason for despair.
Recent theories of unemployment point out that even fully competitive (labor) markets, or at least labor markets that do not suffer from
political interference such as minimum wage legislation, will realize a
situation in which some are involuntarily unemployed while others are
paid more than market-clearing wages for their services. Such theories
are of two kinds: efficiency wage theories explain the existence of
overpayment and unemployment by its positive effect on productivity—workers will be less inclined to shirk if the cost of losing their job
is higher—while insider–outsider theories explain the same phenomenon by the existence of labor turnover costs—"insiders" can claim
higher than market-clearing wages because of the cost of the process of
replacing them (Lindbeck and Snower 1988; Bowles and Gintis 1992).

Hence, workers, due to these or similar special effects of market failure, tend to earn substantially more than they would have earned if the
labor market were to clear, and the difference, according to Philippe
Van Parijs, must be regarded as a "gift" to workers in excess of the sum
that a truly competitive allocation of employment would have allowed
them. That gift can, and should, be taxed away and distributed equally
to each, again without imposing a means test or a willingness-to-work
test, thus swelling the basic income of each to a level that will no longer
be "pathetically low" by any means. Like before, people will be taxed in
such a way as to maximize the yield, and hence basic income, but we
need not fear that we will be taxing more than the employment rents
away, since then, obviously, people will start quitting their jobs, productivity will decline and hence the tax base will go down.

Like resources, jobs can be regarded as external assets and their
unequal distribution is supposedly unjust. In order to get a clearer picture of what distributive justice would amount to, we should extend
the parallel between resources and jobs: jobs ought to be clamshell
auctioned; they ought to be shared and competitively allocated among
all who care to bid for them, and if in an after-auction income-to-job

exchange market the Lazies acquire money without working for it, then this labor-free income consists just of their fair share of the value of employment.

Would this argument for a basic income from employment rents escape the general accusation of being in fact an argument for the legitimacy of parasitic relations? I think not, and there seems to be a quite straightforward way of arguing for this claim. I shall not quarrel with the claim that employment rents can be regarded as a gift, but I will quarrel with the claim that it is a gift that should be distributed among all, and unconditionally. Even as a gift, employment rents exist only in virtue of the preferences, and deliberate choices, of those who receive them. Those who lack these preferences, and knowingly make different choices, are not entitled to them.

In a truly competitive allocation of employment that does not suffer from market failures such as the effects described above, there will be no involuntary unemployment and jobs will not be carrying rent. But a truly competitive allocation of employment does not exclude that some people will be voluntarily unemployed. Some may be extremely Lazy, living off coconuts only, spending their time surfing, others may have incomes from other sources of whatever, and it is not excluded that, given the level of market-clearing wages, some are not willing to work. Now, given that these persons would not envy the others under these conditions, and given that no rent is obtained by the others, there is neither reason nor occasion to turn nonworkers into net beneficiaries of a basic income policy. Suppose next, that due to some market disturbance such as an insider–outsider effect, some of the presently employed workers are expelled from the workforce while those who remain employed now get higher wages.[1] Would that process affect the position of those who had been voluntarily unemployed all along? It would seem not: they are still not prepared to undercut the presently employed, if they could, because they are still not prepared to work at market-clearing wages. That has not changed. So, if we now do turn the voluntarily unemployed into net beneficiaries of a universal basic income, their position must be better than it would have been under a truly competitive allocation of employment. They will receive a share of the rent but relative to the competitive and envy-free allocation of employment the process that produced the rent did not affect them.

The involuntarily unemployed, on the other hand, have been victimized by the disturbance of the labor market, and, arguably, they are entitled to some compensation for their loss of opportunity. So, if we tax rents away and distribute them, it should be among those who are willing to accept jobs at market-clearing wages if offered to them. Insiders receive gifts indeed, but it is a gift that exists and comes forward only as a function of their having a willingness to work. Nevertheless, they get the gift randomly because they are not the only ones who have such a willingness to work. And, therefore, it is justified to regard their gift as a stroke of luck the benefits of which should be shared with others of a similar disposition. Or rather: since the involuntarily unemployed are randomly selected, it is their bad (brute) luck that they have been excluded from the employment they seek. Ex ante the disturbance of the labor market of all employed persons, if rational, would have agreed to share the rents ex post the disturbance. But the voluntarily unemployed would have been excluded from that agreement, since they were not facing a risk of unemployment. They were already unemployed, by choice.

Again, the proposal to turn jobs into items that can be purchased at an auction involves a crucial mistake. The situation is as follows: we observe that, for some reason or other, employment is not distributed in a truly competitive and envy-free fashion. There are fewer jobs than might have been, given demand for labor. Now we regard the jobs that do exist as a scarce asset to which all may bid, including those who would have not taken a job had there been an opportunity to do so in the first place. And, of course, the job shares that individuals end up with after the auction will be tradable, and hence we attract the bids of those who have no independent interest in a job at all, and who only value their shares as merchandize: the usurpers. The person who is not willing to work and who would not, and will not, accept a job at a market-clearing wage will receive a basic income that can only be justified as the real world counterpart of the gain that the usurper makes under the "ideal" procedure of auctioning jobs first and then having a job market between Lazies and Crazies. So there may be a parallel between jobs and resources but if there is the arguments against an unconditional basic income from resources applies equally to a basic income from jobs.

Indeed, I fully side with Stuart White (1997, 2003: 153ff.) in his discussion of this particular argument. White's analysis of the exploitative nature of a basic income from taxing employment, and its violation of what he calls the "reciprocity principle," leads him to adopt a much more conditional mode of redistributing employment rents; he argues that "the receipt of the relevant transfer payments should be made conditional on a demonstrated willingness to work in order to ensure that recipients are indeed unemployed as a matter of brute luck rather than as a result of lifestyle-choice."

And it is precisely this phrasing of the objection against financing an unconditional basic income from employment rent that reveals that it is not only exploitative but also in fact inconsistent with the doctrine that seemed to inspire the whole project from the beginning: the idea that there is an essential difference between a person's circumstances, which result from (bad) luck, and her circumstances as they result from deliberate (informed) choices. So the essence of White's argument is that the voluntarily unemployed person is not affected at all by the "circumstance" of employment rents and that her income situation is entirely attributable to her own deliberate choices.

But there is an interesting and subtle denial of this claim by Philippe Van Parijs, which is brought out when he considers the possibility of realizing the complete elimination of involuntary unemployment, e.g. by "the dismantling of all rigidities that hinder wage flexibility." He agrees that in that case no employment rents can be collected in order to fund an increased basic income. But, he says, since under full employment at market-clearing wages, labor costs would be substantially lower, and productivity higher, than they are at present we may expect the value of other external assets to go up:

> As a consequence, people's per capita share of external assets in the standard sense [such as natural resources] would be greater, and the maximum level of basic income that could be financed by taxing these assets could therefore be expected to be significantly higher than it is with wages as they stand. (Van Parijs 1995b: 112)

The implication of this argument is, of course, that voluntarily unemployed persons, contrary to appearances, are negatively (and brutely) affected in a roundabout way if labor markets do not clear: the value of their equal share of natural resources goes down compared to what it would have been if there had been no involuntary unemployment.[2] And hence it seems that even the voluntarily unemployed person is entitled to a compensation financed through a tax on employment rent. To be sure, but this argument has presupposed all along that the voluntarily unemployed person was entitled to an equal share of the market value of natural resources to begin with. If no such entitlement is plausible, all claims to a share in employment rents must be discarded as well. And hence we are back with the questions about the legitimacy of taxing the productive use of natural resources that I have been trying to answer in chapter 4. Without an unconditional right to resource rent, there can be no unconditional right to employment rent.

To resume, then, those who are entitled to some labor-free income from the productive activities of others must be those who have an independent interest in the assets that make these productive activities possible but have no access to them, and such independent interest cannot exist without a willingness to work.[3] As in the case of natural resources, the amount of compensation that the presently involuntarily unemployed are entitled to should be determined by the actual utility loss they suffer from lacking the opportunity to take a job. Otherwise, they would still be parasites, namely usurers. In other words, they are maximally entitled to a labor-free income that leaves them indifferent between their present unemployed position and a job at market-clearing wages. Any financial gain improving their unemployed position beyond what it would be in a clearing labor market would be usurious. Labor-free incomes from employment rents should be such that no person can take its assured possession as an incentive not to accept a job if offered. It seems that justice in the original "acquisition" of jobs commits us to a "basic income" that is just low enough not to interfere with the competitiveness of the labor market. Highly industrialized "affluent societies" such as ours, in which employment is the main source of income, owe to their members a right of access to employment and to "full compensation" for not having such access. They do not owe to their members a property right in employment and to "market compensation" for not having such property. The solution to the inherent injustice of failing markets can hardly be to adopt policies that reinforce and sustain the failure itself. But this is what we do if we give some people, the Lazies, a positive interest in the existence of rent. The justification of capitalism, if anything, is that people will be compensated for its failures, not that people will be allowed to exploit its failures.

Van Parijs insists that it is a matter of liberal neutrality that the voluntarily unemployed will not be excluded from their shares of employment rent.

> [A]dopting a policy that focuses on the involuntarily unemployed amounts to awarding a privilege to people with an expensive taste for a scarce resource. Those who, for whatever reason (whether to look after an elderly relative or to get engrossed in action painting), give up their share of that resource and thereby leave more of it for others should not therefore be deprived of a fair share of the value of the resource. (Van Parijs 1991: 126)[4]

But, as in the case of natural resources, this is not a happy choice of phrasing. If some people have a taste for employment that I am not interested in so that I do not have to forgo anything if they get it all, then this employment is not scarce between us and their taste for it cannot be called expensive. Even if we agree with authors like Dworkin and Rawls that relatively (and perhaps irrationally) inefficient converters of assets into well-being (or utility) should not end up with larger shares of these assets so as to enable them to reach equal levels of well-being,[5] this does not mean that inefficient converters should be fair game for exploitation. If Crazy's inefficient asset-utility conversion function makes her greedy for assets that Lazy, efficiently living from air and water only, has no interest in, then there is nothing particularly neutral in the idea that Lazy is entitled to some of Crazy's product or income. Again, there may be something to the claim that the efficient should not relatively suffer from the fact that others are inefficient, but that cannot amount to the claim that the efficient should actually benefit from other people's inefficiency. Should the Dutch be taxed for eating raw herrings, which all other people politely decline if offered? Surely the Dutch are very inefficient in making their happiness dependent on the difficult catch of herrings in such numbers as they want them, and, yes, in fact herrings are scarce. Among the Dutch, they are (and perhaps a couple of Scandinavians). But who of the others is entitled to complain about the ordeal the Dutch have to go through, and who would dare to ask them for money on top of that? How unfair the world would be. In chapter 6, I will show how we can avoid such unfairness, while still staying true to our intuition that people are "responsible for their expensive preferences."

Van Parijs's way of posing the "Crazy–Lazy challenge" conceals that the voluntarily unemployed in giving up "their" share of employment are giving up something to which they should not have had a claim in the first place, and that their act of giving it up is not a way of benefiting others, but of stopping to harm others. This is the point: people do not have an unconditional right to a basic income because they have no unconditional right to a share of employment. The right to employment itself is conditional on the willingness to work. Adopting a policy that concentrates on the elimination of involuntary unemployment, or on the more equal sharing of its negative consequences, is not at all biased with regard to the voluntarily unemployed. Of course, people who look after the elderly—whether related or not—may be entitled to payment for their good services, and not only by the elderly themselves but also by all of us who regard the well-being of the elderly as a common responsibility. But the would-be action painter should hope to attract an audience to support her activities. If not, the only just alternative is in the good old parental incitement: go out and do something useful, girl![6]

5.2 Could Jobs Be Like Cars or Concerts?

Other voucher systems, somewhat different in structure from Dworkin's clamshell auction, have been designed with the purpose of organizing and sharing access rights to the job market in a fairer way. Hamminga (1995)[7] proposes to give every person an x number of so-called "Labor Rights," on a yearly basis, but to ask every applicant for, or holder of, a full-time job for a number of y Labor Rights in return for having that job, where y will be exceeding x in the same ratio as the number of "able-bodied" adult citizens is exceeding the number of available full-time jobs. Thus, in his example of "Eu," the country where "the Eunians have truly liberalized the labor market" all individuals will be allowed to hold four Labor Rights (issued by a Labor Bank) and they will have to pay five Labor Rights for taking a job, because there are five million able-bodied adult citizens and only four million jobs. So persons who eagerly want jobs will have to buy one Labor Right from the others who are less eager and who will thus be supplied with an income for which they do not have to work.

This proposal does not seem to suffer from the tension between a Parijsian commitment to a highest sustainable basic income and a commitment to a basic income that matches the "competitive value" of the vouchers—Labor Rights or clamshells. But Hamminga's proposal harbors a possibility for the parasite nevertheless. Consider the employer who, because of the fact of overpayment has only one job on offer where he could have had two were the market to clear. There are three persons. Presently A is employed for a wage of two thousand golden coins, but he would have done the job for one thousand, in which case B would also have willingly accepted a job for the one thousand coins that then remain in the employer's wage fund. And there is also C who does not want a job at all. So there are three able-bodied citizens A, B, and C, and this year there is one job. The Labor Rights bank will issue one Labor Right to each of them for the purpose of "liberalizing" next year's labor market. And the person who wants the job most badly next year—let us presume this is A—will have to buy two Labor Rights, one from B and one from C. Of course, because of the small scale of the example, it is very difficult to determine a price for these two labor rights (except that we know that A cannot spend more than one thousand coins) and I foresee complicated negotiations, but it is also obvious that, whatever the outcome of the bargain, C is going to obtain a parasitic benefit here.

Perhaps C's position in this example is too incredible to give enough practical bite to my argument against unconditional entitlements to labor rights or to shares of job space. For after all: who can survive without some income, so who can be really uninterested in the minimal assets that are needed to produce such an income? Does not every person, given the human condition, automatically qualify for the possession of vouchers or asset shares, and is he not entitled to the full competitive value thereof? The rejoinder, implicit in these questions, is, of course, that the willingness-to-work condition that I am so eager to impose on labor-free incomes is in fact always, be it perhaps minimally, satisfied. Nobody will ever be a 100 percent usurper of his vouchers, since nobody can be 100 percent uninterested in productive opportunities.

But let me, in order to answer, point out a further problem in Hamminga's proposal. That problem is that "for simplicity" he wants to assume that "Eu has only full-time jobs" (Hamminga 1995: 23). The idea, then, of sharing the value of jobs is that one will be forced to choose between working full-time, say: five days a week or not at all. But then, it follows, that the Labor Right system, for the sake of simplicity, would assume the violation of what Dworkin called the "principle of abstraction," which, among other things, "requires . . . the utmost feasible divisibility in the goods auctioned, so that people can bid on indefinitely small units of each resource (though not, of course, on units so small that no single unit can serve any purpose)" (Dworkin 1987: 28). Dworkin's assumption, and I think that it should be shared by Hamminga himself (and by Van Parijs), is "that an auction is fairer—that it provides a more genuinely equal distribution—when it offers more discriminating choices and is thus more sensitive to the discrete plans and preferences people in fact have" (Dworkin 1987: 27–28). The same would hold, without doubt, for a labor market. Now, obviously, full-time jobs are not the smallest possible unit of job space that can still "serve any purpose." It is perfectly reasonable, and actually occurs on an ever-increasing scale in Western industrialized societies with a high rate of labor division, that people want to have part-time jobs of only one, two, three, or four days a week.

It is even true that some types of employment (for instance in high school and university teaching) are sometimes only offered on an hourly basis. Jobs of twelve or even two hours (a week) are no exception. So, it appears that in one important respect the Eunians have to live in a society that is far from ideal, whatever its merits may be otherwise. They have a very limited range of options compared to ourselves who may in some occasions decide to do part-time work.

But Hamminga is not unaware that the Labor Right system ought to be sensitive to the possibility of part-time labor contracts. In an earlier article (Hamminga 1983), he argues that those who get such contracts can easily be incorporated in the market for Labor Rights (called "coupons" there): they just sell the fraction of their Labor Rights that exceeds the proportionate fraction that they need to get access to their part-time employment. So let us say, contrary to the later assumption, that a substantial number of jobs will be available on a daily basis, and not on a weekly basis. Many Eunians can work for one, two, three, or four days every week. Having withdrawn the simplifying assumption we may now see the parasite's opportunity in the Labor Rights market. Think of a "non-needy bohemian"—Hamminga's description of the person whom we already know by the name of Lazy—who is an able-bodied adult member of the five-million-person Eunian community, and let us, for argument's sake, assume that last year there was no job scarcity in Eu: every Eunian who wanted to work had a job. Lazy, who is only a "part-time non-needy bohemian," took a two-day job. The revenue of two days of work and three days of leisure (exceeding the week-end) was exactly the right mix to suit his appetite. It kept him alive and allowed him long surfing hours. This year, however, due to the insider–outsider effect, the total volume of job space has gone down dramatically to only four million times five days of work (equivalent to four million full-time jobs). So, again, Hamminga's Labor Bank starts printing Labor Rights and issues four of those to all able-bodied citizens, including Lazy. For these four Labor Rights, each of them is entitled to four days of work and the resulting income, without being taxed for the benefit of others (except perhaps those who have not been given Labor Rights, say: orphans who are too young to work).[8] But Lazy's preferences for work have not changed. Let us suppose that Lazy renews his two-day labor contract. Lazy is in the same position as he was last year, qua job satisfaction, income, surfing hours, and what not.[9] Except that now he is holding two Labor Rights for which he has no independent productive use. What will he do with those? Indeed, he should sell them! There are many who want a more-than-four-day job, which they cannot afford with their own four Labor Rights. They are willing to buy. And since Lazy is in one of the best positions to sell—he does not have to give up something in selling his spare

Labor Rights, so his reservation price is zero—he will certainly be among those who sell. He will be on the supply side of the liberalized Labor Right market. And there we have it again: Lazy is taking an extra income from "Labor Right rent" on top of his regular earnings from his own two-day job. And this rent is financed by (some of) the people who want five-day jobs. It is exploitative because he acquires the fruit of the labor of someone else, and the benefit of another's pains, without giving up anything he wants to have for himself: a two-day job.

We may describe the problem in Hamminga's proposal as follows: if he does not assume that only full-time employment is available, and distributes Labor Rights equally, then it is obvious that those who have a preference for part-time employment only will take parasitic profits from the sale of their spare Labor Rights. But if he does assume that there is only full-time employment, then we are dealing with the distribution of opportunities in a form that is less abstract than the form in which they actually exist, or might exist.

In order for a Labor Rights system to be just, the number of Labor Rights a specific individual receives should reflect the extension of his preference for labor opportunities, measured by the number of days, or hours, he would want to work. A labor market that makes people end up either working full-time or not working at all may call for compensatory transfer payments to those who have been involuntarily excluded. But where voucher systems are called in, for the purpose of sharing the value of jobs on the assumption that jobs themselves cannot be shared, there we should take a very critical look at the assumption. We should consider the merit of working time reduction and job sharing. For this, we shall return to Philippe Van Parijs.

Could jobs be like cars and concerts? This question is the subtitle of Hamminga's article. Well, could jobs be like cars? I guess they could not, unless cars could be like jobs. If we could chop cars into five or more equally useful pieces, which we could distribute among those wanting them, then jobs could be like cars. But cars, in general, are the smallest unit of car to serve any purpose. Could jobs be like concerts? Well, perhaps it is true in our morally imperfect world that if I, being a very, very thin person get a ticket while you, being a very, very fat person get one ticket too, I may sell half of my seat to you afterwards, but that only proves that one seat is not the smallest unit of sitting space to serve any purpose. Justice requires that I ought to have the opportunity to acquire half of a seat, and you three halves. So, it seems to me, if we get the distributive units right, jobs are not the kind of thing we should be driving (parasitic) bargains with among each other. It is much better to see to it that the actual distribution of job space as job space reflects our preferences for work and leisure as closely as possible within the limits that are imposed by a system of fair sharing.

5.3 A Feminist Case against Highest Sustainability

There is a remarkable response by Philippe Van Parijs to the ideal of job sharing and to the tendency towards the shortening of working hours.

> [T]he very fact that firms choose not to spread employment more evenly among those wanting to work strongly suggests that doing so would run against their concern with maximizing their profits. Compulsory working-time reduction can, therefore, be expected to have a negative impact on profits, and hence on the value of assets and on the maximum level of basic income that can be financed by taxing the transfer of standard wealth. . . . It would therefore diminish the endowments of some of the least privileged, those who, even after jobs have been shared, would have nothing to live on but a basic income. (Van Parijs 1995b: 10)

Here we have a second reference to the interdependency between the value of assets in the standard sense, such as natural resources, and the distribution of employment. But this time I believe we must regard the reasoning as wholly inconsistent even on Van Parijs's own terms, for what he is implying here is that labor should not only be taxed but also be distributed in such a way as to produce the highest yield from taxing assets, even if (some of) the beneficiaries of a basic income would themselves favor a more equal distribution.

Think of the following situation. There is one full-time job, presently done by Crazy, producing a wage such that nine hundred golden coins will be the total tax yield from jointly taxing Crazy's labor and the use of natural assets, and these nine hundred will have to be shared with Moderazy and Lazy on an equal footing, since they are entitled to an equal share of the job's and of the assets' value. Let us ignore the incentive effects for the moment: they all get three hundred. This is fine with Crazy, eager as she is for income and tolerant as she is to work. It is fine with Lazy too, detestable as he finds work. But it is not fine at all with Moderazy. She detests sitting at home all day and would gladly take one-third of the job that Crazy is presently doing. Why? Because the job is one in a factory that builds aircraft, and, ever since childhood Moderazy has been crazy about flying machines. She has chosen an education that reflected that passion and now she wants to "humanly flourish."[10] Not that she wants to flourish the whole week, but about two days of flourishing every week would be just fine. So she demands her fair share of the job, instead of her fair share in the job's present value. "Well, that won't do," says the Treasury, "if you take one-third of the job, and if because of that Crazy will be left with two-thirds of the job, then the tax yield will go down, so much so that I will only be able to pay each of you two hundred instead of the three hundred that you have now. Would you accept that?" Moderazy muses for a while but she finds that yes! she likes flying machines so much that she even prefers an income of two hundred plus one third of a job, to an income of three hundred, which forces her to sit at home all day, all week. But, of course, there are also two protesters. There is Crazy, who is not willing to trade one-third of her present job for a loss of one hundred golden coins and who regards the reduction of her working time as compulsory. And there is Lazy who starts screaming that he is being treated unfairly because the basic income, on which he is still depending (as he does not have a share in the job and does not desire one either), is going down. He feels that we are biased against the voluntarily unemployed, like himself, who suffer terribly from "a repulsion to being bossed around" (Van Parijs 1995b: 110), if we let Moderazy have her way.

But what seems to be surfacing here, again, as in paragraph 4.6, is that the argument for the highest sustainable basic income can interfere with the "primitive" Dworkinian justification for having a basic income at all. Even if we would accept, as I do not, that there is a good argument for some unconditional basic income, it must be obvious that equality of job space does not warrant the highest sustainable basic income. In the present case, the concentration on Lazy's fate, and on the pecuniary value of jobs, victimizes people who value the so-called "intrinsic" quality of part-time employment as an ingredient of a varied life, and who value it over an increase in income. The involuntarily unemployed are forced, to put it bluntly, to accept money instead of all other things that employment might provide because the voluntary bohemians happen not to care for work at all. But as long as those who want entry to the labor market are willing to pay their share of the efficiency loss in per capita productivity, the fact that others are not so prepared, whether Crazy or Lazy, can be no argument against job sharing.

Consider the following parallel. Suppose ninety individuals own a small garden each. The gardens are all bordering on each other and together they cover an area that is quite large. Now thirty garden owners get the idea of combining all ninety gardens to turn the whole area into a football field. However, there are two special circumstances: first, they know that given the limited capacity of a single football field not every person will be able to play, and, second, they know that not every person who owns a garden is a football enthusiast. The thirty football fanatics conclude that they will have to buy the sixty gardens of the others. They consider the case and find that, provided they buy every single garden that is not yet in their possession, they are willing to pay x golden coins per garden. Now, of the other owners thirty consider x coins for a not very interesting garden quite a profitable deal. But the remaining thirty garden owners are not willing to sell at all for x coins; they value their garden much higher than that. Unless the price goes up significantly they will not sell. But the price will not go up significantly because the football fans are not willing to pay more than x coins. Typically, the people who like their gardens so much and who refuse to sell will face resentment from both other groups. The fanatics are frustrated because they will not have a football field and those who are willing to sell have to forgo a profitable deal. Both groups will complain that the value of their initial equal share of the grounds goes down because there are some who refuse to sell. In this parallel playing football is equal to full employment, ninety times x coins to the maximal yield from taxing full employment, a garden to part-time employment, and the profitable sale of a garden to a labor-free income. The principle of abstraction requires that those who want to keep their gardens shall have their way. But the highest sustainable basic income policy is like disowning all garden owners in return for x coins, including those who prefer their garden to the money. They are less than fully compensated.

How likely is it that large groups of people are so disposed that they value part-time work over additional income? I will give some considerations that seem to me to be relevant. First, we should remember that the context of this discussion, as Philippe Van Parijs has stressed repeatedly, is provided by reasonably affluent societies. And in these affluent societies an overwhelming majority of individuals live in couples or families: most incomes are household incomes and generally they are quite high compared to some time ago. What is not so high, generally, is the opinion that many household members have about the division of responsibilities and opportunities. As things are organized now, about half do indoor work only, and the other half of them do out-of-doors work only. Many of the former group, and some of the latter, are thoroughly dissatisfied with this situation. Would they accept a certain loss of income if that went along with a more even sharing of the various tasks and activities? I think many would (I think many of us know many who would). Since income situations are not really critical anyway, it might very well be that many people would value the goods that part-time work can give over the goods that additional income can give. Let me be more precise: from a gender political perspective, and I mean the perspective of both Shazy and Hazy, and perhaps the perspective of their infantazies too, the idea of a highest sustainable basic income might pretty well be disastrous. It would give distinct incentives to reproduce present economic relations between the sexes. Its implementation would destroy all the hope of true social innovation that has been raised by our present affluence.

Marx hoped (and predicted) that the affluence that would be created by communism would do away with the economic necessity of full-time and life-long specialization in one activity. That it would do away, so to speak, with "one-dimensional" men and women, and that it would provide opportunities to engage in a wide variety of interesting activities. As he puts it in a well-known passage, "[communist society] makes it possible for me to do one thing today and another tomorrow, to hunt in the morning, fish in the afternoon, rear cattle in the evening, criticize after dinner, just as I have in mind, without ever becoming hunter, fisherman, shepherd or critic" (Marx and Engels 1970: 53). We have not quite reached that point (hardly, by the way, because we have failed as a communist society), but in some respects we are near the state predicted nevertheless. We can afford not to be full-time employed as either a specialized child raiser and dishwasher or as a specialized out-of-doors moneymaker. We can afford to earn money half a day, raise children during the other half, criticize (each other's performance) over dinner, and do whatever we like in the evening. So why should we not do so if such a mix of activities suits us better than the purchase of yet another turn in the merry-go-round during the weekend?[11] Yet, the luxury of that possibility would have to be forgone if we accept Van Parijs's argument against job sharing and in favor of maximizing the tax yield.

Further, due to more or less recent demographic developments ("baby booms"), it so happens that young people make up a large section of the involuntarily unemployed. Working time reduction and job sharing would better their position on the labor market, but again it might lead to some income losses. Would the youngsters mind that very much, or can they be expected to value the chance to start a career over the certainty of never having one, even if that would mean that they would have to start with a lower income than they would have had otherwise? I think it is not too far-fetched to assume that many would be willing to trade boredom for low income, if that holds prospects of being involved in the labor process, and of the real exercise of those skills and abilities that they were once taught because they so improved their freedom to choose whatever they might wish to do.

So, I believe that there are at least two significant groups of people that tend to be at the "side line" presently, women and youngsters, who can be expected to accept at least some income losses, if only that would restore the control over their rightful equal share of employment. These groups have quite consistently signaled that they value employment for various other reasons than the pecuniary reward. And, of course, there are many others who do so too.[12] If there are some others, either fully employed or voluntarily unemployed, who are not interested in such restoration of original entitlements and prefer high incomes instead, that cannot be a reason to abandon the job-sharing strategy.[13]

Perhaps it will be argued that my observations apply only to certain limited sections of the middle classes, to skilled and well-educated people who have access to the more exciting types of job and can afford to forgo some additional income, while the majority of the workforce, even in affluent societies, is single-mindedly preoccupied with the improvement of its income from jobs that are tedious and boring anyway. But such a rejoinder would be beside the point. Middle-class women and youngsters are persons too. Even if my argument were relevant only to the types of job that carry very high internal rewards— say teaching and research positions at universities—there is no reason at all for rejecting a robust job-sharing policy in that particular area of employment.[14]

All this must hold, I repeat, even if we accept unconstrained equality of external assets as the right view of justice in original entitlements. The highest sustainable basic income in actual fact is not the highest justifiable basic income on the basis of that doctrine. So, in a way, Hamminga's proposal of the Labor Rights market, provided we drop the idea that there can only be full-time employment, is superior to Van Parijs's proposal of a highest sustainable basic income. It is fairer to those who want part-time employment, for two reasons: on the one hand, the Labor Rights system can be made sensitive to people's limited independent interest in employment, thus reducing their opportunities to be a parasite, but, on the other hand, the Labor Rights system allows people to hold on to their job space even if the consequence will be that its pecuniary reward goes down compared to the market price they might otherwise have got. It allows people to accept such losses if they value work for other reasons. If your husband is ready to pay you three hundred coins for your Labor Rights, leaving himself with three hundred as well, while you would only get two hundred if you took the job yourself, you remain perfectly entitled to take your own job. If he now starts complaining that he too will only make two hundred at his job, then you can rightly say that this is his problem and not yours. And if the next-door bohemian thinks he has a valid reason to interfere with the way you conduct negotiations with your husband, then, frankly, you should tell him to mind his own business.

These conclusions remain quite consistent with my main objection against both Van Parijs and Hamminga that you should not be allowed to hold vouchers, or be entitled to an income, if you are such a Lazy that you would not even have worked a single minute under non-scarce conditions. The point in this section is just that equalizing (or maximining) income from jobs is simply not the same thing as equalizing (or maximining) the value of employment. Employment as an ingredient of variety is the source of value other than income. There is no justification for ignoring that.

5.4 Equalized Civic Feudalism?

Just as unconstrained equality of resources would "democratize" the former (and sometimes actual) privileges of the landed aristocracy, by giving everybody an equal right to lease out usurped shares of land in return for income, or to practice usury otherwise, so equality of job space seems to democratize the former privileges of the mercantile city patriciate and its vassals. There are distinct parallels, conceptually, but also historically. As Geert Mak, writing about the history of Amsterdam, tells us about Jacob Bicker Raye, "the prototype of the upper middle class in the eighteenth century":

> Because the stadholders were weak and absent, the regents were at liberty for decades to appoint their friends and relations to the more than three thousand offices the city had to give away. Capacities did not count at all because *the one who got the appointment just pocketed the fee and had someone else carry out the actual work for a small sum.*
>
> Thus, our Jacob Bicker Raye had been able to take over from his brother the office of auctioneer of the "Grote Vismarkt" [Main Fish Market] on the Dam. For that he got two and a half percent of the

turnover of the market, and that might amount to some five hundred guilders a month, sometimes even twice as much. He paid the man who did the real auctioning work four hundred guilders a year. The rest he could put in his own pocket. (Mak 1995: 177; my translation from the Dutch, italics added)

An office came to be regarded as a favor, a fief, a dignity which one could give away and receive—a governmental tradition dating back to the Middle Ages. (Mak 1995: 178)

Likewise, the historian C. R. Boxer observes that "public offices in the Dutch Republic—as elsewhere for that matter, though for different reasons—came to be regarded as private, *more or less negotiable*, family properties" (Boxer 1965: 42; italics added).

And Boxer quotes an anonymous Englishman, then resident in Holland, who concludes that its government is in fact aristocratic and that "the much boasted liberty" of the Dutch is to be understood "cum grano salis."

The striking thing in these passages is not the nepotism referred to by the authors—nepotism is of all times—but the strange phenomenon that people could own jobs with the accompanying fixed pay and could lease them out to others for a substantially lower pay. Given the privileged entitlement to jobs the (legal?) possibility of leasing them out and taking "tenure rent" must have been something of a necessity, since many occupied more jobs than they could possibly carry out themselves (just as aristocrats occupied more land than they could possibly work on), and offices were even assigned to children. Others just had to do the real work. Bicker Raye, the in-name-only auction-eer of the fish market, was also a captain of the local citizen's mili-tia ("schutterij"), collector of taxes on coal and peat, and bookkeeper of the "corn book." And once Amsterdam enjoyed the services of a 5-year-old postmaster (Mak 1995: 156).

Once the nobility lived off large landownership, once patricians lived off large job ownership. Of course, it is true that one of the gross injustices of such a "system" of office ownership, as in the case of land ownership, lies in its inequality and in the circumstance that the right to be appointed to a "rent-bearing" office was in fact a privilege to which one was entitled by birth or status. But inequality is not the whole story about its injustice. The hard core of "civic feudalism" is not affected by introducing equality into the distribution of job space, as philosophers like Van Parijs and Hamminga do, because the hard core of the injustice is that people are allowed to hold ownership rights over

productive opportunities for which they have no independent interest. Equalizing the opportunities for foul play is not the same thing as
removing them. Perhaps it makes the game somewhat fairer but it does
not make the game as it ought to be.

The idea of an unconditional basic income for all has been referred
to by the canvassing slogan "Every one a king."[15] There may be irony
in this expression, but we should understand its serious implication
nevertheless. Its real bite would be best expressed by: "Every one a
liege lord."[16]

CHAPTER 6

AGAINST REAL UNFREEDOM:
EQUALITY AND NEUTRALITY

> And so assigned to every family a parcell of land,
> according to the proportion of their number for
> that end, only for present use.
>
> William Bradford

6.1 On the Move

I have pointed out that the right to exploit one's nuisance value is an
essential element in the argument for an unconditional basic income. If
such a right were rejected, it would not be possible to infer a person's
entitlement to an income without some corresponding obligation to
accept work. In this concluding chapter, I will discuss an argument
that we should nevertheless be committed to equal property rights in
external resources, on account of our (broadly liberal) commitment
to freedom as a fundamental value. In order to demonstrate the problem with this argument, we have to return to the original egalitarian
Robinsonade that was invoked to make the case for basic income.

Assume that, as discussed earlier, our Lazy and Crazy are sitting on
their island with four plots of land, while their constellation of interests
is of B-type: Crazy has an independent interest for three plots, Lazy
only wants one plot for his own use, so that under a regime of equal
and tradable resources Lazy may obtain a benefit from Crazy's pains.
Let us now imagine that a ship comes by, and that the captain of this
ship makes the offer to transport both Lazy and Crazy (and for some
unexplained reason only both of them, not just one of them) to a
nearby island that is exactly alike to their home island in all respects,
except that it has six plots of land, not four. Obviously Crazy would
gladly accept this offer, since on the new island she would have three
unencumbered plots of land without the need to hire or buy additional

resources. Lazy however will certainly want to resist the collective move to the larger island, since there he would be robbed of his convenient labor-free income from Crazy's efforts. Under a regime of equality of tradable resources an extension of the stock of aggregate resources at their disposal would make Crazy better off, while Lazy would be made worse off. Their move to the larger island would not be a Pareto improvement. It seems then that there is no hope for a consensus about what to do. Crazy and Lazy will not agree, but would it be acceptable if a theory of justice would not succeed in ranking large stocks of resources as socially more desirable than small stocks of resources?

Or, to put the question in another light: would such a ranking reveal a bias towards Lazy's interests, a bias that would be unwarranted by the basic concerns underlying equality of resources as a theory of justice? Remember that, until now, this theory, and the real libertarian argument for basic income it enabled, aspired to maintain strict neutrality towards the interests of all who would be affected by distributive schemes, also towards interests that could only be satisfied through parasitic relations. Would such a theory now be forced to maintain its neutrality towards Lazy's present preference to stay (collectively) on the smaller island?

A foreseeable response would be that although equality of resources maintains neutrality towards all interests, it need not be committed to neutrality to all actual preferences. It is man's fundamental interest to have so-called "real freedom." Equality of resources seeks to equi-maximize such freedom, and it would be greater on the larger island. In the following, I will argue that a real libertarian argument that larger stocks of resources are superior to smaller stocks of resources can be successful, but not without incapacitating the real libertarian argument for basic income. So let us turn to Van Parijs's fundamental notion of real freedom.

What exactly is to be understood by real freedom, and why is it desirable or required as the index for interpersonal comparisons in matters of distributive justice? Van Parijs defines real freedom as the freedom to choose to do whatever one might desire (or prefer) to do, and as such he opposes real freedom both to power and to actual freedom. The conception of actual freedom dates back to Voltaire: it is the freedom to choose to do what one actually desires (or prefers) to do. But the conception of actual freedom is deficient for purposes of justice, as Van Parijs argues, because it implies "that a person could be made free, or her freedom be increased, through an appropriate manipulation of her preferences." (Van Parijs 1995b: 18). A theory of justice using actual freedom as its basic index would, therefore, be fatally vulnerable to the phenomenon of so-called "contented-slavery." In a famous article Jon Elster (1983) has pointed out, and illustrated, that persons may show a general tendency to "downgrade" the value of options that they do not have. In other words, they tend to change their preferences in a way that fits their actual possibilities more conveniently, making them more satisfied. Thus, the fox that cannot reach the grapes seeks comfort in the thought that they are sour, so that he does not want them anymore. Similarly, Tocqueville reported 150 years ago that the slaves in the southern states did not seem to suffer at all from their obvious lack of freedom.

Indeed, using the metric of actual freedom for judgments of justice should meet with the very same objection as using the metric of preference satisfaction itself. Amartya Sen states that objection as follows:

> In situations of long-standing deprivation, the victims do not go on grieving and lamenting all the time, and very often make great efforts to take pleasure in small mercies and to cut down personal desires to modest—"realistic"—proportions. Indeed, in situations of adversity which the victims cannot individually change, *prudential reasoning* would suggest that the victims should concentrate their desires on those limited things that they *can* possibly achieve, rather than fruitlessly pining for what is unattainable. The extent of a person's deprivation, then, may not at all show up in the metric of desire-fulfillment. (Sen 1995date: 55)

Now, about the rationality or "prudentiality" of adapting our preferences in reaction to our actual circumstances, as contented slaves seem to have done, a number of knots still have to be untied. The process, on any account of it, seems to contradict John Stuart Mill's observation that we would prefer to be dissatisfied men rather than satisfied pigs, and it seems rather odd if rational agents were to "choose" their conceptions of the good life with a reference to the level of expected success in living accordingly. Yet, as we encountered in chapter 5, there are also those who have defended distributive equality precisely with the argument that rational agents are responsible for their "expensive preferences" implying that those who are distraught without a diet of champagne and caviar (Rawls) or who cannot manage without prephylorexia clarets and plovers' eggs (Dworkin) should have been more cautious in forming (at least the culinary aspects of) their conceptions of the good life. Is it unwise take a bite (or sip) of something you cannot afford? Should we shy away from trying what we cannot have? To my mind there remains a deep question to be answered: how important is it to appreciate what we are missing? I cannot produce a deep answer to that question here. But whatever it would be, it is clear, and I here I agree with Van Parijs, that we have a fundamental interest not only in being able to do the things we happen to value to do but also in maintaining the conditions that protect, so to say, the integrity of the process by which we acquire or form our values. That integrity does not only require the standard liberal political liberties, such as freedom of expression and information; it also requires certain material conditions.

The second opposition, between real freedom and power, is explicated by Van Parijs as follows:

> it suffices to reflect on the following two situations. In situation A, each of us can decide for herself whether to scratch her nose. In situation B, we decide together, in a perfectly democratic fashion, whether nose scratching is permissible. Assuming (plausibly) that variations in nose size can be deemed irrelevant, it can be said that in both situations the weight of each person in decision-making is identical. But surely the freedom to scratch (or not to scratch) is not. Each of us enjoys this freedom in situation A. But there is no such freedom in situation B, where scratching is subjected to collective approval.... Demanding that people be equally or maximally free is not the same as demanding that they be given equal or maximal power. (Van Parijs 1995b: 8)

Real freedom, then, defined as the range of options a person can choose, independently of her actual desires and independently of the desires and decisions of others, seems to be generally required not only as a safeguard against unduly impaired preference formation but also as a warrant for our self-determination. Taken together these two guarantees can be taken to cover our capacity for making autonomous choices. Having real freedom is a condition for the proper exercise of what Rawls has called our "higher order capacities": the capacity to form and revise our conceptions of the good, and our capacity to pursue such a conception.

Now, external resources, says Van Parijs, are the "substrate" of real freedom. To the extent that people have a protected and fixed right in them under the rule of law, they will be able to determine for themselves what combination of goods, leisure, and income, they will obtain, that is: how hard they will work and for what purpose; and in as far people are not relatively deprived of such rights their conceptions of the good need not suffer from contented-slavery effects.

Conceived as such, it would seem that real libertarians should have no trouble in deciding that larger stocks of resources, equally distributed, are better than smaller stocks. Would not larger shares of resources simply represent greater extensions of real freedom for all? This is, of course, the intuitive conclusion we would all want to share.

Unfortunately, Philippe van Parijs cannot yet help himself to this conclusion, as Lazy would be happy to point out. The source of the trouble is in the way he argues for the significance of the tradability of resources. Given that we have equal shares of resources, why should they be tradable? Here is the answer:

> Endowing... Crazy and Lazy with equal plots of land certainly constitutes one non-discriminatory allocation of real freedom between them. But if this endowment is not tradable, if they are both stuck with it, this allocation cannot be optimal from the real-libertarian standpoint. It will not give either Lazy or Crazy the highest attainable level of real freedom. (Van Parijs 1995b: 98–99)

Introducing tradability will increase the real freedom of all. And this is why the real libertarian cannot unambiguously rank higher stocks of resources as more desirable than lower stocks.

Assume a fairly large population living on an island with a restricted supply of resources, allowing each an equal share that it is just sufficient to work only half of the available time. Were such shares not tradable each would be "stuck" with a certain restricted range of *leisure/income bundles,* or LIBs, to choose from. Now, in all likelihood, given the variety of preferences for LIBs among the population, introducing the tradability of resources for income would result in an extended LIB set for each, reflecting an equilibrium price per unit of land. And, according to Van Parijs's argument, this should be considered as an extension of their real freedom. The new freedom set fully includes the old one, since the liberty not to sell or buy resources and to continue to work one's own equal share will remain intact. So clearly it is superior. Everybody will be freer to choose combinations of leisure and income, as he or she might desire.

Consider now that this population could be moved in its entirety to a nearby island, similar in all respects except that it has twice as much resources, so that an equal distribution will now give each a share that enables one to work to full capacity—the whole week. This means that, whatever the preferences within the population, nobody could have any use for additional resources and demand for them will be zero. Therefore, making resources tradable for income on the larger island will not change the real freedom sets of either the Lazies or the Crazies. Nothing could be gained by selling shares of resources and consequently basic income on the larger island would be zero.

So given the tradability of resources each person's (equal) real freedom set as it would be on the larger island only intersects with her
real freedom set as it is on the smaller island. Therefore, it cannot be
ranked as superior: some LIBs are only available on the smaller island,
e.g. to enjoy full-time leisure on revenues at the level of basic income,
and some other LIBs are only available on the larger island, e.g. to
work full-time on unencumbered land in return for a high income.
This analysis can be generalized. The real libertarian cannot maintain
that larger stocks of resources will give everybody more real freedom.
With larger stocks the commercial value of resources will go down: the
shape of the resulting freedom sets will change, adding opportunities
to work on unencumbered land but excluding those LIBs that were
only attainable through the selling of resources at a high price per unit.
There is no decisive argument either way, and therefore a ranking of
larger stocks of resources as socially more desirable than smaller stocks
cannot in itself be a matter of real libertarian justice, and seemingly
reveals an unjustified bias against Lazy.

Such, at least, would be Lazy's favored conclusion. But can this
annoying result be avoided, while we still keep a commitment to the
"higher order" concerns that real libertarianism is rightly anxious to
protect: the concern for (what I have called) the integrity of preference formation, and the concern for (what I have called) the capacity
for self-determination? I think we can produce a better result, implying indeed that greater stocks of resources are always better, but the
improvement comes with a serious price for the real libertarian project
as envisioned until now. What has to be given up is the view of original
rights to resources as property rights, essentially involving the right to
buy and sell. The cause of the trouble is the idea that the commodifi-
cation of natural assets realizes an extension of people's real freedom,
and indeed that idea can be demonstrated to be wrong, also on real
libertarian terms. Tradability does not increase people's real freedom as
it was originally defined.

Recall the discussion of our freedom to scratch our noses. A person
is only free to scratch his nose if it is he, and only he, who can decide
(independently of the desires and permissions of others) whether or
not to engage in scratching. The point was not that the permission
to actually scratch one's nose would somehow not be forthcoming
once the matter were left to "perfectly democratic decision making."
It seems unlikely that, in that event, some majority (qualified or not)
would be sufficiently interested in the unscratched condition of our
noses, so as to actually issue a scratch prohibition. As far as I know,

not even the most collectivist democracies have ever imposed a nose-scratch tax. Van Parijs's point, correctly it seems to me, is rather that the very need for such permission would already be an infringement of our real freedom.

More formally, then, if a person has real freedom with regard to doing or having x, it means that his choice or decision to do or have x will not merely be a necessary condition for her actually doing or having x but also a sufficient condition. But on this account of real freedom, it should be clear that the introduction of the possibility of market relations between individuals by allowing them property rights over shares of resources could not really create an extension of their real freedom. It is simply not true that Crazy's right to buy Lazy's land creates Crazy's real freedom to use that land, without Lazy's permission, and independently of Lazy's preferences or desires. And likewise, Lazy's right to sell his land to Crazy does not lead to Lazy's freedom to determine all by himself, without Crazy's permission, whether or not he shall have access to some income that is generated by Crazy's labor. In such cases some decision of Crazy (or Lazy) is necessary, but no decision is sufficient, to create an actual opportunity for Crazy (or Lazy).

Markets may create great opportunities for gain for each of us, and indeed great extensions of what we may choose to do or have, but not without the permissions of others, and not independently of the desires of others. Indeed, markets subject our opportunities as much to the tastes and whims of the millions as democracies (of the indicated intrusive nature) would. It takes a very specific constellation of the desires of many other people as producers and consumers to create our opportunity to purchase a chocolate bar at the (attractive) current rate. That rate is certainly not a matter of the self-determination of the individual who wishes to consume chocolate. Elsewhere (Van Donselaar 1998) I borrowed a couple of terms from G. A. Cohen (who in his turn borrowed them from the Medieval schoolmen). There is freedom *in sensu composito*, and there is freedom *in sensu diviso*. The first means that all can do what each can do; the second means that this not the case (Cohen 1983: 14). Now, markets generally provide freedom *in sensu diviso*. Each of us can buy that chocolate bar at the current rate. But the current rate would not be the current rate if demand for chocolate went up significantly: we cannot all buy chocolate at the current rate.

Likewise, my freedom to choose to leisurely live off basic income would be vitally dependent on there being sufficient others sufficiently eager to work (and not too many others who, like myself, desire to cash in the rent of their spare resources). The opportunity, then, to live off basic income would be freedom *in sensu diviso*. Not all can have it. If all would be fully satisfied with their initial equal shares of resources, basic income would be naught, and nothing in this respect would be left to be determined by myself.

By contrast, the LIBs that are attainable through secure access rights to resources belong to our freedom *in sensu composito*. How long we will work on our equal share, and in return for what income, is to be fully determined by ourselves, independently of what others decide to do with their own shares. And this time all can do what each can do. And naturally that freedom increases as shares of resources increase.

Real freedom, I submit, should be conceived as freedom *in sensu composito*. If not, we would be blurring the essential distinction between self-determination and bargaining power (Van Donselaar 1998). Bargaining power is still power: there is no way to define it without referring to the desires and decisions of others. But the extent of our capacity for self-determination should characteristically be identifiable without such a reference. The tradability of resources, then, and their status as property rights, is not a condition by which real freedom for all will be maximized.

The Pareto improvement that tradability allows is desirable in its own right, but not on account of our commitment to real freedom. Once this confusion is eliminated from the real libertarian theory there should no longer be any hesitation about the collective move to the larger island. A true commitment to the equi-maximization of real freedom proper would require it, even though some LIBs that were available on the smaller island will then be lost. Those lost LIBs were not part of people's real freedom set to begin with, while the newly gained LIBs on the larger island are part of their real freedom set. On the larger island, all can choose to work on larger shares of resources, even though the Lazies would not care for that. This should silence Lazy's complaint.

6.2 The Rule of Maimonides

The good news resulting from our refutation of Lazy's complaint is that, since a commitment to equal real freedom does not imply a commitment to equal property rights in resources, neither are we morally required to accept exploitation on account of the value of real freedom and the underlying concerns it protects. Of course, no sane doctrine of justice will deny that Pareto optimality in the distribution of LIBs is independently desirable. But introducing the tradability of rights to resources, thereby changing those rights into property rights, is just one way to achieve Pareto optimality, and not one we should be committed to simply in virtue of being committed to equal real freedom itself. The commitment to equal real freedom does not preclude that we consider alternative ways of achieving Pareto optimality.

In the following, I will attempt to sketch an alternative distributive principle of resources, not involving an allocation of property rights, and not allowing exploitative relations on the basis of such rights, yet achieving Pareto optimality in the distribution of LIBs, meanwhile robustly reflecting an equal protection for each of the higher order interests that we identified.

Consider what seems to be (at least the beginning of) such a principle, call it: the *principle of equality-based progressive satiation*:

> Each person shall have an equal share of the available resources, unless she needs less than an equal share for the achievement of her favorite leisure/income bundle, call this her "satiation level of use." In that case the part that exceeds her satiation level shall be equally shared by all whose initial equal shares did not yet secure their own satiation. If by this transfer some persons acquire shares in excess of their satiation levels, then there will again be a transfer of the surpluses to those not yet satiated. This procedure will be repeated, until finally, if there are any, those whose favorite LIBs require the very largest shares of resources will have to remain less than fully satiated.

For short, this principle may also be called *Maimonides' Rule*. It is an iterated application of the adjudicating principle that was once developed by the famous medieval philosopher and physician from Cordoba:

> Give an equal amount to every claimant or the full amount of his claim, whichever is smaller.

Maimonides developed his rule for the (Talmudic) legal context, e.g. for the case where rival claims to an inheritance were due to inconsistencies in a testator's will. We however identify a person's "claim" with the share of resources that is required for her satiation and apply the rule to the distribution of external resources.

The rule obviously makes short work of the possibility of exploitative relations on the basis of (what I called) usurpation. As no one would be in the position to maintain rights to shares of resources for which she has no private use, no independent interest, such shares will not be marketable. Moreover, since those who would otherwise be demanding resources on the market will now be freely supplied with additional shares in excess of equality, demand can be expected to down anyhow, even if not, perhaps, to exactly zero.

But the attentive reader will have noticed that the rule of Maimonides, even if it is applied to the fullest, may still not achieve complete Pareto optimality, and that it may still allow exploitative relations of the usurious kind. Some Crazies not yet satiated might still put a high value on parts of the shares that the Lazies hold, sufficiently high perhaps to induce some Lazies to sell. So the principle would require some modification in order to deal with usury. I will not attempt such a modification here, but not to worry: the principle of progressive satiation is merely meant to indicate the lines along which we may try to reconcile our commitment to equal real freedom, our objection to exploitation, and Pareto optimality in the distribution of LIBs.

How does Maimonides' Rule secure maximal equal capacities for self-determination, independent of other people's decisions (or permissions)? As long as people do not require larger than equal shares of resources in order to achieve certain favored combinations of leisure and income, as would be allowed by using these resources, each is perfectly free to make her own decisions and live accordingly, independently of what others may or may not prefer, or permit, her to do. The principle specifies that the extent of a person's freedom of choice, or real freedom in Van Parijs's original sense, only meets a constraint where it would not be compatible with a similarly extended freedom for others. It is only when one aspires for "life styles" that require more than equal shares of resources (and if therefore one could be said to entertain "expensive preferences"), that one becomes dependent on the tastes and preferences of others, though not in such a manner as to become an object of their exploitative intentions. Additional opportunities for work, beyond equality, would only be available when (sufficient) others willingly decide, based on their own independent trade-offs between leisure and income, that they need less than equal shares of resources. These additional opportunities, then, would not belong to one's real freedom set proper, just like additional opportunities that originate from market relations do not belong to real freedom.

Next: the demonstration of the principle's insensitivity to adaptive preferences proceeds along similar lines. Preference adaptation can only occur as a response to (reduced) sets of real freedom, that are themselves fixed independently of one's preferences. I may come to prefer to stay home (and take pleasure in the small mercies my home provides), once I know that the door happens to be locked. But if my preference for going out determines whether or not the door will be locked

I can hardly adapt my preferences to it being locked. Our worry about contented enslavement is not per se that the slave's options precisely fit his actual wants, e.g. that he is not able to move to another place while he has no desire to do so. The worry is that he would not be able to move even if he did want to do so. The lack of his ability to move is unconditional on his desires, and it is this unconditional absence of options that disturbs the real libertarian. Correctly so. But as we saw, it leads the real libertarian to the thought that he should be committed to the unconditional presence of options, in order to prevent contented enslavement. Indeed, the nonconditionality of basic income can be traced directly to this nonconditionality of the options the real libertarian wants to distribute equally. The essence of the strategy considered here however is to counter contented enslavement, and as we may say: to avoid "real unfreedom," by providing the conditional presence of options.

This is what Maimonides' rule intends to achieve. Up to equality the amount of resources one shall acquire for one's own use is simply a strict function of one's desire for them, and this is true for each. The conditions of preference formation are not given by access rights that are somehow fixed and restricted in advance; the only fixed condition is the principle itself and it is equal for all. There is nothing to adapt one's preferences to. Maimonides' rule cannot be vulnerable to the contented slavery objection. But again, access to opportunities beyond what equality of resources would allow, cannot be secure, since, as I argued, the opportunity of such access will depend on the whims of others. This means that developing an appetite for LIBs that require larger shares of resources may be hazardous in a way that developing "modest" preferences is not. Those with such demanding appetites will be at the back end of the queue for full satiation. It might make for frustration. In this sense, then, the principle of progressive satiation can be said to recognize that, as a matter of justice, agents should be held "responsible" for their expensive preferences, whatever we mean by that precisely.

Let me rehearse some of my findings. First, the principle of progressive satiation, Maimonides' rule (or some modified version of it dealing with usury, which I said could not be developed here), allows us to think of ways to reconcile a commitment to equi-maximize people's ability to make autonomous choices with a concern for Pareto optimality in the allocation of LIBs that results from their choices. The principle has the merit, contrary to the basic income proposal, that it does not allow, or invite, parasitic relations, and that it does not have to face up to the embarrassment that it cannot rank larger stocks of resources as more socially desirable than smaller stocks of resources (without violating liberal neutrality). Moreover, though there is no articulate tribute to Dworkin's so-called "non-envy test," the proposed principle is robustly egalitarian in that it realizes equality in people's conditions both for the formation and the pursuit of their values. Finally, it captures the "anti-welfarist" intuition that the modest should not loose out on behalf of the eager.

6.3 The Libertarian Librarian

No doubt I should anticipate objections to the "impracticality" of Maimonides' rule for policy purposes in the complicated economic reality of our modern societies. But that is to put things in the wrong order. Recall, Van Parijs's proposal was offered as a principle of justice itself, not as a proxy for justice. What I hope to have demonstrated is that even if we were to solve the problem of distributive justice under the ridiculously primitive circumstances of Dworkin's island there would not be a principled argument for basic income, based on the paramount need for property rights. The idea that there would be such an argument is what started it all.

The objection might continue that my alternative still would create all kinds of measurement problems leading to inapplicability, even in Dworkinistan. But frankly, it seems to me that measurement problems are there to inspire the creativity of the measurers, not to determine our sense of justice. If justice requires us to measure x, then we should find ways to measure x. It is not the other way around: if we are only able to measure z, then justice must be about distributing z. Well, the rule of Maimonides tells us what to look for in the darkness of the attic. It is now for the economist, or the psychologist, to develop a flashlight.

More substantial however, is this: suppose A wants to take an exam in political philosophy next week while today B rushes ahead to the library to borrow the last copy of the *Second Treatise* only to hire it out to A for a handsome figure. Then, in my view of it, B would be abusing his borrowing rights, and he would be abusing A. He would be morally wrong in doing so. This is what the book argues. Are there any fatal measurement problems to obstruct this conclusion? For the librarian, perhaps. Now, I myself have been a university librarian for a good part of my career and I would certainly have suppressed such a practice, had

I been aware of it, either by excluding B from my services—which he, being a real libertarian, would have found unfair—or by extending the stock of copies of the *Second Treatise*, which he, being a real libertarian, would also have found unfair.

But, whatever the plausibility of the educated guess (about B's independent interests) underlying a librarian's policies, in the above scenario there is at least one person who does not have a fatal measurement problem. And that person is B himself. It is difficult to see why the librarian's want of a flashlight should affect B's sensitivity to the arguments in this book.

In other words: the function of principles of justice is not at all exhausted by the way they may inform policy makers or legislators. They are also the principles of a social morality that is shared by citizens who have a sense justice that may well go beyond the defective legislative capacities of their government, to which they may appeal in dealing with each other, and which they may consult in making their own decisions. The rule of Maimonides would not suffer from any measurement problems when just people applied it to themselves.

NOTES

1. But it is by no means the first instance of its formulation, as is sometimes assumed. The decision of the Colmar court could have been a direct application of seventeenth-century town law of the ancient Dutch town of Tiel, which says that "one may build as high as one wants, unless there is a servitude, or if it is done only from spite and anger, in order to torment one's neighbor, without one's own use or profit" (*Stadsrecht van Tiel*, quoted in Van den Bergh 1979: 62; my translation). In fact *Neidbau* (spite building) had already been prohibited by the *Münchener Bauordnung* as early as 1489 (Voyame, Cottier, and Rocha 1990: 26).

2. Throughout this book I will use the words "parasitism" and "exploitation" interchangeably, but the reader should keep in mind that the indicated type of relation is distinct from the relation that socialists call "exploitative." In the next chapter, I discuss this distinction.

3. Another forceful attempt to argue from the general principle of equality of opportunity to substantial unconditional financial provisions is *The Stakeholder Society* (1999) by Bruce Ackerman and Anne Alstott. Their proposal is not to provide an unconditional basic income in regular installments, but to provide a capital grant (a stake) to all upon reaching the age of maturity, financed by a tax on inheritances, thus rectifying the inequalities in starting positions that result from inequalities in parental wealth. The proposal will not be discussed in this book, but elsewhere (Van Donselaar 2003) I tried to point out the analogies in the arguments for unconditional basic income and for the unconditional stake, and I argued that they should, therefore, meet with similar objections. In his reply Ackerman (2003) politely pointed out that the view I attributed

to him was (at least partly) inaccurate. This I have to admit, and I should have been more careful. But nothing much in my argument depended on this error. A stake with "no strings attached" allows exploitation.

Chapter 2

1. Luce and Raiffa (1956: 124–42) is still a useful discussion of the alternatives. For a recent, and hostile, comment on the merits of MRC compared to its rivals, see Binmore 1993.

2. See, for instance, den Hartogh 2002 and Sugden 1993.

3. See also Hausman 1989.

4. It is not excluded per se that omissions, not doing something, can count as an expression of will. Consent can be tacit. Nor is it excluded that certain acts that are not intended to be an expression of will are nevertheless so taken, and hence constitute a legal obligation. If I raise my hand during an auction, if only to wave to a friend, I have actually made a bid.

5. I am aware that here I am going rather quickly through a body of complicated, and sophisticated, theory. However, the complications need not detain us. What matters is that the natural distribution is the utility distribution that rational agents will reach as long as they do not cooperate.

6. In the appendix to this chapter, I give a further interpretation of the idea of social disintegration through economic progress.

7. A "solitary" life would be "poor," but perhaps less "nasty, brutish and short" than a life in the company of other wolves.

8. The claim itself might be subjected to a criticism like the one I give to Steiner and Wolff in chapter 4: the disposition not to comply with Pickles's demands is perhaps relevantly similar to the disposition to act "spitefully" in the ultimatum game (it violates sub-game perfection), and the rationality of such dispositions is a matter of controversy. However, here I am not commenting on the validity of the no-invitation argument per se; my point is rather that even if it were perfectly rational to act from spite, the natural distribution and the Lockean proviso would still not establish the same initial bargaining point.

9. I shall not comment on this claim itself. Just note that it has been pointed out that the "equal rationality" argument for MRC is similar to the, very controversial, so-called 'symmetry argument" for the rationality of cooperative choices in the Prisoners' Dilemma. See Sugden 1993: 164ff.

10. Of course, neither can we have a guarantee against parasitism without fixed rights in internal resources.

11. For a criticism of Gauthier along these lines, see Grunebaum 1990: 556ff. Grunebaum takes Gauthier to employ an efficiency argument per se; he does not consider the fact that efficiency is a necessary condition for the non-violation of the Lockean proviso.

12. For a critical analysis of the development of Spencer's doctrine, see Miller 1976: 193–98.

13. The definition is "somewhat simplified" mainly because the amount of a person's labor effort is not just a function of the number of hours she labored, as not all labor is equally "intense" or strenuous. One hour of sitting alongside a river angling for fish is not the same thing as one hour of "wrestling with greasy mud" to make it produce yams. Yet, for the moment, I will abstract from these differences.

14. I discuss John Roemer's response to a similar analysis of unequal labor exchanges in section 4.7.3.

Chapter 3

1. In the appendix at the end of the chapter, I have included some considerations and materials that were not essential to the arguments presented, yet, perhaps, interesting enough (to students of Locke) not to throw them away.

2. Waldron's reading is supported by Clark Wolf who claims that "while the proviso has often been taken as a necessary condition for legitimate appropriation, the context here implies that Locke regards its satisfaction as sufficient" (Wolf 1995: 795).

3. Waldron 1988: 209–18.

4. See also the appendix to this chapter, sections 4 and 5.

5. Perhaps a third reason: parties in a conflict are also biased in exacting punishments for trespasses. Victims, left to themselves as punishers, are inclined to take two teeth for one, or an arm for a hand. Society needs its executioners as well as its umpires to be unbiased. In short, the whole of law enforcement is best invested in the state.

6. This judgment is based on Den Hartogh's representation of Tully's position.

7. Locke 1970: 477. See for the editorial significance of the Christ's copy: appendix, section 2.

8. English and Irish fishermen rather sympathized with the Canadians. They even started flying Canadian flags on their vessels.

9. Think of them as Switzerland and Austria, having no access to the ocean.

10. Empirical claims that have been contradicted by some who spoke with more authority. Compare the epigraph to this chapter.

11. Since "Robinsonades" are popular in political economy, islands are so too. You will find them in the work of almost every author I discuss in this book. Gauthier even invents a whole archipelago in order to explicate the consequences of his theory.

12. This answer strikes me as at least a bit strained, for why is it not the retailer's own responsibility, in choosing a site for his business, to find out whether or not his future customers will be willing to accept an atmosphere of racial discrimination as part of their bargain for his products? Is he entitled to the expectation that they will? I do not think so. Nevertheless, I will accept Mack's maneuver, for the sake of argument.

13. Of course, as Peter Vallentyne pointed out to me, the people who feel they are the victims of the "atmosphere" of racial discrimination need not only be the people who are the victims of the discrimination itself.

14. I would prefer to say "extortionist." A blackmailer is the special type of extortionist whose (threat of) harm consists in the revelation of a shameful or even criminal fact about his victim.

15. And this is Nozick's reason for defending a state monopoly on the use of violence to protect the rights of its citizens. Roughly his argument runs as follows. If people who would create a nuisance to others are prohibited to do so, they ought to be compensated for the prohibition, but only in so far as the prohibition constitutes a disadvantage to them. Now, people who prepare for self-defensive acts by carrying guns around, and Bazookas, explosives, surface-to-surface missiles, or by keeping "well-trained" pit bull terriers, and what not (the examples are mine) do create a nuisance to others, since they create a general atmosphere of fear on account of the risk that the explosives might go off unintentionally, or that the pit bull may prove not to be that obedient after all. So, their activities may be prohibited but only on condition that they will be compensated for the disadvantage. And the state does compensate those who are disadvantaged by its monopoly on the use of violence if it extends its services as a protective agency to all.

16. My view is supported Van Zetten's Dutch translation of *The Second Treatise* (Locke 1988: 79)

17. See Mohlhuysen 1905: 38, 39; Mohlhuysen 1921: 443, 462, 210*, 211*; *Icones Leidensis*, entry 2.

Chapter 4

1. Most of my quotations from Van Parijs's work will be from this book. Sometimes however, I have quoted from other publications when I found the formulations there more concise.

2. Goodin 1992: 210: "So at root, the reason we should cherish the target efficiency of basic income strategies is simply that it guarantees that we will, through them, be able to relieve human suffering as best we can."

3. My references in this chapter are to Dworkin's original essays on equality. They have been reprinted in Dworkin 2000.

4. Yet, I feel confident in doing so because all through *Real Freedom for All*, and in many of the other texts, this is also the arena Van Paris's himself favors. In order to make good his claims about the idea of sharing the value of resources, he too begins by tentatively abstracting from differences in internal endowments.

5. Compare Van Parijs 1991: 112–13, where the text has "resources" instead of "assets."

6. Of course, simplifications like these may present special problems and ambiguities, but I do believe that they serve to bring out certain peculiarities that might have been lost in a more general treatment. Again, I feel confident

in this approach, since Philippe Van Parijs also uses it in the explanation of the more qualitative aspects of his justification of basic income.

7. I follow Van Parijs in his choice of these two names, but we should take care to appreciate the irony. Monks in contemplative orders or people "who get engrossed in action painting" (Van Parijs 1992: 126), or indeed surfers, may get up very early and go to bed late, quite exhausted from their activities; they are not lazy in the usual sense of the word. The point is that in order to be able to do only the things they want, they must benefit from (or are dependent on) the activities of others, while these others, by assumption, are not benefiting from the activities of monks, action painters, and surfers. The analysis in this chapter does not make a judgment on the inherent worth or desirability of the goals and purposes that "lazy" people set themselves, it only comments on how the realization of such goals and purposes relates to their claims on shares of resources.

8. Would this constitute a case of violating Lock's non-spoilage proviso, on top of his enough-and-as-good proviso?

9. In the next chapter, we will meet with a proposal to do exactly what I am suggesting here, this time with regard to the labor market. Hamminga (1995) proposes to issue "Labor Rights" (vouchers that give access to job space) to all able-bodied citizens, and then organize a market where Labor Rights can be exchanged for money. We do not sell the things we originally appropriated; we sell the right to originally appropriate those things.

10. I have adapted this example, and the figures used in it, from Young 1994: 155–56.

11. Note that our condemnation of envy-freeness in scenario B is not in any way inspired by an interpersonal comparison of anything, not of the glasses of favorite mixes they consume, not of the utility or welfare they derive from that consumption. It is intrapersonal comparisons, in terms of better or worse, which render the verdict "parasitic."

12. Roemer 1985: 52ff.

13. Bas Kist in NRC Handelsblad, 22.11.1995. This article also tells that "The Body Shop" has withdrawn from Israel for similar reasons, and that McDonald's is considering legal steps against a shrewd "trademark broker" in South Africa.

14. Of course, everyday life provides us with many interesting parallels: what if I rush to the library to borrow the book I know you need to pass your next examination in political theory, and then say to you: "sure you can borrow it from me—for one hundred coins"? What if I, having my own garage, park my car on one of the few public parking places in the neighborhood and declare myself prepared to remove my car in return for payment? What if I buy hundreds of tickets out of the limited stock for a football match, or for a concert, with the purpose of creating and exploiting a black market? All these are clear instances of a parasitic abuse of access rights that should be counteracted.

15. This parallel shows, I believe, that at least in one case, which has always been an intuitively powerful case, of "building fences" between "spheres of

justice" (the fence between the market and politics) that fence is not really a fence between two things at all. The prohibition to sell votes is not justified by a difference in the "shared understandings" or "social meanings" of two radically different goods (see Walzer 1983: 9), but by a principle of justice that rules and structures one single area: the market. The selling of political influence cannot be anything else than a parasitic exploitation of the scarcity of a good—always displacing opportunity costs on others and that is, or ought to be, prohibited throughout the transaction practice we call the market, regardless of the "nature" of the good that is distributed. In this sense Walzer's fence between two spheres is more like one of the "edges" of a multidimensional realm, and we ought to be on our guard against other claims about radical distinctions in our social perceptions. Close inspection might always reveal that there is a coherent "deep structure" of normative principle underlying various areas that superficially appear to be governed by radically different rules of distribution.

16. For a discussion, see Binmore 1998: 23–29.

17. This result could be prevented if something like Gauthier's no-invitation argument were valid (see chapter 2.8).

18. It should also be clear that the general idea that public services should be self-supporting, which seems to inspire the recent trend of privatizing publicly owned enterprises, is far too simple. Turning public transport companies into private profit-seeking enterprises will backfire on those who do not want to use their services. Where public supply of x will relieve those who want to use y, privatization of the supply of x will be detrimental to the interests of all.

Chapter 5

1. Of course, I am using quasi-historical drama here to compare two types of situation: with or without an insider–outsider effect. In reality outsiders cannot be portrayed as insiders that are expelled. Outsiders are those who can never get in, in the first place.

2. Of course, this remark sits uneasily with the efficiency wage explanation of unemployment, which assumes that productivity, and profits, will go up, not down, at higher than market clearing wages.

3. This is even truer about jobs than about resources. We can be independently interested in the natural beauty of resources and prefer them not to be processed into consumer goods. But a spontaneous appreciation for the natural beauty of an unfulfilled job rather strikes me as odd.

4. Van Parijs 1991: 126. Reference to the action painter is dropped in the corresponding passages in Van Parijs 1995b: 109–10.

5. For a discussion of (egalitarian) welfarism, see Dworkin 1981a and Rawls 1972: 90–95. For an interesting criticism of Rawls's argument against welfarism, see Rijpkema 1995: 235–44.

6. Now, these are harsh words, but perhaps the would-be action painter may find some consolation in the idea that there may be other good reasons for

financing her efforts. Dworkin (1986) points out that liberal societies may have a legitimate interest in supporting more or less experimental artistic activities that actually fail to attract sufficient demand. The reason is that contributions to "high culture" have a tendency to "spill over" to popular culture (for which there is much demand). Supporting new and unpopular art forms may be seen as a sort of long-term investment in the quality of culture generally. Unfortunately, there will not be much consolation in this idea for the surfers who want to be fed.

7. In this article the author resumes an argument already presented in Hamminga 1983.

8. Why does Hamminga exclude non-able-bodied persons from holding Labor Rights? Is it not odd to deny those to people who cannot work, but not to those who do not want to work?

9. In fact he is in a somewhat better position than last year since his wage has gone up.

10. This is the way she puts it because she has read Aristotle. The point is that exercising her skill as a trained aero-technical specialist gives her a strong sense of accomplishment.

11. Gauthier (1986: 333–34) complains that Marx's view is utopian, of course, but more seriously he objects that the life that Marx depicts as an ideal is in fact impoverished. To really get the sense of self-realization or accomplishment from a given activity, we need the "full commitment" to that activity that is excluded by the "dilettantish" way in which we can do (and be) all things at once. There may be something to this objection but surely it must be a gross exaggeration if Gauthier means to say that one cannot be a "self-realizing" technician or teacher or even neurosurgeon (Gauthier's example) or, for that matter, parent for a few days in the week. After all, there must be some middle way between the "unbearable lightness" of Marx's ideal and the ideology of the guild system according to which you were born as a specialist, lived as a specialist, and died as a specialist, without ever allowing you the luxury of changing or spreading your commitments.

12. I hope it is clear that I am not professing a work ethic here. It is not I who claim that "working is good for people"; rather I point out the empirical evidence that many people perceive work as good for themselves—apart from the pay.

13. Note that, along similar lines, a green case can be made against the highest sustainable basic income. Obviously, many natural resources are not income-productive resources only. Uncultivated land can be turned into farmland, but it can also be appreciated as a thing of beauty in its unaltered state. Whales can be turned into lamp oil and perfume, but many people are perfectly ready to do without these "goods" because they find it a sad idea that no whales will be left in the oceans in the long run. Considering the spontaneous public support for conservation policies and initiatives—think of Greenpeace—it is not at all obvious that most people would be willing to accept cash in return for their equal shares in "nature as it is."

14. Especially not as we can observe that the insider–outsider effect is not at all absent in that sphere.

15. Indeed this slogan is the title of Walter van Trier's profound study on the theory of basic income during the interbellum (Van Trier 1995).

16. Some time ago a modern equivalent of civic feudalism surfaced in Dutch society, this time the privileged job space holders are "legal residents" and their victims "illegal immigrants." In order to get a temporary job through one of the special "temp" agencies that are popular, for instance, in the cleaning business one has to identify as a legal resident of Holland. Sometimes such residents enable illegal immigrants, who are desperate for work, to get a job by letting them use their passport. Fees are then paid to the account of the legal resident who, on a monthly basis, passes on some of the money to the person who does the work in actual fact (*Het Parool*, 6.2.1996).

BIBLIOGRAPHY

Newspaper articles are referred to in the notes and not included in this list.

Ackerman, Bruce. 2003. Radical Liberalism. In *The Ethics of Stakeholding*, ed. Keith Dowding, Jurgen de Wispelaere, and Stuart White, 94–113. Houndmills.

Ackerman, Bruce, and Anne Alstott. 1999. *The Stakeholder Society*. New Haven.

Binmore, Ken. 1993. Bargaining and Morality. In *Rationality, Justice and the Social Contract: Themes from Morals by Agreement*, ed. David Gauthier and Robert Sugden, 131–56. Ann Arbor.

——— 1998. *Game Theory and the Social Contract II: Just Playing*. Cambridge, Mass.

Bowles, Samuel, and Herbert Gintis. 1992. Power and Wealth in a Competitive Capitalist Economy. *Philosophy & Public Affairs* 21: 324–53.

Bottomley, Stephen, and Stephen Parker. 1997. *Law in Context*. 2d ed. Sidney.

Boxer, C. R. 1965. *The Dutch Seaborne Empire 1600–1800*. London.

Brecht, Bertolt. 1961. *The Caucasian Chalk Circle (1944–1945)*. English version by Eric Bentley and Maja Apelbaum. In *Seven Plays by Bertolt Brecht*, edited with an introduction by Eric Bentley, 495–587. New York.

Buchanan, James M. 1975. *The Limits of Liberty: Between Anarchy and Leviathan*. Chicago.

Coase, Ronald. 1960. The Problem of Social Cost. *Journal of Law and Economics* 3: 1–44.

Cohen, G. A. 1983. The Structure of Proletarian Unfreedom. *Philosophy and Public Affairs* 12: 3–33.

Den Hartogh, Govert. 1990. Tully's Locke. *Political Theory* 18: 656–72.

——— 2002. *Mutual Expectations: A Conventionalist Theory of Law.* Dordrecht.

Dowding, Keith, Jurgen de Wispelaere, and Stuart White, eds. 2003. *The Ethics of Stakeholding.* Houndmills.

Dworkin, Ronald. 1981a. What is Equality? Part 1: Equality of Welfare. *Philosophy and Public Affairs* 10: 185–246.

——— 1981b. What is Equality? Part 2: Equality of Resources. *Philosophy and Public Affairs* 10: 283–345.

——— 1986. Can a Liberal State Support Art? In *A Matter of Principle,* by Ronald Dworkin, 221–33. Oxford.

——— 1987. What is Equality? Part 3: The Place of Liberty. *Iowa Law Review* 73: 1–54.

——— 2000. *Sovereign Virtue: The Theory and Practice of Equality.* Cambridge, Mass.

Ellickson, Robert C. 1991. *Order without Law: How Neighbors Settle Disputes.* Cambridge, Mass.

Elster, Jon. 1983. *Sour Grapes: Studies in the Subversion of Rationality.* Cambridge.

——— ed. 1986. *Karl Marx: A Reader.* Cambridge.

——— 1989. *Solomonic Judgements: Studies in the Limitations of Rationality.* Cambridge.

Gauthier, David. 1986. *Morals by Agreement.* Oxford.

Gauthier, David, and Robert Sugden, eds. 1993. *Rationality, Justice and The Social Contract: Themes from* Morals by Agreement. Ann Arbor.

Goodin, Robert E. 1992. Towards a Minimally Presumptuous Social Welfare Policy. In *Arguing for Basic Income. Ethical Foundations for a Radical Reform,* ed. Philippe Van Parijs, 195–214. London.

Grunebaum, James O. 1990. Ownership as Theft. *The Monist* 73: 544–63.

Hamminga, Bert. 1983. Opstaan voor Iemand Misstaat Niemand. *Maandschrift Economie* 47: 395–405.

——— 1995. Demoralizing the Labour Market: Could Jobs be like Cars and Concerts? *Journal of Political Philosophy* 3: 23–35.

Hausman, Daniel M. 1989. Are Markets Morally Free Zones? *Philosophy and Public Affairs* 18: 317–33.

Icones Leidensis: De portretverzameling van de Rijksuniversiteit te Leiden. 1973. Leiden.

Hobbes, Thomas. 1968. *Leviathan.* Edited with an introduction by C. B. Macpherson. N.p.

Lindbeck, Assar, and Dennis Snower. 1988. *The Insider–Outsider Theory of Employment and Unemployment.* Cambridge, Mass.

Locke, John. 1740. *The Works of John Locke, Esq.* 4th ed. 3 vols. London.

——— 1755. *Du Gouvernement Civil.* Par Mr Locke: Traduit de l'anglois. Cinquième Edition exactement revue et corrigée sur la 5 Edition de Londres & Augmentée de quelques Notes, Par L.C.R.D.M.A.D.P. Amsterdam.

—— 1764. *Two Treatises of Government by Iohn Locke.* London.

—— 1924. *Two Treatises of Government.* Introduction by W. S. Carpenter. London.

—— 1966. *The Second Treatise of Government (An Essay Concerning the True Original, Extent and End of Civil Government)* and *A Letter Concerning Toleration by John Locke.* Edited with a revised Introduction by J. W. Gough. Oxford.

—— 1970. *Two Treatises of Government.* A Critical Edition with an Introduction and Apparatus Criticus by Peter Laslett. 2d ed. Cambridge.

—— 1980. *Second Treatise of Government.* Edited with an Introduction by C. B. Macpherson. Indianapolis.

—— 1988. *Over het staatsbestuur.* Vertaling F. van Zetten. Inleiding G. A. den Hartogh. Amsterdam.

Luce, R. Duncan, and Howard Raiffa. 1956. *Games and Decision:. Introduction and Critical Survey.* New York.

Mack, Eric. 1981. Unproductivity: The Unintended Consequences. In *Reading Nozick: Essays on Anarchy, State, and Utopia*, ed. Jeffrey Paul, 169–90. Oxford.

Mak, Geert. 1995. *Een kleine geschiedenis van Amsterdam.* Amsterdam.

Manza, Jeff. 1995. Review of Van Parijs (ed.) 1992a. *Theory and Society* 24: 881–89.

Marx, Karl. 1975. *Das Kapital: Kritik der politischen Ökonomie.* Karl Marx, Friedrich Engels, Werke, 23, 24, 25. Berlin.

Marx, Karl, and Friedrich Engels. 1970. *The German Ideology.* Ed. C. J. Arthur. New York.

Miller, David. 1976. *Social Justice.* Oxford.

Mohlhuysen, P. C. 1905. *Geschiedenis der Universiteits-bibliotheek te Leiden.* Leiden.

—— 1921. *Bronnen tot de Geschiedenis der Leidsche Universiteit,* V: 10 Febr. 1725–8 Febr. 1765. Den Haag.

Nozick, Robert. 1974. *Anarchy, State, and Utopia.* Oxford.

O'Sullivan, Richard. 1955. Abuse of Rights. *Current Legal Problems* 8: 61–73.

Rawls, John. 1972. *A Theory of Justice.* Oxford.

Rijpkema, Peter P. 1995. *State Perfectionism and Personal Freedom.* Amsterdam.

Roemer, John E. 1985. Should Marxists Be Interested in Exploitation? *Philosophy & Public Affairs* 14: 30–65.

—— 1989. What is Exploitation? Reply to Jeffrey Reiman. *Philosophy & Public Affairs* 18: 90–97.

Sen, A. K. 1995. *Inequality Reexamined.* Oxford.

Spencer, Herbert. 1893. *The Principles of Ethics,* vols. I, II (A system of Synthetic Philosophy, vols. IX, X). London.

Steiner, Hillel, and Jonathan Wolff. 2003. A General Framework for Resolving Disputed Land Claims. *Analysis* 63: 188–89.

Sugden, Robert. 1993. Rationality and Impartiality: Is the Contractarian Enterprise Possible? In *Rationality, Justice and the Social Contract: Themes from Morals by Agreement*, ed. David Gauthier and Robert Sugden, 157–75. Ann Arbor.

Van den Bergh, G. C. J. J. 1979. *Eigendom: Grepen uit de geschiedenis van een omst-reden begrip*. Deventer.

Van Donselaar, Gijs. 1998. The Freedom-based Account of Solidarity and Basic Income. *Ethical Theory and Moral Practice* 1: 313–33.

———— 2003. The Stake and Exploitation. In *The Ethics of Stakeholding*, ed. Keith Dowding, Jurgen de Wispelaere, and Stuart White, 94–113. Houndmills.

Van Parijs, Philippe. 1991. Why Surfers Should Be Fed: The Liberal Case for an Unconditional Basic Income. *Philosophy & Public Affairs* 20: 101–31.

———— 1992. Competing Justifications of Basic Income. In *Arguing for Basic Income: Ethical Foundations for a Radical Reform*, ed. Philippe Van Parijs, 3–43. London.

———— 1995a. De solidariteit voorbij: Over de ethische transformatie van de ver-zorgingsstaat. In *Het Basisinkomen: Sluitstuk van de Verzorgingsstaat*, ed. Van der Veen en Pels, 53–78. Amsterdam.

———— 1995b. *Real Freedom for All: What (if Anything) Can Justify Capitalism?* Oxford.

Van Trier, Walter. 1995. *Every One a King: An Investigation into the Meaning and Significance of the Debate on Basic Incomes with Special Reference to Three Epi-sodes from the British Inter-War Experience*. Leuven.

Voyame, J., B. Cottier, and B. Rocha. 1990. Abuse of Rights in Comparative Law. In *Abuse of Rights and Equivalent Concepts: The 1990 Principle and its Present Day Application*, 23–55. Proceedings of the Nineteenth Colloquy on European Law, Luxembourg, 6–9 November 1989, Strasbourg.

Waldron, Jeremy. 1979. Enough and As Good Left for Others. *Philosophical Quarterly* 29: 319–28.

———— 1988. *The Right to Private Property*. Oxford.

Walzer, Michael. 1983. *Spheres of Justice: A Defense of Pluralism and Equality*. New York.

White, Stuart. 1997. Liberal Equality, Exploitation, and the Case for an Uncon-ditional Basic Income. *Political Studies* 45: 312–26.

———— 2003. *The Civic Minimum: On the Rights and Obligations of Economic Citi-zenship*. Oxford.

Wolf, Clark. 1995. Contemporary Property Rights, Lockean Provisos, and the Interests of Future Generations. *Ethics* 105: 791–818.

Young, H. Peyton. 1994. *Equity: In Theory and Practice*. Princeton.

INDEX